Japan, Internationalism and the UN

Japan's position in world politics is a curious one. It has huge economic muscle and yet is politically weak. Since the Cold War, and especially since the Gulf War, there has been a fierce debate regarding Japan's role in the world. After years of being a loyal junior partner in an alliance with the United States the question of whether Japan should now adopt a far more assertive role within the UN is being raised.

These were the issues that prompted Ronald Dore to write this book, originally in Japanese for a Japanese audience. This translation is accompanied by some of the responses the book evoked from leading Japanese academics, journalists and officials, making it a valuable source book for those who want to understand the deep structure, political and emotional, of Japanese foreign policy, and not just its geopolitics.

Ronald Dore provides a unique insight into Japan's foreign policy and related domestic politics. In particular he explains the paradox that it is the least chauvinistic and most internationalist of Japanese who have tended to be the most opposed to any Japanese involvement with the UN and its peacekeeping.

Ronald Dore is a Senior Research Fellow at the Centre for Economic Performance, London School of Economics and Political Science.

The Nissan Institute/Routledge Japanese Studies Series
Editorial Board
J.A.A. Stockwin, *Nissan Professor of Modern Japanese Studies, University of Oxford and Director, Nissan Institute of Japanese Studies*
Teigo Yoshida, *formerly Professor of the University of Tokyo, and now Professor, Obirin University, Tokyo*
Frank Langdon, *Professor, Institute of International Relations, University of British Columbia, Canada*
Alan Rix, *Professor of Japanese, The University of Queensland*
Junji Banno, *Institute of Social Science, University of Tokyo*
Leonard Schoppa, *University of Virginia*

Other titles in the series:

The Myth of Japanese Uniqueness, *Peter Dale*
The Emperor's Adviser: Saionji Kinmochi and Pre-war Japanese Politics, *Lesley Connors*
A History of Japanese Economic Thought, *Tessa Morris-Suzuki*
The Establishment of the Japanese Constitutional System, *Junji Banno, translated by J.A.A. Stockwin*
Industrial Relations in Japan: the Peripheral Workforce, *Norma Chalmers*
Banking Policy in Japan: American Efforts at Reform During the Occupation, *William M. Tsutsui*
Education Reform in Japan, *Leonard Schoppa*
How the Japanese Learn to Work, *Ronald P. Dore and Mari Sako*
Japanese Economic Development: Theory and Practice, *Penelope Francks*
Japan and Protection: The Growth of Protectionist Sentiment and the Japanese Response, *Syed Javed Maswood*
The Soil, by Nagatsuka Takashi: a Portrait of Rural Life in Meiji Japan, *translated and with an introduction by Ann Waswo*
Biotechnology in Japan, *Malcolm Brock*
Britain's Educational Reform: a Comparison with Japan, *Mike Howarth*
Language and the Modern State: the Reform of Written Japanese, *Nanette Twine*
Industrial Harmony in Modern Japan: the Invention of a Tradition, *W. Dean Kinzley*
Japanese Science Fiction: a View of a Changing Society, *Robert Matthew*
The Japanese Numbers Game: the Use and Understanding of Numbers in Modern Japan, *Thomas Crump*
Ideology and Practice in Modern Japan, *Roger Goodman and Kirsten Refsing*
Technology and Industrial Development in pre-War Japan, *Yukiko Fukasaku*
Japan's Early Parliaments 1890–1905, *Andrew Fraser, R.H.P. Mason and Philip Mitchell*
Japan's Foreign Aid Challenge, *Alan Rix*
Emperor Hirohito and Showa Japan, *Stephen S. Large*
Japan: Beyond the End of History, *David Williams*
Ceremony and Ritual in Japan: Religious Practices in an Industrialized Society, *Jan van Bremen and D.P. Martinez*
Understanding Japanese Society: Second Edition, *Joy Hendry*
The Fantastic in Modern Japanese Literature: The Subversion of Modernity, *Susan J. Napier*
Militarization and Demilitarization in Contemporary Japan, *Glenn D. Hook*
Growing a Japanese Science City: Communication in Scientific Research, *James W. Dearing*
Architecture and Authority in Japan, *William H. Coaldrake*

Japan, Internationalism and the UN

Ronald Dore

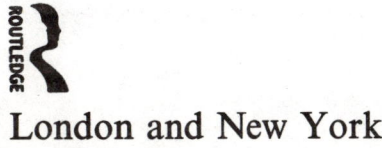

London and New York

JZ
1745
.D67
1997

First published in the UK 1997
by Routledge
11 New Fetter Lane, London EC4P 4EE

Simultaneously published in the USA and Canada
by Routledge
29 West 35th Street, New York, NY 10001

Originally published as *Kō shiyō to ieru Nihon*, Asahi Shimbunsha, Tokyo, 1993

© 1997 Ronald Dore; Part 2 the contributors

Typeset in Times by
BC Typesetting, Bristol

Printed and bound in Great Britain by
Mackays of Chathm PLC, Chatham, Kent

All rights reserved. No part of this book may be reprinted or
reproduced or utilized in any form or by any electronic,
mechanical, or other means, now known or hereafter
invented, including photocopying and recording, or in any
information storage or retrieval system, without permission in
writing from the publishers.

British Library Cataloguing in Publication Data
A catalogue record for this book is available from the British Library

Library of Congress Cataloging in Publication Data
Dore, Ronald Philip.
    Japan, internationalism and the UN/Ronald Dore.
       p.   cm. – (Nissan Institute/Routledge Japanese studies
series)
    1. Japan–Foreign relations–1989–   2. United Nations–Japan.
I. Title. II. Series.
JZ1745.D67   1996
327.52–dc21   97-14241
                                                                      CIP

ISBN 0–415–16646–2
      0–415–16647–0 (pbk)

Contents

Series editor's preface   vii
Preface to the English edition   ix
Preface to the Japanese original   xxxii

Part I The argument

1 Philosophies of history   3
2 The early stirrings of internationalism   16
3 The birth of the United Nations   29
4 The use of armed force   37
5 The enactment of Japan's Peace Constitution   52
6 From the world's United Nations to the United Nations as no man's land   60
7 The revival of the UN   81
8 Japan's international role and the Constitution   95
9 A UN-centred foreign policy and bilateral relations   112
10 The restructuring and strengthening of the UN: A survey of the issues   126

Part II Other points of view

Wanting to throw off a nasty burden, but suppressing the urge
Midori Yajima   143

Contributions, yes, but geared to the complex needs of a complex world
Yutaka Kōsai   148

To die for high principle?
Shinsuke Yoshimura   156

Economic and cultural rather than military contributions
Shinji Fukukawa   160

The need to wait for a generation change
Yukio Matsuyama   162

Limits on the spirit of self-sacrifice
Shijurō Ogata   169

The advantages of diversity
Masahiko Aoki   171

The fork in the road
Kazuo Chiba   176

Notes   178
Index   185

Series editor's preface

Japan in the latter half of the 1990s is the dominant economic power of the Asia-Pacific, which in turn is the most dynamic economic region of the contemporary world. Japan's dominance remains in place even though its economic growth remains sluggish; reform of the political system is needed but slow in coming; and public alienation from the ruling establishment has become uncomfortably high. Other parts of the region, such as South Korea, Taiwan and Thailand, have borrowed much from the Japanese model and exhibit economic dynamism of a high order; while China, despite its many problems, has moved decisively in the direction of economic growth. Japan remains by far the largest economy in the area, and globally second only to the United States. In a world set free from the constraints of the Cold War, Japan is playing a role consistent with its own interests in a region where, however quietly, it has become a dominant (though not *the* dominant) power. In so far as it is possible to discern a clear direction in Japanese external policies, they are premised on a need for global and especially regional stability, and a concern for security of markets and sources of supply.

The Nissan Institute/Routledge Japanese Studies Series seeks to foster an informed and balanced, but not uncritical, understanding of Japan. One aim of the series is to show the depth and variety of Japanese institutions, practices and ideas. Another is, by using comparisons, to see what lessons, positive or negative, can be drawn for other countries. The tendency in commentary on Japan to resort to outdated, ill-informed or sensational stereotypes still remains extraordinarily strong, and needs to be combated.

There have been many books on Japanese foreign policy. Most of them focus on the long and tortured debate which has taken place since the late 1940s about constitutional inhibitions on Japan acting as a 'normal nation', creating what would formally be recognised as armed forces and participating fully in the military–strategic aspects – as well as other aspects – of world affairs. The Gulf crisis and war of the early 1990s represented something of a turning point in this debate, and increased the influence of those in Japan who advocate a more active international role for the world's second largest economic power. This book, originally published in Japanese, analyses in perceptive detail, and from several points of view, the ways in which Japanese decision-makers and commentators try to tackle these issues. Its originality lies in the fact that it explores a possible way forward, whereby Japan might make an adequate contribution to global and regional stability and progress while still operating within the essential spirit embodied in the peace clause of the 1946 Constitution. Advocacy of a UN-centred diplomacy is no doubt unfashionable in the aftermath of Somalia and Bosnia, but those failures should not obscure the potential that the UN contains for establishing a stable world order now that the Cold War is a historical memory. This book could not have been written by a Metternich or a Kissinger, but Ronald Dore and his Japanese colleagues, fully sensitive to the importance of power in international affairs, have nevertheless mounted a cogent challenge to the assumptions about the ruthless exercise of power on which such thinking is based.

J.A.A. Stockwin

Preface to the English edition

THE BACKGROUND TO THE BOOK

It is hard, in writing this preface, to recapture the mood of optimism (optimism, that is, for anyone with world-federalist leanings) which prevailed in 1992 when I wrote the original version of this book. It was intended as a contribution to Japan's perennial 'Our place in the world' debate. Coming not long after *The Japan that Can Say No*, the notorious Ishihara–Morita 'time to shake off the American yoke' book, my Japanese title was *The Japan that Can Say 'Let's Do This'* (which does not sound quite as clumsy in Japanese). It sought to encapsulate the idea that Japan might be less preoccupied with equality in its relationship with the United States and, if it wanted in some sense to prove itself, might take initiatives in other fields.

The nuances of that 'place in the world' debate are well captured in the responses to the book's arguments of the friends and acquaintances – journalists, academics and officials – which are included in this volume and constitute the chief reason for thinking an English edition to be worthwhile. But, if less vividly and more schematically, it is worth briefly reviewing the background to that debate.

But how far back to go? More than a millennium, perhaps, to the time when energetic youngsters of the Imperial family were busy recasting Japan's political and social institutions in direct imitation of those of Tang China – the country's first reshaping after imported foreign models, accompanied even then by a good deal of psychological discomfort. Was taking another country as a model not a form of subordination, and was that subordination not an affront to national pride and identity? That experience, and the ambivalent reactions to that experience, foreshadowed the second great remodelling after Japan was 'opened' to the West in the middle of the nineteenth century. This was a much more fundamental institutional restructuring – it had to be, given all the guns on the warships off Japanese shores and the propensity of Europeans to use them. It was a restructuring aimed at achieving defence security and a place in the international system by bringing what at the time was called 'civilization and enlightenment' to Japan (a process which came to be called 'modernization' only in the middle of this century). Once again, there was ambivalence, deeply rooted in the low-status subordination to the countries which provided the models, a subordination far more clearly institutionalized than in the tributary missions to China of the eighth and ninth centuries. It was made apparent in the overtly 'unequal treaties' whose revision required a quarter-century's diplomatic effort, in the expressions of racial contempt or condescension which individual Japanese experienced when they travelled abroad, or treated with foreigners on their own soil, in the debate at Versailles which resulted in the defeat of Japan's proposal that a declaration of racial equality be inserted into the preamble of the peace treaty. Most Japanese carried within their own skins something of the tension between pride and necessity, symbolized at the extremes (as in so many late-developing countries) by the clash between the mature rationality of the reformer who acknowledges his country's 'backwardness' on the one hand – recognizes the need to learn and accepts that the learning pupil has to defer to his teachers and if necessary tolerate their insults – and, on the other hand, the impatience of the nationalist for whom no insult, no denial of equality, should ever be tolerable and who cannot wait for the day when the strategy of 'Western techniques and Eastern values' (*necessary* Western techniques and *superior* Eastern values) would allow the tables to be turned and the oppressor to be oppressed.

That tension, the different strands differently expressed by different groups, lay at the heart of Japanese debates about foreign policy from 1890 to 1945. As Japan did become stronger, economically and militarily, the inferiority complex/superiority complex balance shifted; the nationalists grew in voice and fervour; the heirs of the reformers – both the new class of calculating businessmen and the 'liberals' whose attachment to ideals of justice, peace and international harmony drew on older Confucian as well as on modern Western traditions – slowly lost both strength and courage. Inexorably through the 1930s, the nationalists gained control of the ideological airspace and denounced their opponents as mercenary traitors and as blasphemous detractors of the sacred ideals embodied in Japan's imperial polity. They – and the American reactions to their posturings – thus succeeded in creating the atmosphere in which the nation could be dragged, almost without overt protest, into a war which it had no rational hope of ever winning.

Which led to the third great remodelling, this time in the image of democratic and peace-loving America, an image which (see the contribution by Matsuyama in this volume) survived America's conversion to Cold War belligerency (the transition is reflected in the debates of the UN's Military Staff Committee analysed in Chapter 4 of this book) and the subsequent Vietnam War. The reforms carried through under American military occupation touched every aspect of society – the land reform, the reform of the justice system and of the civil code governing family and inheritance, electoral law reform and the establishment of democratic accountability, the protection of trade unions which set the seal on the wartime transformation of the corporation and created Japan's 'employee sovereignty' capitalism. But the reform of greatest relevance to current debates was 'reform' of Japan's armed forces, i.e., their total abolition and the prohibition on their resuscitation contained in Article 9 of the 1947 Constitution. (The background to the enactment of which, and the way in which it reflected contemporary views about the nature of the postwar world and Japan's role in it, are the subject of Chapter 5.)

Once again, there was intense ambivalence towards the nation which provided the reform models, this time intensified by the bitterness of defeat, by the far greater density of contacts in the new world of the aeroplane, the telephone and more recently the fax and Internet, and by the fact that Japan gained its peace treaty only by agreeing to accept American guarantees of its defence and, concomitantly, the continued stationing of American troops on Japanese soil. And once again the postwar tensions over external policy which this ambivalence created can be summarized crudely as a reproduction of the triangle of forces out of which the war had grown – the triangle, that is, whose three sides were the 'economic maximizers' – the 'economic animals' of 1960s polemics – the 'liberals', and the 'nationalists'. But the balance among them was very different. Defeat, military impotence, and the fixed geometry of the Cold War meant that the 'foreign affairs' to be attended to just were not all that salient – a circumstance which allowed the economic maximizers to have their head. And that meant not only spectacular growth of the economy, but increasing dependence on the American market and dependence on the friendly intervention of the State Department to suppress the protectionist reactions which the avalanche of Japanese exports was apt to provoke in Congress.

As for the post-war heirs of 'the liberals', now more often Marxists or Marxisant intellectuals, they dissociated themselves completely from Japan's past – Japan's modern history was written off as a one hundred per cent history of aggressive imperialism – and were devoted above all to the preservation of the postwar reforms. They had good reasons for this in the 'reverse course' days of the 1950s and 1960s, but, as the serious threat of anything like a return to prewar militarism receded to a vanishing point, they were increasingly driven back to defending the 'Peace Constitution' against the combined forces of the nationalists and of the Americans who wanted an increasingly rich Japan to do more to 'share the burden of defending the free world' in Asia. Their stance of total devotion to the letter of the *American*-inspired Constitution thus derived ironically both from fears of a revival of Japanese militarism and from animosity towards America – towards contemporary American culture, and towards America as Asian hegemon and adversary of communist regimes with which they sympathized.

They were frustrated by all the devices described in Chapter 8 which provided the constitutional reinterpretations enabling Japan slowly to build up one of the most powerful military forces in Asia. That build-up had no obvious military objective in view. There was no intention of using them as instrument of any expansionary policy (1945 really did put a stop to that), nor even from any strong consciousness of a security threat. It was motivated, in part, to appease American demands for 'burden-sharing' and, in part, as expression of the same macho notion that only strength gains respect, which makes Britain and France so insistent on their nuclear deterrents.

The third group, the nationalists for whom that macho notion was a major preoccupation (the anti-capitalist, national–socialist strains of prewar fascist radicalism having been largely inherited by the Marxists), were mostly of a conservative or nostalgic ex-radical kind and they were mostly to be found, along with the economic maximizers and friends of economic maximizers, in the Liberal Democratic Party. Once the first impetus of the 'reverse course' 'correcting the excesses' of the postwar reforms was spent in marginal changes in local government and educational administration, their concerns had primarily to do with symbols – gaining control over school textbooks to make sure that history teaching reflected a sense of patriotic pride, flying the national flag in schools, refusing to apologize for the war in any way that impugned the motives of those who led Japan into it, even claiming that Japan had fought, and unfortunately lost, a noble and just war to liberate Asia from the European colonial yoke.[1] See Matsuyama's witty characterization of these 'accidental liberals', the 'pro-American hawks' in his contribution to this book. Like their counterparts in other countries, they were the ones in favour of greater defence expenditure but, given Japan's particular circumstances, they were forever beset by the dilemma that rearmament in response to American pressure for 'burden-sharing' served only to reinforce the appearance of servile subordination ignobly accepted as a means of buying export market access, and hence was hardly a satisfactory way of demonstrating national pride.

But, nevertheless, it seemed to be the only way open to them. The sense of frustration that Japan was not playing a role – was not cutting a figure in the world consonant with its real economic strength and its cultural achievements – grew in the 1980s as that economic strength spectacularly increased. Japan pulled ahead of the United States in many fields of technology and production. In America the rapid Japanese penetration of its domestic markets prompted, on the one hand, belligerent complaints about unlevel playing fields and, on the other, anxious self-questioning at the reasons for America's loss of preeminence. Serious journals on both sides of the Pacific speculated about Japan becoming 'Number One', about the possibility that Herman Kahn's prediction that the twenty-first century would be the Japanese century might be true, about whether Japan had the moral qualities necessary to make the coming Pax Japonica as benign for mankind as the crumbling Pax Americana had been.

And yet, in the Great Affairs of Men, in the events which made the headlines, the nuclear negotiations between the US and USSR, the Iran–Iraq war, the many confrontations between Islamic fundamentalism and the West, Japan was nowhere in sight, neither in public UN debates nor in the chambers where the real dealing took place. Ever since it came back fully into the international organizations in the 1960s, Japan had steadily increased its contributions to the United Nations and its agencies. It became the second largest, and well on the way to becoming the largest aid donor, and yet seemed to have little influence over the way UN agencies spent its money and to earn little gratitude for it. 'Economic giant, political pigmy' became an overused cliché, and it rankled, for even the most drily calculating of economic maximizers is more likely in Japan to share common ground with the nationalist. For all the reasons set out in Chapter 8, Japan's circumstances make the Japanese more concerned than most other peoples with the first of what I subsequently learned also to be Thucydides' classification of the aims of external policy, or at least of the reasons people go to war – honour, fear and interest.[2]

But what brought that rankling discomfort to the forefront and prompted open debate about Japan's role in the world was the Gulf War. Once the American-led multilateral force got under way, Japan, the world's largest importer of Middle Eastern oil, was under pressure to make a contribution. To send fighting men would have been a big jump beyond any 'reinterpretation' of Article 9 of the Constitution ever contemplated hitherto. All official statements had unambiguously and repeatedly declared that, in earnest of the purely defensive nature of the Japanese armed forces, they would never be sent beyond Japan's shores. And what, anyway, would happen to a government which allowed peace-loving Japanese to die in a war more commonly seen as an American move to protect its oil sources and maintain its dominance in the Middle East than as an expression of mankind's determination to punish aggression? In the end, Japan sent a team of doctors and, after the war was over, some of its navy's minesweepers. *And* paid $13bn – far more than the expenditure borne by the Americans themselves. The sum was partly raised by a gasoline tax (which no American administration dares contemplate), partly by squeezing departmental budgets – cutting the 4–5 per cent contingency item from university budgets, for instance. But the caution, confusion and indecision betrayed by official government statements, the daily reports of the to-ings and fro-ings between the American Embassy and the Secretary-General of the government party, the sophistry of the Government legal representatives' interpretations of the Constitution in endless Diet hearings, and the reluctance with which the sum offered as contribution was raised under pressure to the final figure of $13bn, won the government no friends at home and Japan no friends abroad.[3] The unkindest cut of all was when the Kuwait Government took a full-page advertisement in the *New York Times* to thank all the countries which had contributed to its liberation and did not list Japan among them.

The anguishing did not end with the Gulf War. In the debate that followed, a fairly widespread concern was to avoid earning such opprobrium, so expensively, if something like the Gulf War were to happen again. But it was also an expression of longstanding unease at the 'economic giant, political pigmy' jibe, catalysed into overt debate by the experience of that war. The most forward position was that of those who wanted Japan to bcome a 'normal country' – if changing the Constitution was too difficult, to find some other formula which would allow Japanese troops to fight alongside Americans in any future multilateral force. ('Normal country' was a phrase popularized in the political testament of Ozawa Ichiro,[4] the Liberal Democrat Secretary-General who had pushed hardest for Japan's involvement in the Gulf War, and whose breakaway from the Liberal Democrats brought an end to the Liberal Democrats' monopoly of power in 1993.) Far more common was the more cautious view that Japan should find some way of squaring its Constitution with participation in UN peacekeeping operations in ways which gave full evidence of Japan's willingness to do its bit ('international contribution' became one of the most commonly used phrases in newspaper headlines at the time) without giving the impression, particularly to its Asian neighbours, of a Japan anxious to revive the martial virtues and get back into the business of 'using armed force as a means of settling international disputes'.

It was not always clear whether 'international contribution' meant keeping America happy, or furthering the ideals of world order for which the UN was created. The popular debate often drew no distinction between a peacekeeping force under UN control, and a Gulf War-type multilateral force whose actions were sanctioned by Security Council resolutions. But among the officials and politicians who took the initiative, it was the dominant view that only something which was clearly compatible with Japan's claims to have a 'UN-centred' foreign policy could, at that stage, be an acceptable enlargement of the Constitution's interpretation, and restriction of participation to operations under UN command was clearly spelt out in the legislation which eventually emerged from this debate, the International Peace Cooperation Law of August 1992.[5]

The Law permitted only assistance in the implementation of peace agreements already arrived at – with total impartiality and the consent of the parties to the agreements. There is a detailed list of activities which a Japanese contingent might engage in, six items of which, it was agreed in the final compromise with a fiercely dissenting Socialist opposition, should be not removed from the bill but retained only as 'frozen' items which the Diet might in its wisdom one day 'unfreeze'. Weapons were restricted to small arms, and were not to be used to exercise any pressure on contending parties. They were for the individual protection of the peace-keepers and individual meant strictly individual. If a platoon were to find itself in danger, its members could fire, but the platoon leader could not give the order to fire – which, as the Prime Minister who presided over the enactment of the Law subsequently remarked, poses something of a problem for people who are trained to obey orders, particularly where firearms are concerned.[6] So restrictive are the guidelines that, when in Cambodia the doctors attached to the 600-man Self-Defence Force battalion of engineers were asked to treat the soldiers of other peace-keeping contingents, a Cabinet order was required before they could do so.

It was these debates which prompted me to embark on this book. To someone like myself who had grown up with the idea that the United Nations was a Good Thing, that the loss of its founding ideals in the nakedly confrontational politics of the Cold War was deplorable and that the revival of those ideals was the only way, in the long run, that we could avoid blowing ourselves up in some nuclear holocaust – and someone who, as I explain at length in Chapter 7, saw the glimmerings of such a revival in the developments since 1987, culminating in the Security Council summit of January 1992 and the publication of Boutros-Ghali's *Agenda for Peace* the following summer – it seemed to me a paradox that in Japan it was nationalists, preoccupied with Japan's power and prestige, who were promoting this attempt to take part in the building of a UN-based security system, while the Socialist party and my academic friends who were most resolutely opposed to nationalism – and one would have thought most prone to entertain internationalist ideals – were so fixated on 'defence of the Peace Constitution' that they saw embarking on peace-keeping as yet one more concession to American attempts to subvert it.

Hence the book's arguments, which can be simply summarized:

Those internationalist ideals have a long and noble history; they are worthy; they may not be wholly unrealizable. Many Japanese feel deep ambivalence about their nation's subordination to the United States but fear that the only alternative might be international isolation. As a way of making Japan an independent force which counts in the world, why not try what one might call the super-Scandinavian option – making Japan the champion of the UN, giving priority in its foreign policy to the objective of strengthening the UN security system and the establishment of the international rule of law even at the expense of other diplomatic objectives, thus giving substance to its frequent claim to have a UN-centred foreign policy? The UN's fiftieth anniversary is likely to provide the occasion for a lively debate about revising the Charter, bringing it into line with present-day realities, making it capable of accommodating in future to changes in those realities, and, above all, modifying those elements which make it still, in many ways, so obviously a victors' charter. Japan has a chance to play a prominent role in this debate if it shows a constructive concern for making a better world, and not just for whether it gains a seat at the Security Council high table, or gets the references to 'enemy countries' removed from the UN Charter. This may involve some clashes with the UN's rival as alternative world policeman, the United States, but standing up to (saying 'no' to, as Ishihara and Morita would have it) America, not simply in the continuous 'national interest' bickering over trade in semiconductors or auto parts, but on matters of real principle, would do wonders for the national ego. In order to do that, however, Japan would have to clear the decks for such a policy by revising the Constitution, replacing the tatters of Article 9 with a real (and this time wholly voluntary) peace manifesto declaring that Japan's armed forces are to be used only for defence and for participation in UN operations.

The book sold half the edition and disappeared without trace – a lesson to interfering busybodies, though Japanese readers are probably more apt than most to accept the arguments I use at the beginning of Chapter 8 in justification of a non-citizen's involvement in internal debates. I did, however, get some interesting reactions from a number of Japanese friends and acquaintances, and this prompted the idea that if I got them to write their reflections down and translated the original it could add up to a thought-provoking dialogue on the nature of international 'society' and Japan's place within it. Given the 'dialogue' intention, it seemed sensible to reproduce here in this translation exactly what it was the Japanese commentators were reacting to. But although I have not 'cheated' by changing anything, I have added 'translator's notes' where some statement looks particularly questionable, naive or outrageous in the light of what has happened, or what I have learned since.

THE OUTLOOK FOR THE UN

What I have learned since is about the ephemerality of hope. I knew already how quickly the international climate can change – from, if from nothing else, the story of the UN's Military Affairs Committee which is detailed in Chapter 4 (which, along with the story of the enactment of Japan's 'Peace Constitution' in Chapter 5, are the only two parts of the book which come close to being original research). As an unreconstructed social evolutionist it still seems to me probable that in the long run, short of some ghastly nuclear accident, the world will end up with a single agency exercising a monopoly over the means of serious violence – some kind of world federal government. Also that the choice is between getting there the way the US federation came into being, through agreement by nation-states, or getting there by conquest, the ultimate hegemon being the nation with the most powerful military technology (the most obvious candidates for some such ultimate confrontation being, at the moment, the US and China). I do take Aoki's point, in his comments, about the advantages of diversity, not just because tolerance is a major virtue or because respect for cultural traditions is an important part of the social cement (a world federal government, in the 'monopoly of legitimate violence' sense could still tolerate far greater diversity than, say, that between Arizona and Vermont), but also because a diversity of mediating institutions may be the best way of solving conflict-of-interest problems. True, and the point is met in part by Chapter 8 of the UN Charter about regional collective security organizations, by the effectively independent Bretton Woods institutions and the WTO, etc. However, in the end, it seems to me that a stable order depends on some consensus as to what constitutes legitimacy in the use of force, and the best chance we have of arriving at that consensus by agreement rather than by conqueror's imposition does lie in improving the institutions ostensibly created for that purpose in 1945, albeit that they were also created to establish the legitimacy of the victors' victory. ('*Kateba kangun*' – 'the army that wins becomes the government army' – is the neat Japanese description of the process.)

But if my long-run perspective has not changed, my short-run expectations most certainly have. When I finished the book in the spring of 1993, it was still possible to believe that the chances of that improvement in UN peace and security institutions had never been better. Boutros-Ghali's *Agenda for Peace* and Brian Urquhart's proposals for a UN volunteer force were still being taken seriously; graduate students of international relations were beginning to be told by their supervisors that, even in the age of neo-realism, the United Nations was an acceptable subject again; the UN's peace-keeping operations were rapidly expanding; in Somalia, what an American initiative had started looked like turning into a new kind of collective colonialism – benevolent, albeit paternalistic, collective nation-building colonialism – akin to the declaration of President's rule in federal India for states which had fallen into chaos. The speeches of President Clinton at the start of his administration seemed to promise a greater willingness than at any time since the war to accept the need to work through the UN as a constraint on American policy.

But within six months of the book's publication there came the dramatic change of mood in the United States as the Somalia operation sank deeper into incompetence and futility and culminated in the death of eighteen US Rangers, and the sight, on television, of the body of an American airman being dragged through the streets of Mogadishu. The Presidential decision paper which was to govern American future involvement in UN operations was rewritten – more to reassure the American public of future American disengagement than to promise the world greater involvement. Then came the morass of Bosnia, with the US acting more to disrupt than to aid UN operations until it finally elbowed the UN aside and ordered NATO into action. And Rwanda, in which the UN was totally ineffective except in providing relief for refugees.

This is no place to describe this sea-change in the reputation, authority and prospects of the UN as our best hope of saving 'succeeding generations from the scourge of war', as the UN Charter has it. That has been better done by others, not least by Rosemary Righter under the apt title *Utopia Lost*.[7] It may be useful, however, to conclude this preface with a brief description of developments in Japanese debates about foreign policy, particularly policies towards the UN, over the last three years.

JAPANESE FOREIGN POLICY

It is easy enough to summarize the trend in official policy. In security matters – ever-closer ties with the United States, and acceptance of US leadership and the need for US approval even for major developments in relations with its close neighbours, Korea and China (over, for instance, relations with North Korea). In UN matters – a continued 'good neighbour' stance: generous financial contributions (though its financial accounting system periodically puts it some months in arrears on its dues), responsiveness to requests for Japanese participation in such peace-keeping activities as the Peace Cooperation Law allows (Angola, Mozambique, Zaire–Rwanda, most recently in the Golan Heights),[8] and continuous lobbying for the proposal to give Japan, with Germany, a 'permanent member' seat on the Security Council. (The last objective, always seen as something primarily dependent on American goodwill and initiative, has been pursued with diminished vigour since the US lost interest in the UN, the Charter's fiftieth anniversary came and went, and the deliberations in the General Assembly's Charter amendment committee ran into the sand.) Otherwise, a cautious attitude towards other conflicts in which Japanese interests are not directly involved, except when pressed by the Americans for some specific endorsement, e.g., over the continuation of sanctions against Iraq, which France and Russia were trying to modify. Needless to say, there has been precious little of the constructive world-order-building initiatives of which this book talked; if anything, Japan has cooperated more in efforts to cut the UN down to size than on support for the UN reform efforts advocated by, for example, Urquhart and Childers.[9] Government statements welcomed Boutros-Ghali's retreat from the earlier *Agenda for Peace* proposals for the UN to develop a peace-enforcement role; if the UN sticks to traditional impartial peace-keeping, Japan is closer to being able to play a full part and hence enhance its chance of a Security Council permanent seat. Boutros-Ghali in visits to Tokyo explicitly said that he saw no reason why the limitations Japan imposes on its participation in UN operations should be an obstacle to Japan joining the Security Council as a permanent member. But the decision is not his. In a magazine discussion the recently retired Japanese ambassador to the UN answers calls that Japan should take a lead in proposing UN reform by saying that, first, one cannot lead reform without a record of taking 'actions that are respected by other countries, like participating in peacekeeping, accepting refugees and actively [governmentally?] developing NGOs.' Second, that Japan could not begin to have a beneficent influence until it became a member of the Security Council.[10] Policies are not yet formulated, it seems, as to what direction that beneficent influence might take.

One inhibition on their formulation which cannot be easily ignored is described by Fukukawa in his comment in this book: 'Japan is still not internationalized enough, and we are not quite confident enough in our grasp of world affairs to be able to [take such initiatives] well.' International organization, the international diplomatic system is a product of Western history, deeply imbued with ideas and conventions of European origin, conducting its more intimate affairs – the affairs that count – in European languages, resorting for rhetorical devices to European and American aphorisms and proverbs. Newcomers who do not share that history, and learn those conventions only in their teens or their twenties, are bound to 'punch below their weight' as compared with those whose confidence and self-regard reflect the fact that they have been cocks of the world's walk for several centuries and who, as Chiba (drawing on a lifetime of diplomatic experience) notes in his comments are still inclined to look on the initiatives of 'newcomer nations' as presumptious. The author of a cool and well-informed book about the UN – a lecturer at the Defence University who stresses the limitations of the UN and believes it neither likely nor desirable that it should ever grow into anything like a world government – stresses in his final chapter the importance of having people who, in the words of Akashi, the Secretary–General's Special Adviser in Bosnia whom he quotes, 'have an internationalism which has been tempered in the searing heat of the nationalist ideology and nationalist sentiments of the developing countries' and whose 'internationalist loyalty consists ... in bringing the best elements of their national cultures to their work in the UN'. And he goes on to give figures which illustrate the shortage of such people in Japan; in 1994, Japanese occupied only 91 of the 5,000 professional staff posts in the UN system, compared with a 'quota' entitlement of 165–223.[11]

Japan has not sought to rearm. Defence budgets remain modest and, since the end of the Cold War, slightly reduced as a proportion of GNP. The switches in expenditure – more for air defence, supposedly in response to North Korean developments, and more for large transport aircraft and ships with peacekeeping operations in mind[12] – have also been modest. Any observer of Japan has to take seriously the point, made by both Ogata and Yoshimura in their contributions to this book, that the present generation has come a long way from their grandfathers' martial spirit, their propensity to be aroused by flags and brass bands and the prospect of battlefield glory. Some doubt whether even the Self-Defence Forces would have much stomach for fighting if push came to shove.

Former Prime Minister Miyazawa, making exactly the same point in his reminiscences, draws the distinction, however, between a taste for battlefield gore and the clinical pressing of remote-delivery buttons. The Japanese are no less sensitive to the attractions of nuclear weapons as status symbols than the British or the French. However, Japan's support (after initial hesitations) for the indefinite extension of the Nuclear Non-proliferation Treaty would seem to answer suspicions that its nuclear reactor choice and its plutonium store reflect a determination to keep the nuclear option open. Though, to be sure, treaty regimes do not always last. Miyazawa, who was Foreign Minister at the time of the ratification of the Treaty in 1975 and Prime Minister from 1991 to 1993, is interesting on this point. He recalls that although he had considerable doubts about the Treaty – because it was an unequal treaty and because it closed off options – he nevertheless took strong issue with Kissinger over the latter's prediction that Japan would prove no exception to the rule that great economic powers inevitably seek to translate their supremacy into military domination, and that the day would come when Japan too would have nuclear weapons. He then goes on:

> If the environment changes and Japan starts thinking in more relaxed terms about armaments, then I imagine the nuclear question would come up. Conscription wouldn't become an issue, but nuclear weapons would. It's the cheapest option, and technically there'd be no problems. You could always represent them as being purely for self-defence, and if siting them on land is a problem, you can put them in submarines. If you're thinking in 'normal country' terms the question is bound to come up.

That this is not an off-the-cuff remark but something to which he has given some thought becomes clear in what follows. The problem, he suggests, would be maintaining control; Japan being neither a dictatorship nor a country with deeply rooted democratic traditions but a country where 'for good or for bad politics tend to be swayed this way and that by considerations of popularity' (so unlike other democracies!). This, he says, was what went through his mind when Bush had his famous vomiting attack on television and Barbara Bush sat on at the dinner table after he had left the room, remarking to Miyazawa that it would 'send the wrong signal' if she left. 'Some discipline, I thought. There may be an end to the Cold War, but the President is still the man with his finger on the button. It's no cake-walk having nuclear weapons.'[13]

REVAMPING THE US–JAPAN SECURITY TREATY

But, to repeat, all questions of Japanese foreign policy are referred back to one central, axial criterion: what would be the effect on Japan's alliance with the United States? Even its UN policy – far from the suggestion of this book that championing the cause of the UN might prove for Japan a viable alternative to its uncomfortable dependency on US goodwill – is evaluated primarily in the perspective of that alliance. The well-informed journalist author of a 1995 book on the UN was probably reflecting official opinion in this, as well as in other matters, when he writes of the recent revamping of the US–Japan security arrangements, 'this expanded US–Japan cooperation can be developed into a world strategy if Japan were to come to sit beside the US as a fellow permanent member of the UN Security Council.'[14]

That revamping of the alliance, culminating in the joint declaration 're-defining' that relationship announced during a visit of President Clinton to Tokyo on 17 April 1996, represents the most significant milestone in the development of Japan's defence posture after the end of the Cold War, and the removal of the Russian threat which gave the US–Japan Security Treaty its original *raison d'être*. Like the persistence of NATO, the unchallenged continuation of the defence arrangements, despite the disappearance of the situation they were intended to meet, is to be explained primarily by organizational inertia, but the 1996 amendments to existing arrangements were specifically a response to: (a) the crystallization of American long-range Asian defence policy in the so-called Nye Initiative of 1995 – the clear declaration that the United States would maintain a force of 100,000 troops in Asia for at least the next ten years, deeming this to be an essential element in the region's stability; (b) growing concern about the 'self-assertiveness' of Chinese policy and its slowly growing military capability, a concern heightened just before the April accords by the China–US threats and counter-threats in the run up to the Taiwanese elections; (c) less important than the latter, but more openly talked about, the danger that a desperate North Korea might try some Samson-and-the-temple act; (d) the long-standing American demand for more Japanese 'burden-sharing' – if anything intensified by Japan's rather clear 'victory' in trade talks where, with the support of European and WTO opinion, it rejected American demands for import targets. Japan was pressed for clearer commitments of support – diplomatic, logistic and, if possible, fighting military support – for any use of its 100,000 troops that the US might deem it necessary to make, and also access to Japanese proprietary technology which might have military relevance; (e) a major preoccupation of the final six months: the need of the Japanese government to respond to a public opinion outraged by the rape of an Okinawan schoolgirl – not to mention the remark of the subsequently dismissed Admiral in charge that it would have been cheaper for the two marines involved to have gone to a brothel than to hire the car they used for their calculated rape.

Of such stuff are defence agreements made. The 17 April 'redefinition' of the alliance, said one Japanese commentator, represented a bargain which was not unreasonable but, as in the Okinawan reversion negotiations in 1970, one in which the clever Americans got more than they gave.[15] Japan got American promises of withdrawal from some of its more obtrusive Okinawan bases and a less noisy use of its airfields there, and in return promised logistical and other support for American operations in 'Asia and the Far East' – well beyond the previously narrowly defined Japan-defence-line limits of the immediately surrounding waters and their approaches. Separate agreements concerned the sharing of defence technology in, for example, the joint development of a new fighter.

An alternative evaluation, reputed to be that of the Prime Minister, is that these 'concessions' to the Americans are not concessions at all, but a way of edging Japan back to 'normal country-hood'; the creation, under the excuse that it was the only way to gain American concessions, of *faits accomplis* which further nibble away at constitutional taboos. The agreement is widely interpreted as involving clear abandonment of the hitherto established doctrine that Japan is precluded from entering into 'collective security arrangements' which are deemed, like sending troops overseas, to impugn the constitutional legitimacy of the Self-Defence Forces, based as it is on the claim that they really are only for self-defence. Under a collective security arrangement, the Japanese might find themselves embroiled in American operations in defence of Taiwan, for instance. 'So they might, and not a bad thing either; Japan must pull its weight if we are to turn the alliance into a more equal relationship' is what counts as the hawkish position apparently held by the Prime Minister. 'So they might and that is why the agreements are disastrous and a further step on the road to perdition' is the position of the dwindling band of traditional doves. 'So they might on one reading of the agreements, but it is not clear that this constitutes a collective security arrangement, and so it would be wrong to admit that the agreements, in themselves acceptable, do so involve ending the ban on such arrangements' is the tortuous position reportedly taken by the Socialist Party and the New Harbinger Party within the governing coalition, which have the problem of squaring their established positions with the need to maintain the coalition and postpone the election which will probably send them into the wilderness. As this is written the argument between them and the Prime Minister has prevented any clear government statement on the question whether the agreements do, or do not, represent a collective security arrangement.

There is no hint in the accords of what might constitute the alliance's potential enemy. All the emphasis is on its providing a guarantee of international stability, an argument which most Asian countries greet, if not with enthusiasm, at least with tolerance. And that includes, if with increasingly explicit reservations, the Chinese, if for no other reason than that they would rather have the Japanese tied to the Americans than left to defend themselves and thus given an excuse for dangerous rearmament. (Statesmen do tend to assume that it is the pattern of the last war which is most likely to repeat itself.) During his visit to Japan in November 1995, Joseph Nye did, however, at a news conference specify one potential enemy – North Korea. A mistake, in the view of one Japanese defence expert, because it would mean the alliance could disappear when the North Korean problem is solved, and 'everybody knows that the real enemy is China'. Not for nothing have the US–Japan joint manoeuvres which used to have as their object repelling an invasion of Hokkaido by a 'red army', been switched to Kyushu, where the invaders are known as the 'brown army'. The American summoning of not one but two aircraft carrier fleets to counter Chinese missile-firing bluster at the time of the Taiwanese elections provided scenario-writers with material for depicting the sort of situation in which

Preface to the English edition xxiii

Japan might in future be called upon to demonstrate its loyalty to the alliance.

On the complexities of Japanese attitudes to China I cannot do better than refer the reader to Kōsai's subtle analysis in this book (written in 1994). On my reading of present-day majority opinion, confrontation with China would, indeed, be seen as very deplorable and awkward, but not a disaster because the US has such an overwhelming military superiority. If anyone is speculating about the relative strengths of China and the US in ten or fifteen years' time – as opposed to short-term developments such as China's designs on the Spratly Islands or its intention to acquire an aircraft carrier or two – they seem not to do so in public.

Much less does anyone discuss the possibility that China might one day overtake Japan as America's closest rival in defence technology. There is no reason to exclude that possibility, however. With ten times Japan's population, China probably therefore has ten times the number of first-class brains. She is devoting considerable resources to their scientific education, and is animated by the same sort of unsatisfied nationalism as drove Japan to war in the 1930s, a nationalism which might provide the political will and the physical resources to mobilize those brains for war games – building the next or the next-but-one generation of missiles or anti-missile defences – rather than the Sega or Nintendō electronic games that keep Japan's electronic experts occupied. That, as I argued in Chapter 8, is one very good reason why we *need* a United Nations that counts – to provide a multilateral arena in which the bilateral tensions, which are inevitable as China's economic and military power grows, can be diffused by being played out in the presence of disinterested – or less interested – equal-status mediators. The former Japanese ambassador to Washington gave an illustration of the dialogue gap between China and its interlocutors which can be allowed to exist – with all the possibility of exacerbating rather than defusing tensions – as long as the UN does not count. He recalled discussing with the Americans in 1994 the possibility of sanctions against North Korea if it did not give nuclear assurances. They would have to be outside the UN framework because, he said, they could not risk taking the matter to the Security Council; nobody in Washington or Tokyo knew how the Chinese would react to a sanctions resolution.[16]

AND ASIA?

I accept the point made by Kōsai in his comment that in this book I do not give adequate weight to Japanese concern with, and to some extent deference to, Asian opinion. The emotion generated in the run up to the Diet 'peace resolution' to mark the fiftieth anniversary of the end of the war and over the nature of the apology for Japan's past to be contained therein is one sign of this. So also is the fact that mention of Japan's participation in Cambodian peace-making is so frequently followed by the observation that public opinion in many Asian countries, taking its cue from the opposition within Japan, at first condemned the plan as a dangerous sign of resurgent militarism, but, by the time the expedition was over, had come round to full approval. Japan does indeed pay considerable attention to mending its Asian fences. As Wolf Mendl points out,

> Japan has already replaced the United States as Asia's principal market, source of investment and provider of development assistance. It has begun tentatively to stake out its political leadership with a claim to protect regional interests, especially as spokesman for ASEAN in the Group of Seven and through various attempts to mediate in regional conflicts, and it has played a leading role in the development of the Asian Regional Forum.[17]

None of which is in conflict with existing close relations with the United States. *Ajia-shugi* – 'Asianism' – however, as a recognized, if ill-defined concept in Japanese foreign policy discussions, has different connotations. As a strategic option it has hardly any clearer definition than 'an alternative to close reliance on the United States', spelt out in no more concrete form than in the America-phobe follow-on to *The Japan that can say 'No'*, written by one of the authors of that original, the maverick novelist-right-wing MP, Ishihara Shintarō, together with the Malaysian Prime Minister, Mahathir, following the latter's tough stand against including the United States in Asian regional organizations (*The Asia that can say 'No'*). But Asianism is not so much a strategic option as an 'ism' that is more sentiment than philosophy, more an exasperated reaction to what is seen as an overbearing, uncomprehending and culturally alien America (a feeling encapsulated in the early 1990s by the word *kembei* – dislike of America, as opposed to traditional *hambei*, anti-Americanism) as it is an assertion of cultural affinity with Asian civilizations. It drew some strength from Huntington's thesis about the next century's conflicts being inter-cultural conflicts (though in his scheme he tactfully made Japan a culture *sui generis* instead of making it a part of the Confucian cultural sphere); it prompted a certain amount of cultural exchange activity – study groups of Osaka business men looking for the Confucian roots of Asian economic growth, for instance; and it was admitted, if grudgingly, to the realm of respectable discourse, after a much-quoted article by Japan's ambassador to Thailand. Enough, at least, for rebuttals to be written asserting that this rise of Asianism could be dangerous if it implied in any way that Japan had any reasonable alternative to its close military alliance with the United States. Don't repeat the tragic blunder of the Greater East Asia Co-prosperity Sphere – the last attempt to shut the United States out of Asia.[18]

To say that Asianism is more a matter of sympathies than of strategies is not by any means to dismiss its possible importance in some future crisis situation. One should not underestimate the 'cultural affinity' effect on journalists and diplomats of those television pictures during the Vietnam War of wizened peasant ladies who might have been their own grandmothers, eating rice out of a bowl with chopsticks, and living in fear of powerful Americans. Nor the fact that *hakujin* (white man) and *yokomeshi* ('getting indigestion through having to talk English over a meal'), while rarely appearing in print, are common expressions in the conversation of the Japanese elite. At the same time, one should not forget that Japanese officials and intellectuals at the end of the century are one more generation removed from their peasant roots, and contain far more people who feel at home in Los Angeles than could ever happily settle down in Beijing or PhnomPenh.

NON-OFFICIAL OPINION

At any rate, today it seems fair to say that the government's determination to found Japan's foreign policy on the US alliance has the backing of a broad spectrum of business and media opinion. In what was probably a good representation of the Tokyo consensus view, one of the two main business associations, the Japan Association of Corporate Executives (Keizai Dōyūkai, formerly known in English as the Japan Committee for Economic Development), published a report by its Defence and Security Committee about a week before the Clinton visit in April 1996.[19] The purpose seems to have been primarily to express support for the accords which were about to be announced. It makes no bones of its desire to see a 'rethinking' of the ban on collective security arrangements in order that Japan should be able to cooperate more vigorously with its ally 'with whom it shares universal values'. (Other references to the United States are 'a state based on international cooperation and humanism, and founded on the values embodied in the Japanese constitution – freedom, democracy, human rights and peace' and 'a state which is supported by a citizen society which respects individuals' individuality and allows the principle of individual responsibility to flourish', also as a 'free capitalist system operating under the rules of a market economy'.) The report also proposes that there should be some 'flexibility' in the interpretation of the rules which at present keep Japan out of the arms trade where the 'importing country is an allied or friendly country whose use of the arms can be trusted'. (There is also a call for a 'clear vision' of the future of the defence industry for the sake of the 3,000 firms said to be involved in it.) The report makes a point of the fact that the Committee members consulted foreign opinion during their deliberations. A footnote indicates that nine of the eleven persons consulted were American.

The hostility of the traditional left to this tightening of the alliance with the United States has been blunted since the deal which led to the birth of the bizarre tripartite coalition (Liberal Democrats, Socialists, and New Harbinger parties) with the Socialist Party leader, Murayama, as Prime Minister – until he could take the anomaly of his position no more and made way at the end of 1995 for the Liberal Democrat, Hashimoto. Murayama's conversion, as a condition of the arrangement which made him Prime Minister, to a) acceptance of the legitimacy of the Self-Defence Forces, b) acceptance of the necessity, indeed, desirability of the Security Treaty with the United States, and c) acceptance of the fact that close ties with the United States had to be the basis of Japan's external policy – all of which the Socialist Party had hitherto fiercely opposed – deprived the anti-consensus left – an aging body of university intellectuals and journalists – of any kind of parliamentary representation, except for the less fastidious who maintained contact with the outcast Communist Party. (Outcast in a curious way; it is as if they were not admitted to polite society, people about whom one lowers one's voice to speak. In none of the possible combinations considered in forming recent coalition governments has the inclusion of the Communists ever been discussed.)

FOREIGN POLICY AND THE CONSTITUTION

The 'dwindling band of doves' continues to dwindle – and to age. One wing very explicitly rejects the idea of the UN itself deploying, or acting as a forum for the deployment of, armed force in the settlement of international disputes, and pins its hopes for a future world order on the institutions of civil society. Two recent expressions are, first, a book by the former Vice-Rector of the UN University who comes out of a couple of decades' experience of conferences with NGOs – the more vociferous feminist, environmentalist and human rights groups as well as the humanitarian aid ones – convinced that somehow or other they are capable of creating, in the teeth of state power, a moral order which will pull the world away from its addiction to free trade and free market economics, redistribute the world's wealth and usher in an era of non-interventionist world peace. Japan should concentrate on using its power in the World Bank and the IMF and the WTO to bringing this about, and abandon all thoughts of becoming a member of the interventionist Security Council.[20] The other, a much more scholarly and analytically sophisticated book, draws its inspiration from Kant and Tolstoy and Richard Falk to argue similarly for a peaceful global anarchy, but contrives in two hundred pages to avoid any mention of Japan or what its policy should be.[21]

A rather more down-to-earth group, predominantly of political scientists, did however squarely address the issues which actually confront Japan in setting its UN policy, namely what to do about the Constitution and what role for the Self-Defence Forces. Their suggestion, in a manifesto produced in 1993, was for the enactment of a Basic Peace Law as a means of adapting to the reality that it is beyond the bounds of political feasibility that the Self-Defence Forces should ever be dismantled, while at the same time not taking the unthinkable course of abandoning the *goken* – Protect the Constitution – slogan which for forty years had been the central rallying point of the left.[22] Much of the manifesto is concerned with abstract argument about the right of self-defence, whether it is inherent or contingent, and if the latter, contingent on what. Concretely, the SDF would be reconstituted (renamed?) as a National Guard, and what it might or might not do would be spelled out, while a separate organization would be created to provide contingents to UN forces, though under tight restrictions similar to those provided by the present bill. (The softening of political divisions consequent on the Murayama prime ministership was symbolized also by the fact that one of the leading authors of this initiative became one of the sponsors of the private trust set up with government blessing to collect funds to provide compensation to the Korean wartime 'comfort women' – a means of doing something about a troublesome political issue without opening the door to a flood of wartime compensation claims.)

A rather similar line was taken in a major statement by the *Asahi* newspaper on Constitution Day, 3 May 1995, of which one of the contributors to this book, Yukio Matsuyama, was formerly senior editor. Its motives for being firmly against revision of the Constitution are somewhat similar to his, but it also makes a strong argument for the flexible interpretation of Article 9 as having no intention to deny the right of self-defence, whatever Prime Minister Yoshida may have said at the time of its enactment. 'As long as there are countries which would not hesitate to use force, unfortunate as it may be, the power to defend oneself may not be denied, and the Japanese people would not feel safe relying simply on unarmed resistance or a popular uprising.' Article 9 has served however to keep nuclear weapons out of Japan, to maintain the ban on arms exports, to prevent conscription and to stop the enactment of an Official Secrets Act, a Martial Law Act or the establishment of Military Tribunals. The statement goes on to outline in great detail a plan for transforming the weaponry of the SDF by the year 2010 so that it shall be in unmistakable conformity with its purely defensive role.

Let it be said however, to put this in perspective, that the dominant emphasis of this *Asahi* statement is not on military matters, but on the need for Japan to play a positive international role – to become, as Professor Inoguchi puts it, 'a global civilian power, rather than a traditional great power'.[23] The statement is in six equal parts (in terms of wordage). The first concerns international contributions – improvement in quality and quantity of aid, initiatives in the environment, etc. The second concerns peace-keeping operations; the third is the section on Article 9 just discussed. Fourth comes the transformation of the SDF; fifth, the problem of security in Asia and the need to build something like the Organization for Security and Cooperation in Europe while winding down the American alliance; and finally the need for Japan to take a leading role in initatives to reform the United Nations – with an emphasis on 'democratizing', giving more power to the little nations in the General Assembly and reducing the dominance of the Security Council's dominant members.

In the second section on the key controversial issue of participation in peace-keeping, the statement takes a view similar to Yajima in her contribution to this book: Boutros-Ghali's *Agenda for Peace* ambition to develop peace-enforcement activities was quite mistaken. The UN should confine itself to the traditional peace-keeping activities which do not require the application of force and in which, therefore, Japanese can take part in good conscience. The model should be the Finns in Suez in 1973 who, when the Israelis tried to overrun their inspection post, put down their weapons, made a human wall, and outfaced them. (How this squares with the rejection of unarmed resistance as a means of national self-defence is not spelt out.) But participation in peace-keeping should be the job of a specialist organization, a Peace Cooperation Corps of about 2,000 men and women.

It is probable that the *Asahi* statement represents a reply from left-of-centre to a rather remarkable initiative taken by the right-of-centre *Yomiuri* exactly six months earlier.[24] It was remarkable in showing that the nostalgics – the politicians of the 1950s who first pushed for constitutional revision as part of their 'reverse course', wanted the army revived and the Emperor declared the 'head of state', not the 'symbol of the state and of the unity of the people' – no longer make the running among the advocates of Constitutional reform. Which is not to say, as Shinsuke Yoshimura argues in his comment in this book, that 'constitutional revision' has ceased to be inextricably associated, in the Japanese public consciousness, with such intentions.

To my knowledge, this is the first attempt in recent years to offer a comprehensive agenda for constitutional change which addresses problems in local government, the operations of the Diet and the administration, etc., which fifty years of experience have revealed. The years 1993 and 1994 saw the publication of a number of concrete proposals for the revision of Article 9, beginning with the political testament of Ozawa Ichirō[25] cited earlier. Ozawa was the main negotiator with the Americans at the time of the Gulf War and now the leader of the opposition Renewal Party. In his realist view of the world, any attempt to distinguish between just wars and aggressive wars is nonsense; what the UN decides is what goes, and Japan, if it is to become a normal country, should take part in any wars it approves of. Hence add a third paragraph to Article 9 to say that nothing in the preceding renunciation of military force shall prevent Japan from having a 'Self-Defence Force which acts to procure peace' and which may *also* play a part in any standing army the UN might create. The directions in which an Ozawa army might procure peace are rather clearly indicated by the way in which his chapter on foreign policy begins with, and is predominantly devoted to, the US alliance as the absolute cornerstone of Japan's foreign policy. It gets round to the UN only later in the chapter.

There were one or two other suggested redrafts in reports issued by business groups, including the Japan Association of Corporate Executives whose April 1996 manifesto was discussed earlier. It is fair to say that in all of them, accommodation to the exigencies of the US alliance takes precedence over any 'building world order' considerations, and some show an overt interest in an easing of the ban on weapons export and greater collaboration with the US in defence technology.

The *Yomiuri* draft, however, is not embedded in any discussion of foreign policy, but the result of a review of the whole constitution. Its distance from traditional constitutional reform movements is made clear in its handling of the definitions of sovereignty and the Emperor; shifting the declaration that sovereignty lies with the people, that it is exercised through their elected representatives and that the definition of a sovereign citizen is determined by law, from the preamble to Articles 1–3, and shifting the Emperor – still a symbol – down to Article 4. The first part of Article 9, renouncing war or the threat of war as a means of settling international disputes, remains intact, apart from changing 'renounce' to 'does not recognize' – presumably because the Japanese word *hōki* means 'give up' and you cannot give up what you do not have. It does make a subtle difference, however; in the original it was the Japanese people who 'gave up' the use of force, regardless of what others did. 'Does not recognize' applies to others too – including the United Nations. The exegesis does not make clear whether this was intended.

The second paragraph of Article 9 – renunciation of the right of belligerency and the declaration that no armed force shall be maintained – obviously disappear. In their place is a renunciation of 'inhuman and indiscriminate weapons of mass destruction', while a separate article declares that an organization for self-defence will be formed, that its commander-in-chief shall be the Prime Minister and that there shall be no conscription. As for the vexed question of peace-keeping activities, a separate chapter on international cooperation first declares Japan's intention to eliminate human calamities from the earth – including both those caused by military activity and natural disasters – and secondly that the Self-Defence Forces may cooperate with *kakuritsu sareta kokusaiteki kikan* (established international organizations) in those activities. It appears that the English text published in the *Daily Yomiuri* said 'the relevant well-established and internationally recognised organizations'. The latter sounds like the UN, but the Japanese, particularly since it uses the *teki* to qualify 'international' could equally well cover Gulf War-type *ad hoc* multinational organizations. Whether the translation was a deliberate ploy to give foreigners and Japanese a different impression, there is no way of knowing. But about the draft's intention there can, however, be little doubt. Ex-Prime Minister Miyazawa, again:

> Their redraft of Article 9 looks quite moderate and can be read as an explicit statement of what we were doing with the PKO Law, but I gather from talking with the drafters that it doesn't stop there. We

have traditionally held that Japanese troops should never be engaged in the use of force overseas, but although the wording in this draft is obscure, the spirit of it is that Japanese troops *could* be involved in using force if it was with the UN in the cause of peace. It is the collective security notion... which it seems can also be applied to security relations beween two countries. I asked them: 'Does that mean that if we rewrote the Japanese–American Security Treaty so that, if America were in danger of war we would take that as a danger for Japan also and be entitled to use force' and they answered: 'We wouldn't exclude that.'[26]

The relevance to the debate about 'collective security' set off by the April 1996 redefinition of the Japanese–American Security accords will be obvious. Not accepting the collective security principle even apropos of UN arrangements is a bulwark against being persuaded into obligations towards the US which even politicians as wedded to the alliance as Miyazawa are not prepared to contemplate.

TOWARDS MORE OPEN DISCUSSION?

The striking thing about these various proposals is that they never seem to lead to any serious debate either between the 'no constitutional reform, ever' doves, the Miyazawas who want to continue (at least for some time) to avoid any possibility that Japanese soldiers could shoot people outside Japanese territory, and the Ozawas who want to be in there when the Americans organize the next multinational force. The *Asahi* took three weeks to comment on the *Yomiuri*'s draft – which was by any reckoning a major political event – and then dismissed it, hinting that the wholesale revision exercise was merely window-dressing to cover the proposals to subvert Article 9, and going on even to question the propriety of the *Yomiuri*'s decision to publish. Of course, it said, free speech is a sacred right, and the *Asahi* too will actively promote discussion of the Constitution. But not produce drafts: 'self-discipline is required of any organ of public opinion dedicated to objective and fair news coverage'.

This coyness about entering into direct debate may seem evasive and unhelpful, but it has its own logic, expressed in the closing sentence of Matsuyama's contribution to this book. The time will come for debate about constitutional reform – but not until those driven by nostalgia for prewar Japan vacate that particular debating arena. Because, the implication is, they are still capable of making the running and gaining widespread support. He was writing before the *Yomiuri* published its draft, and I am not sure whether he would count it, and some of the other proposals coming from business groups, as the emergence of the 'conservative radicals who have broken loose from the prewar value system', further evidence of what Kōsai in his comment calls the 'growing body of people in Japan who, although conservative, are also capable of taking a stand on democracy and internationalism'. That there is a considerable fund of altruistic concern ready to be mobilized in an international cause, especially among young Japanese, was demonstrated by the reaction to the death of a young Japanese election monitor working as a UN volunteer in Cambodia. His father declared that in his son's memory he would devote himself to the cause of the UN and international solidarity. He wanted the world to know that there were people in Japan motivated 'not by national interest, but by global citizenship, by the ideal of sharing global solidarity with the people of other countries.' And in the following two months there were 5,000 applications for the volunteer corps, the highest ever.[27]

Shifts of opinion – on whether Japan should take part in peace-making operations, for instance – can occur quite rapidly in Japan, but shifts in the basic values and world-views that constrain those movements of opinion – the emotional and conceptual levers that opinion-formers can pull – occur at a more tectonic pace. (There are, rarely, generational watersheds such as divide those who completed their schooling before 1945 and those who were brought up on the postwar curriculum.[28]) This book reflects the preconceptions of someone who started listening in on Japanese foreign policy arguments in 1950–1 when the 'peace camp' was first acquiring its organization and identity in the debate about the peace treaty: whether Japan should accept the San Francisco settlement or wait until a peace treaty which Russia too would accept could be negotiated. Whether by the standards I have learned to apply to these debates, younger generations will prove better or worse remains to be seen. At least they are bound to be different.

Preface to the Japanese original

In a recent issue of the Japanese Foreign Office's PR journal, *Gaikō Forum*,[1] Haruo Sakamoto (formerly head of the MITI Hokkaido office) remarked in a transcripted discussion:

> What I want to see above all in Japanese foreign policy is evidence of a 'sense of participation'. At the time of the Gulf War, for instance, it seemed to me that everybody in the Foreign Office had no thought but 'how on earth do we get out of our predicament on this one?' It's the same with the debate about Japan joining in peace-keeping operations. You don't get the sense that anybody is thinking: 'Japan wants to see this kind of a world; therefore we should make this kind of contribution.' That's the sort of philosophy one needs.

That 'sense of participation' is what this book is all about.

The image of Japanese foreign policy in the world today is polarized. There are some who see it simply as an obedient follower of the United States – either because of the overwhelming importance of American markets to the Japanese economy, or because ever since the days of the American occupation the elder brother/younger brother complex has been bred into the bone. It is said that the reason the British and the French so much resisted Japan becoming the Number 2 power in capital contribution and voting in the IMF was because it seemed tantamount to giving the US both the leading positions.

The alternative image is of a Japan whose inner sentiments are clearly betrayed by the book *The Japan That Can Say 'No'* – particularly the contributions of Shintarō Ishihara which made up the bulk of the subsequent English-language version. (Never has an unpublished book acquired such wide circulation since the samizdat of *Dr Zhivago*. I was once offered a copy of the Pentagon's pirate translation by a factory manager in a suburb of Bologna.) This is the image of Japan as threat, a Japan under whose veneer of good neighbourliness and fine sentiments lies not just emptiness, but resentment and hatred, directed not just at the Americans but at all the 'white race countries', a Japan likely to become unpredicatable if it ever achieves self-confidence again, a Japan full of scholars endlessly pursuing the identity question: 'What is the essence of Japaneseness?', 'What are the special characteristics of Japanese society?', in ways that seem reminiscent of the 'National Essence' debates of the 1930s.

That is an image of Japan held by not a few people in Europe and the US. A country always saying 'Yes, yes', or at most 'Well, we'll have to see', wanting desperately to say 'No', but holding back until the time should be ripe – that was the image reinforced by the incidents at the beginning of 1992 when, first the President of the Lower House and then the Prime Minister made not-intended-for-reporters remarks about the quality and the morals of American workers which were, however, reported – and the embarrassed and ungracious apologies which followed.

Both 'No' and 'Yes' are passive reactions to the initiative of an active other. Economists draw a distinction among market-participants between oligopolistic 'price-makers' and the 'price-takers', the small operators who have no power to set prices. Japan, for the last fifty years has in fact been an 'existing international environment taker'; for so long in fact that most Japanese thinking about the world is predicated on the assumption that Japan cannot be anything else.

That assumption comes across clearly in the speeches and leading articles one constantly reads in Japanese papers on the subject of Japan's 'international contribution'. Leave aside the most simple-minded of them who clearly show that the question for them is: what tribute do we have to pay to appease the Americans? Even the more sophisticated never question the unchangeability of the *status quo* as the starting point.

Is it not time that Japan stopped seeing itself as a minor in an adult world? A Japan that can say not just 'Yes' and 'No', but also 'Why don't we do this?', a Japan that can make proposals concerning the management and the restructuring of the international system – proposals which are more than just self-serving, a Japan in other words that sees itself as an 'international environment maker'; I do not think I am alone in hoping to see the emergence of such a Japan.

In the economic sphere one can already see signs of such a Japan emerging. One example is the mechanism for dealing with Third World debt – originally a Japanese initative, later hijacked by the US State Department and Treasury as the Brady Plan. The initiatives Japan has recently taken on the World Bank Executive Council have also been widely commented on. The urgings of the Governor of the Bank of Japan and other Japanese representatives that bank policy was far too much dominated by American free market ideology, backed by the doctrines of neo-classical economists, and that as a consequence the conditions attached to loans were often counter-productive because they were driven by an ideological prejudice against any kind of state intervention have – to Japan's great credit – aroused a lot of flutterings among the dovecots of the American-dominated staff at the World Bank and the IMF.[2]

It is true that there was, in Mr Watanabe's speeches, just a tiny element of self-righteousness – 'That was the way Japan grew, so it must be the right model'. But the point is that this was an example of a Japanese representative being willing to incur hostility by speaking out in an international forum, not in order to promote some Japanese interest, but for some other motive which has to do with convictions about how the world can be made a better place. And that this seemed to observers a relatively new – and much welcome – phenomenon.[3]

THE MAINSPRINGS OF FOREIGN POLICY

The purpose of this book is not confined to promoting 'the sense of participation' or 'the art of getting yourself disliked in a good cause'. I take the liberty of going on to say in what direction I personally, as a foreigner, would hope that Japan's initiative-taking might lead it.

As a rough generalization one might say that the objectives of the foreign policy of sovereign states are three-fold. (In spite of the way in which the internationalization of the economy and the growth of international organization have eroded sovereignty = freedom of action, I suppose one can still talk about sovereign states.)

1. To safeguard the security of the country.
2. To promote its people's economic welfare. ('People' of course begs all sorts of questions. Its multinationals? Powerful interest groups? Particularly vocal minorities? The great majority of its citizens?)
3. To give its people a sense of pride. To make sure that when its nationals are in contact with foreigners, or read in the newspapers about some foreign reaction to their country, they have reason to think, 'I'm glad I'm an XYtanian.'

In short, the desire for security, the desire for profit, the desire for pride.

The dissatisfaction which many Japanese seem to feel with their country's foreign policy – whether one is talking about the Shidehara policies of the late 1920s or policy at the time of the 1991 Gulf War or today – seem to me to focus on the third – the desire for pride. Once, during the Iran–Iraq war, there emerged the faint possibility that Japan might play an effective role as mediator. The manoeuvres were hardly mentioned in the European or American press. But in Japan it was top-headline news for several days. That seems to me evidence of the strength of this unsatisfied 'desire for pride'.

It does seem to me likely to be true that it is a factor which plays a much larger part in determining Japanese foreign policy than in, say, that of the other six nations of the G7 group. This has nothing to do with any specifically Japanese 'national character' but can easily be explained by two particular factors.

1 When we members of the other six countries meet foreigners we are most commonly meeting people who physiognomically look just like us, and whose gestures and body language derive from the same common Mediterranean culture as ours. Consequently, we are not so constantly reminded of our Englishness, our Frenchness. But the proportion of Japanese foreign encounters which is with people whose physical experience and manners and body language are quite different from those they have grown up with is very much higher. The frequency with which they are made conscious of their Japaneseness is much higher, and, consequently so the extent to which that sense of their Japaneseness is deeply embedded in their sense of self. Pride in country, therefore, feeds more directly into personal 'self-respect'.
2 One can in a loose sort of way talk about a country's 'standing' or 'status' in the world community. The people of countries whose status is stable are not likely to think about it much. They can take it for granted. It is countries whose status is shifting – up or down – which are the most sensitively on the lookout for signs which will tell them 'where we are now'. Among the two most mobile countries in the world are upwardly mobile Japan and the downwardly mobile US. Get the two most status-sensitive nations negotiating with each other, and it's not surprising that you get 'frictions'.

THE ARGUMENT OF THE BOOK

The main purpose of this book, however, is not to analyse past Japanese foreign policy. It is, rather, with all due diffidence, to make suggestions about the future which may be summarized as follows.

1 One of the best ways in which the 'desire for pride' can be satisfied is by getting rid of the image of a Japan that can only say 'Yes' or 'No', and creating a different image – of a Japan which can – and frequently does – make positive proposals.
2 Those proposals might best be not the sort of forceful assertion of Japan's national interests advocated by Shintarō Ishihara, but rather proposals which go beyond Japan's own interests, ideas about how mankind can move forward to a more rational world order. Japan surely does not want to repeat the history of the 1930s when Shidehara's policy aimed at evoking respect and friendship from the rest of the world gave way to the army's bitter alternative: 'the hell with friendship; we'll *make* them respect us'. I certainly would not like to see my friends in Japan go through that sort of experience.
3 Irrespective of Japan's role, there is a great task to be performed – the restructuring, relaunching, of the United Nations.
4 Why now? Because the ending of the Cold War has presented us with an opportunity to resume the work of building ever stronger international

institutions, work which has been more or less suspended for forty years. Getting it wrong now might have untold ill-consequences for the future. The time has come to look again at some of those initiatives which were being taken in the period immediately before the intensification of the Cold War made them unthinkable – in particular the moves to give the UN a military role which would, if successful, allow the UN to take over from the United States the role of world policeman – a policeman *for* and not just of the world.

5 The Gulf War showed up the need for restructuring the UN. The nineteenth century Japanese reformers talked about *wakon yosai*, 'Japanese spirit, Western technology'. One might borrow the phrase. A world order based on 'American spirit, Japanese money' – more accurately 'Anglo-Saxon spirit, German–Japanese money' – is satisfactory to no one and unlikely to prove stable. Even less so, probably, as the superior efficiency of German–Japanese capitalism widens the wealth gap with the Anglo-Saxon economies. (I find it hard to believe, either that there will be a sea-change in the efficiency of the British and American economies as they learn to imitate the Japanese model, or that the Germans and the Japanese are going to slide into inefficient indolence[4] in the near future.)

6 Why so unstable? Particularly because of China. Only special circumstances made it possible for the Gulf War to take place, not as a UN operation but as a US-controlled operation legitimated by UN resolutions. The economic problems which dictated Russia's consent are likely to be long lasting, and provided that Russia does not slide into fascist dictatorship, and provided there is no intensification of US–German 'sphere of influence' rivalry over the territories of the former Soviet Union, Russia's need for economic assistance will make it ready to give the same support to US initiatives as the Soviet Union gave at the time of the Gulf War. But China is a different matter. China's need to support the US was dictated by her economic need to extract herself from the pariah status she had acquired following the Tienanmen incident. But there are not always going to be reasons of that telling sort. Think too of the likelihood that as China's economy grows US–China trade frictions are likely soon to dwarf those which now bedevil relations between the US and Japan.

7 Those among the G7 countries which are likely to perceive a coincidence between the restructuring of the UN and their own national interest are Japan, Germany and Italy – together, possibly, with Canada if economic frictions should seriously harm relations with the US. The US, France and Britain do not wish to surrender their positions as permanent veto-wielding powers on the Security Council – positions which were justifiable in 1945 in that they recognized the power balance at the time. Once open up the question of the structure and function of the UN however, and it not only becomes apparent that their privileged position does

Preface to the Japanese original xxxvii

not sit well with the power realities of the world today; the competition among the other powers which seek to share their privileges opens a whole Pandora's box of troubles. Particularly troublesome would be policy towards a Japan which – until now at least – seems unable to say anything about the UN except to complain: 'Here we are paying out all this money to the UN and you won't even give us a permanent seat on the Security Council.' It was clear that the speed with which the Soviet Union's seat was given to the new Russia reflected not so much any love for Yeltsin as a desire to put the lid on what could turn into an unsavoury discussion. It became apparent at the beginning of 1993 that the new Clinton administration had decided it was worth incurring the wrath of Britain and France for the advantages to be gained from expressing sympathy with Japan's aspirations, but it is doubtful how far it will be prepared to go.

8 Of the three countries mentioned, the one which shows most interest in the UN, the one in which one not infrequently hears the phrase 'a UN-centred foreign policy', is Japan. Japan has the potential to take a strong initiative in proposing a restructuring of the UN, and if it did so it could hope to get support from the other 'excluded' countries. There is, however, one essential condition. The plan should clearly be one which is animated, not by resentment at Japan's own mistreatment, but by the constructive desire to lay the foundations for a world order whose animating ideal is a perception of the fundamental unity of mankind.

9 Such a plan is not something to be put together in a week's work. To devise something that can command the famous Japanese consensus requires the commitment of sizeable research resources both inside and outside government, lively and widespread discussion in newspapers, radio and television, and all that takes time. That is why the task is urgent and a start needs to be made now. The sense of 'the potential for a New World Order following the end of the Cold War' will not last for ever.

10 What should be the main points which such a plan should address?

This is the final theme of the book, but to highlight one or two main points:

a) The balance between the one-country-one-vote 'democratic' ('ethnocratic'?) principle of the General Assembly and the oligarchic principle of the Security Council with its privileged veto powers. Is that balance right given the way in which the globalization of the economy and of environmental problems is slowly eroding the sovereignty of nation-states?

b) The Security Council's composition; the status of permanent member and the veto power that goes with it are designed to ensure the continued control of the victors of the Second World War. If it were to be restructured to function as a genuinely representative global executive council what composition and powers would be appropriate? It is only realistic to accept that the UN will be unable to act if it ignores the most militarily powerful of its members, but there are many other ways of realistically recognizing the unequal world division of power other than through the device of a permanent seat with veto power.

c) How to secure finance for the UN? How should national contributions be set? Can the UN find some source of income other than annual member contributions?

d) What sort of foundation stones can one lay which would ensure that eventually – not in the near future, perhaps, but eventually – there will be a UN which has the military resources and the moral authority to be able to act even in a way contrary to the wishes of its militarily most powerful member? The role of the Secretary-General, build-up of the UN's own intelligence-gathering capacity (its own spy satellite, for instance), a rethinking of the recruitment and career structure of international civil servants, are all elements which will affect the long-term outcome.

These are formidable problems.

11 There was once a Japanese Confucian military strategist called Yamagata Daini. A friend of mine, the philosopher Ichii Saburō once wrote a book about the role of 'key persons' in history, and among his special heroes was Daini. Daini was unsparing in his criticism of the oppressive and incompetent rule of the Tokugawa as the second half of the nineteenth century began. But he was not fool enough to switch to 'Revere the Emperor' monarchic restorationism. He coined the slogan; *Tenka wa tenka no tenka nari.* The nation (though *tenka* – 'all under Heaven' – can mean 'the world' too) is the nation's nation. That would not be a bad slogan for a Japan which took the initiative in seeking reconstruction of the UN. It would make the point that a 'world order' cannot be America's order. What constitutes and what does not constitute aggression cannot be left to one country to decide. A world order should be *the world's* order.

I am sure it would be a great pleasure for many Japanese to be able to have furious arguments with Americans, not over such tiresome haggles as the volume of car exports, but over matters of principle and the creation of a lasting international system, but as I argue in Chapter 9, a UN-centred foreign policy need not necessarily mean a policy which leads to deep antagonism in relations with the United States.

THE STRUCTURE OF THE BOOK

Chapter 1 asks how should one view the future; should one, like Paul Kennedy, see history as a cyclical affair constantly repeating itself, or should one believe in a steady process of social evolution? I make clear my own evolutionist position.

Chapter 2 looks at the evolution, from Grotius to the collapse of the League and the formation of the United Nations, of international law, of thinking about world order and of actual world institutions.

Chapter 3 tries to get into the minds of the people who drew up the UN Charter, and to ask what were their hopes and assumptions about the future course of history? What compromises did they have to make?

Chapter 4 traces the history of attempts to implement Chapter 7 of the UN Charter to create a 'UN reserve army', and how those attempts foundered as the Cold War got colder.

Chapter 5 examines the Diet debates on Article 9, the Article which renounces the maintenance of armed forces in the 1946 Japanese Constitution, and advances the thesis that this clause can only be explained if one understands the hopes and assumptions which prevailed generally in the world in the immediate postwar period.

Chapter 6 looks at the 1945–1987 history of the UN arguing that, Cold War notwithstanding, it showed some progressive evolution – in the creation of Peace-Keeping Forces, its slow intervention in human rights issues, its work on development.

Chapter 7 looks at the reawakening of the UN which came with the switch in Soviet policy in 1987 – marked especially by the latter's cooperation with the US in bringing an end to the Iran–Iraq war. It concentrates in particular on the clash between Russian proposals – at the time of the Gulf Patrol in 1987 and again at the outset of the 1990 Gulf crisis – for a unified UN command, and American insistence on American action as a free agent acting in the UN's name.

Chapter 8 tries to answer the question: what would it mean for Japan to 'adopt a UN-centred foreign policy'? Necessarily this leads to the question of the need to revise the Japanese Constitution, as a pre-condition for Japan to seek to play the role of 'champion of the UN'.

Chapter 9 takes up the question: would a 'UN-centred foreign policy' necessarily mean clashing with the alternative world-policeman, the US? It also considers the implications for Japan's relations with Russia and with China.

Chapter 10 reviews the restructuring agenda; what would a plan for revitalizing the UN have to cover?

Japan's foreign policy today seems to me to be formed against a background of three opposing forces – 'workers for peace' (their own term) of an extreme degree of introversion; economic animals, so concerned about US markets that not upsetting the Americans becomes the sole criterion of foreign policy; and would-be self-assertive nationalists who would happily quarrel with America as well as Russia if only they could make Japan a force that *counts* in the world.

And therein lies a strange – albeit historically explainable – paradox. Those Japanese who react most sensitively to any hint of national chauvinism, those whom one would have expected, in principle, to be the most internationalist, namely those on the left who describe themselves as 'workers for peace' (*heiwashugisha*), are the most indifferent to the United Nations, and most hostile to Japan's involvement with it.

It is strange. And it seems to me not only strange, but unnatural and regrettable. That is why I set out to write this book, hoping thereby to 'throw a stone in the pool'.

Part I
The argument

1 Philosophies of history

CYCLICAL REPETITION OR EVOLUTION

'Philosophies of History' may sound slightly pretentious. Most of us manage to live our daily lives without one, and so indeed do most historians who nevertheless succeed in providing fine analytical descriptions of particular concrete events and societies. The philosophy of history, one might think, is something one can safely leave to interested specialists.

However, not so. Most of us do in fact have, however unconsciously, some kind of philosophy of history. That unconscious view of history tends in some way or other to colour our perceptions of social and political issues, be they matters of education policy, policies towards crime, the danger of war or the possibilities of strengthening the United Nations. Perhaps it has to do with basic personality tendencies towards gloomy pessimism or cheerful optimism; at any rate most people are, one might say instinctively, history-as-decline theorists, history-as-cycles theorists or history-as-evolution theorists.

For example, one frequently hears people in Britain describe Thatcherism as a reaction against the excessive egalitarianism of Labour governments and predict that sooner or later there will be an egalitarian reaction against the excesses of pure marketism under the Thatcher regime. Or one hears people saying the history of education is a story of alternation between periods of authoritarian emphasis on disciplined instruction and periods of permissive freedom and now we are at a turning point.

Economists are frequently cycle theorists. Those who study business cycles are primarily interested in uncovering the mechanisms which cause the transition from boom to recession and are not often concerned with the question whether *this* recession now differs structurally from the recession fifteen years ago. The followers of Kondratieff are even more extreme in their belief that one can discern, as a result of successive waves of introduction of new technology, long-term 50–60 year cycles in the economy. They assume, in other words, that capitalism 'as a system' has basically remained unchanged for two hundred years.

4 The argument

Before the industrial revolution, in the seventeenth and eighteenth centuries cyclical theorists predominated among philosophers of history. Among the most explicit, Vico and Condorcet are the most famous. In the Far East, the Confucianists who saw history as a succession of periods of Ji and Ran – of stable order and disorder – and the popular Buddhism, well expressed by the author of the opening words of the Gempei ballad: 'The bell of Gion tolls out the message: the potentates of today are the broken men of tomorrow' – these too were cyclical theorists. In recent times Arnold Toynbee won fame and popularity in the United States and Japan – less so in his own country – for his panoramic vision of the rise and fall of successive civilizations.

The cyclical theorist sees human societies as passing through time, but with no particular direction. Both the theorists of decline and the theorists of evolution would disagree. In its vaguest form the history-as-decline view expresses itself in the complaints of the disgruntled old, forever reminiscing about the good old days of their youth, and muttering about 'the way young people nowadays...'. But, until the Middle Ages, it was in many societies an explicit doctrine of revealed truth. The age of Yao and Shun in China, Eden, the High Plain of Heaven of Japanese mythology, the Grecian Golden Age – the original human society was an ideal paradise created by the Gods. The appearance of original sin, the growing strength of baser instincts – since then it is all a story of continuous decline.

Equally insistent on the notion of a 'direction' in history, but giving it a very different evaluation, are the social evolutionists; or one should rather say the theorists of social progress. 'Progress' and 'evolution' need to be distinguished. The former means movement in a *desirable* direction whereas 'evolution', in principle, contains no evaluative overtones and simply means 'proceeding in a given direction as a result of determinate mechanisms'. In practice, of course, most of the nineteenth-century thinkers described as social evolutionists – Hegel, Kant, Spencer, Morgan, Marx – all had a firm belief that mankind was steadily progressing – or at least, in the case of Marx, if not steadily at least through the leaps of revolution.

In the twentieth century, having seen two world wars costing tens of millions of lives; having seen the rise of a Nazi Germany which elevated genocide to the status of national policy, we are not so sure about progress. From the simple believers in ineradicable original sin to more complex theorists of the essential nature of science, men and women, disappointed in Man, have come to reject the optimistic nineteenth-century theorists as naive victims of wishful thinking; and those who deny progress for the most part are likely to deny also evolution. History is more likely to be seen as meaningless; a continuous directionless flux in which elements of progress mix with elements of reaction.

THE VARIOUS DIMENSIONS OF SOCIAL EVOLUTION

I believe that is mistaken. I would summarize my own view of history as follows.

Proposition 1

Toynbee is right that most of recorded history is the story of the rise and fall of civilizations. It often happened that when a civilization disintegrated the knowledge that its members had accumulated – their material inventions like water-wheels or their social inventions like the secret vote – became completely lost. Much had to be reinvented by succeeding civilizations. It took about a thousand years before Renaissance Italy could get back to the level of Rome at its peak.

Proposition 2

Since the Renaissance, however, and especially since the scientific revolution of the seventeenth century and the industrial revolution which followed, the means of recording, accumulating and diffusing technological knowledge have fundamentally changed and – short of a nuclear war which threatens the very existence of mankind – it is hard to think of the possibility of this rapidly accumulating stock of knowledge being lost.

Proposition 3

It is precisely this accumulation of knowledge and technology which conditions the evolution of society. By 'condition' I do not mean 'determine'. The accumulation of material and social techniques serves to enlarge the scope of human choice. Different countries, different people, make different choices. However, human nature and human drives are not all that heterogeneous. Hence, when choosing from the menu of 'possibly usable alternatives' offered by the accumulated technology, human groups – individuals, business firms and states – tend to make choices which are not all that diverse. It is this which gives a fair degree of universality to the 'directioned' nature of history. Consider, by way of illustration, the way in which countries of the Third World seek to 'modernize' – to become like the 'advanced' industrial countries; or Eda Saburō, the leader of Japan's Socialist Party in the 1960s, setting his targets for Japan: 'an American standard of living, the Welfare State of a Sweden, the culture of a France'.

Let me give some examples of the similarity in choices among 'usable alternatives' – of the way, that is, in which the accumulation of technology conditions but does not determine social structure.

Mankind (or at least that part of mankind which lives in Europe, America and Japan) has accumulated the technology necessary for making splendid television sets. In some respects the organization for using that technology – the business firm – is everywhere very much the same. The machines used, the layout of the workplace, the staging of the productive process most obviously, but also organizational structure, the division of labour among production workers, foremen, drivers, researchers and developers, telephone operators and directors, even the accounting methods and the organigrams of the production department and the sales department look very much alike in Germany, in China, America or Japan. But nevertheless, in some dimensions of very great importance to society – whether the labour market is in continuous flux or there is something like lifetime employment; the wage differentials corresponding to different roles in the division of labour, the balance of rights between the shareholders who provide capital and the workers who provide labour; whether the business firm is generally viewed as a kind of community or as a piece of property of the shareholders – in all these things there can be very wide differences amongst societies. That is one example of the way in which technology constrains but does not completely determine social outcomes.

There are some who believe that eventually social institutions will be so conditioned by the need to make efficient use of technology that the world will eventually become more or less homogenized. It is certainly not difficult to believe. One of the important consequences of technological advance is the spectacular cheapening of transport and communication of the last forty years. The markets for raw materials, the markets for manufactured products, especially electrical and electronic products and automobiles, even markets for insurance, education and medical services have been very largely internationalized. One consequence is that, within individual countries, the conflict between those who gain from foreign trade and those who seek protection has grown fiercer. It may be that the protectionists will gain the upper hand and the process will slow down, but the prospects are that this process of the internationalization of markets, continuously spurred by further developments in communication and transport, will continue at a growing pace.

In most kinds of markets it seems as if it is not American-style capitalism with its emphasis on individual freedom and self-realization, but Japanese-style capitalism with its emphasis on group cooperation and the setting of common (national or industry-wide) objectives which has the competitive edge – not the capitalism which emphasizes short-term gains, but that which seeks market dominance over the longer term. In any open market competition, as a result of processes of natural selection, the most efficient system, that is to say the Japanese system – should become dominant, and thus become the universal world system. At least that seems like a plausible argument.

Unlike biological natural selection, moreover, which operates through the single mechanism of genetic inheritance, the natural selection processes of social institutions involve a dual mechanism. One is, indeed, the perishing of weak organizations and the survival of stronger ones. The other is revitalization – raising the efficiency of existing organizations through adaptive learning. One can see both mechanisms at work in the American automobile industry. On the one hand, while American automobile manufacturers are closing factories at a fast rate the investments of Japanese companies are opening new ones. But at the same time, the American and British firms remaining in the industry are rushing to adopt Japanese-style quality circles, total quality control, and just-in-time manufacturing methods; they are building security into their labour contracts, creating employee councils, and establishing stable relations with their suppliers. Things have even got to the point where the great success-story hero Iacocca is being criticized for the size of his salary.

Nevertheless, it would be a mistake to jump to the conclusion that, because of what has happened in the last ten years, by the year 2030 the whole world will have converged on Japanese-type capitalism. Quite apart from the possibility of a surge in nationalist protectionism, the Japanese people's own value system might change. They might begin to value individual freedom and self-assertion more than the satisfactions of group cooperation; the number of Japanese who feel more admiration for an Iacocca-type hero than for the austere, ascetic industrialist of the older Japanese generation, like Dokō, may increase. As a consequence the efficiency of Japanese-style organizations may diminish. All of which is to say one must never forget that the choices people make among the 'usable alternatives' are inevitably infused with judgements of value.

Proposition 4: Technology and values

But are values not, themselves, partly formed by technology? In the Japan of a hundred years ago when the technologies of agriculture and of industry were best adapted to family production, words like 'the ancestors', the *ie* (the family, 'the house of...' as in 'the House of Windsor'), 'the ways of the family', the *yome-san* (the imported bride of the eldest son, mistress-to-be of the household) were common everyday words, and duties towards the *ie* were at the core of everyday ethics. But as technology has vastly outgrown the ability of small family units to cope and large corporations have come to dominate the economy, both the vocabulary and the reality have changed. These words are rarely heard in today's society of dependent employees. This is but one illustration of the way in which technology influences values and ethical systems, and how changes in the one have a direct causal relationship with changes in the other.

In broad terms one can say the following: there is a distinct pattern in the *degree* to which social institutions are subject to the constraints of technology. Most closely constrained is the division of labour in the production process: next most closely constrained is the legal property structure which facilitates that division of labour. Next in the ever-widening circles of constraint come the family system and the education system, while least directly influenced of all is the value system, religion and the arts.

This is not to say that religion and the arts are uninfluenced by the accumulation of technology. Marxists have a clear and simple story about this: religion and the arts are simply part of the superstructure which maintains the hegemony of the ruling class by justifying the unequal distribution of wealth and power entailed by the production system and the property system. (The myth that any American can become an Iacocca; the message shared both by Christianity and by Salvationist Buddhism that it is the poor that are privileged in the afterlife.) But highly mobile fluid industrial societies lose their homogeneity; neither state nor church have the power to impose narrow ideas of justice and morality on the whole society. There are other mechanisms much more important than the efforts of the ruling class to maintain their position which link on the one hand the accumulation of technology, and on the other the directions of change in morality, ideology and the arts. One might suggest two.

1 As the Analects say: 'When clothing and food suffice, then can Men come to know the *li*' – that all embracing concept variously translated as rites, as propriety, as ethics. As technological advance brings greater affluence there is a steady increase in the number of specialists in the *li* – professional artists and musicians, professional teachers of philosophy or of the history of thought. With the improvement of communications and transport these specialists increasingly go to study in other countries, go to international congresses. There they mix with fellow specialists whose education has been conditioned by different social systems and different cultural traditions. They come to form a kind of international professional quasi-community. One sees in formation a kind of global professional culture divorced from the cultural traditions of particular states or ethnic groups. This process is most advanced in fields where language is not important and there is a high degree of commercialization of the products the specialists produce – in fashion and advertising for instance. It is at its weakest in fields like philosophy where language is all-important and even the most famous can sell only a few thousand books. But even among philosophers for instance, there is today a similarity in the topics they tackle, their methods, and their criteria of truth, whether they be in China or Germany or the United States, which would have been unthinkable a hundred years ago.

2 In affluent societies the struggle for survival becomes less severe. The 'coming to know *li* when clothing and food suffice' phenomenon affects the ordinary citizen too. Just think how our world of birth control and anaesthetics, a world of lifespans approaching eighty years in which children grow up with little confrontation with death, differs from the world of a hundred years ago when most people who reached the age of twenty had had the experience of seeing brothers and sisters dying

before their eyes, and often in great pain. It would be strange if there were not some general change in sensibilities. The cruel atrocities inflicted by Wellington's troops in the Peninsular War at the beginning of the nineteenth century were not reproduced on the same scale in any of Britain's subsequent wars. It is unlikely that Japan's Self-Defence Forces could be persuaded to behave with the same ruthlessness as their grandfathers showed when they 'moved into' China fifty years ago.

Proposition 5: The cumulation of social technology

Along with a tendency towards more 'tender' sensibilities there is also an accumulation of social technology. It may not be so obvious as accumulation of material technology, but it should not be underestimated. Consider the proliferation of regulations – the difference between the first publication in Japan of the 'Compendium of the Six Laws' and the mass of publications one finds in Japanese bookstalls today – the Six Laws for Agriculture, the Six Laws for Education, the Six Laws for Small and Medium Industries and all the rest. It is not simply a matter of quantitative change, but also of progress in quality – the reduction in ambiguity, the specification of various alternative contingencies, the diversification of administrative devices. 'You call that Progress!' is the likely response, not only of anarchists but also of the free marketist followers of Hayek, Friedman and Thatcher. But they are surely wrong. No one in his right mind would maintain that every bit of these accumulated social technologies contributes either to efficiency or to human happiness. But it is equally undeniable that over the last century, in the production of public goods like health and education systems and defence, and in the maintenance of order, and in the concern for fairness, and hence for the minimization of conflict, there has been a steady process of social invention.

Proposition 6: The formation of international professional quasi-communities

The increasing density of administration and (provided that the pursuit of self-interest by the administrators can be kept under control) its increasing efficiency, is not confined to individual countries. There has been a vast growth of international organizations and international administration. It is only seventy years ago, in the early 1920s, when Nitobe Inazō and Maeda Tamon went to what was then, for Japanese, the strange and distant town of Geneva to become the first Japanese members of an international organization. Today, the number of Japanese in international organizations are counted in their hundreds, and soon in their thousands, and two of the United Nations organizations are headed by Japanese nationals. These organizations provide the focal point for many of what I call international professional quasi-communities. Meteorologists, experts in infectious diseases, maritime administrators, members of voluntary organizations dealing with refugees, environmentalists – all create their own transnational organizations and develop common value systems.

Proposition 7: International law

One of the most important of these professional quasi-communities is that of the lawyers and international relations experts with the International Court of Justice as their focal point. There is a slow development of a consensus about the universal principles of justice – principles transcending the traditional value systems of individual countries – to be applied in the settlement of cross-border disputes, between individuals, between business firms, and between countries. It is the slow development of this consensus which is creating the basis for global order, for international rule by law.

Proposition 8: Gleams of the emergence of 'world government'

Within individual countries there is one indispensable condition for judges to do their job of objectively adjudicating disputes and reaching acceptable decisions as to who is right and who is wrong, who wins and who loses. It is the existence of a police force capable of intervening when disputes reach the level of violence and capable of ensuring, if necessary by physical coercion, that the judgements of courts are carried out – the existence of a policing system which forestalls violence before it happens and discourages anybody from taking judgements lightly. The realization that this principle, demonstrated in the history of every individual country, means when applied to international affairs that dispute resolution needs not merely an international court and an international law but also an international policing system – that realization has been steadily growing among political leaders since the nineteenth century. That much is evidenced in the uncertain steps towards such a goal which the world has produced – the Hague convention of 1899, the founding of the League of Nations and, in 1945, the creation of the Security Council of the United Nations.

Proposition 9: The evolution of consciousness

I wrote 'that realization has been steadily growing'. It is not too difficult to predict that it will grow further for there is a clear interrelationship between this growing realization and the trends of change discussed above, rooted in the accumulation of technological knowledge – and of the capital goods in which that knowledge is embodied. Both are products of the evolution of human society.

THE ODD POPULARITY OF CYCLICAL THEORIES

I like not to consider myself a particularly dogmatic person, but the above propositions about social evolution seem to me so patently obvious, it is odd that there can still be cyclical theorists in the world and that, indeed their books, not mine, should become best sellers. A good example is Paul Kennedy's *Rise and Fall of Nations*. His account of the rise and fall of hegemonic powers, especially his description of the rise and decline of the Pax Brittanica and the Pax Americana in the last two centuries is persuasive and backed by a wealth of historical detail, as one would expect from such an able analytical historian. But the conclusion seems to be that there is an invariably repeated pattern. To maintain its power the hegemonic country inevitably runs down its economic strength; eventually it is overtaken by a more vigorous power riding on the strength of a more vital economy and the locus of hegemony shifts. The suggestion is that this is a kind of historical law many times repeated in the past and bound to be repeated in the future. It is not surprising that the book elicited great interest in both the United States and Japan. 'So America's problems are not temporary troubles, but signs of a secular decline. So where is the next hegemonic power coming from? Which is the most likely candidate, if not Japan?' With dire anxiety on one side of the Pacific and happy cheerfulness on the other it became a popular theme of the intellectual and the not-so-intellectual magazines; earnest articles discussed the exact scenarios through which the law that economic power must eventually turn itself into military power would be enacted, and the form that an eventual Pax Japonica might take.

What the Kennedy thesis, in its usual interpretation, ignores is the process of secular evolution in international affairs. Think back to the time when Britain was establishing its hegemony, to 1863 for instance, when a British fleet shelled Kagoshima in retaliation for the murder of an Englishman. Until the turn of the century, in Asia and in Africa, it was possible for Britain to send warships and troops anywhere to protect – and advance – its interests – provided it avoided frontal confrontations with other great powers. Today the United States, with a destructive power thousands of times greater than Britain ever possessed, gave sufficient importance to 'international opinion' to deem it prudent to get the support of the Security Council before it sought to move against Iraq. America did, for reasons which world opinion could see as having a certain grain of justification, move unilaterally against Grenada in 1983 and against Panama in 1989, but it did not venture to attack Cuba, its enemy neighbour for thirty years. There it was not only world opinion, but also the existence of another superpower, the Soviet Union, which provided an important constraint – a constraint which no longer applied at the time of the Gulf War. Think also of the ending of the Gulf War. It is said that the reactions provoked by the CNN's worldwide broadcasts showing fleeing Iraqi soldiers being mercilessly gunned down by American planes were one factor in the decision to cease fire – one more illustration of the link between technology and formation of 'world opinion'. We have come a long way from the London *Times* printing the first dispatches from the Crimean War in 1855 or even from the days when news of the Japanese troops' rape of Nanking gradually seeped out through primitive film taken by American missionaries. Nowadays, the formation of a first-reaction world opinion takes twenty-four hours.

There are other ways in which hegemonic countries become less able effectively to deploy military force. One factor is the ability of even small countries to acquire weapons of a destructiveness unthinkable half a century ago and, if cornered, to inflict unacceptable damage even on a hegemonic power. Another is the way in which the Western ideology of nationalism and ethnic self-determination has spread throughout the world. Both Vietnam and Afghanistan show that the attempt to maintain colonial rule by military strength – albeit nominally through 'aid' to a local independent government – is no longer an easy proposition.

Given these secular changes in the conditions for exercising hegemonic power it is hard to see how anyone can still hold to the notion that there are unchanging historical laws which govern the rise and fall of great powers.

EVALUATING EVOLUTION

The reader – let us imagine a reader who might call himself Mr Realist – might well answer as follows: All right Mr Idealist, let us for the moment accept your evolutionary argument and let us accept your definition of the way the world is going in the long-term towards a situation in which there is either a peaceful settlement of disputes through a body like the Security Council or, if it is necessary to use military force to deal with transgressors against the international rules, in which a monopoly of that coercive force is held by such an international organization. But that is a state of affairs belonging to the far far distant future; something whose shape one can only dimly perceive way over the horizon. Look at the world today. Look at the way nationalism is flaring up in violent manifestations all over the world. Do you really believe that in the near future nation-states are going to do what the Japanese Daimyō did in 1870 when they surrendered their sovereignty and military independence to the central government? Do you think that nation-states are going to give up their sovereignty in military matters in favour of an international organization? Are they going to accept national emasculation? An independent army is the quintessential symbol of national sovereignty. It will take centuries of your kind of evolution before states are prepared to give it up. That will only happen when the integration of the world's economies, when the erosion of national sovereignty in favour of international organization, has proceeded in the non-military dimensions to a far greater degree than is forseeable in the near future.

Meanwhile, until that happens, the only way in which any kind of semblance of international order can be maintained among armed nation-states is either through the traditional mechanisms of the balance of power or through the coordinating control of a hegemon. That is why one should, for instance, welcome the thinking behind the Pentagon's long-term strategy document which was leaked to the press in March 1992 – the document which said that, as the only remaining superpower, 'the United States must accept its role in the maintenance of international order and ensure that it is always prepared to act alone when coordinated international action is not possible or there is an urgent need for a speedy response'.[1]

What is wrong with that? Particularly since the same document goes on to say that the United States must 'take full account of the interests of the other advanced industrial countries' when acting alone. Otherwise there would be a danger of 'upsetting' the existing political and economic order.

Just think back to history, Mr Realist might continue. The unification of China under the first Han emperor, of Britain and of France – the creation of unified kingdoms where once power was decentralized among endlessly warring fiefs. Or think back to the two-and-a-half centuries of peaceful order created by the Tokugawa, bringing an end to the sixteenth-century internecine wars. Every time the pattern is the same: the centralizing force – king, emperor, shogun – is someone who has won out over his rivals in the struggle for power. He wins out but, recognizing that the feudal barons still have the power to 'upset the political and economic order' he accepts that he cannot wield his supreme power in an arbitrary way. He asks for their cooperation. The famous Magna Carta was exactly that; an agreement on the rules by which King and Barons would constrain each others' power. From this bargaining emerges organizations – parliaments – to set and enforce the rules, and out of these grows the rule of law and the institutions of democracy.

If this is the common pattern in the creation of individual nation-states why should the future creation of a global state proceed any differently? And what would be wrong with that anyway?

A lot would be wrong with it, replies Mr Idealist. Your 'realism' is not only over-pessimistic; it also overlooks important aspects of history. First of all, unification through the power of a single hegemon is not by any means the invariate pattern. Think of the establishment of the Meiji Government in Japan. It was a coalition of four powerful fiefs which overthrew the existing hegemon and supported the creation of a formally absolute imperial government subsequently transformed over a couple of decades into a constitutional monarchy.

Nor should one overlook the development of technology. A lot has happened in the four hundred years that separates us from the battle of Sekigahara which confirmed Tokugawa supremacy, and it is not only that the muskets the Portugese introduced to Japan have given way to the hydrogen bomb. In the time it took for the great Lord Maeda to march post-haste from his castle town in Kanazawa to meet Hideyoshi in Osaka, Secretary of State James Baker could make several trips between Washington and Jerusalem and have long conversations on the plane with a dozen other foreign secretaries while on the way.

Nor should one overlook the evolution of ideas, the evolution of man. At the time of the battle of Sekigahara, in the reign of Louis XIV, the world did not contain people who called themselves 'pacifists'. There was no such concept as 'the rule of law'. One should not overlook the importance of the existence of a growing number of people who can think beyond the duty of loyalty to nation-state with military force as its expression. If you are fond of history, continues Mr Idealist, what about this for a historical fact? In 1946 the United States Congress passed a resolution the sense of which was that American military forces which, it was anticipated, would be assigned to duty with the United Nations as a result of the progressive implementation of Chapter 7 of the UN Charter, could be committed to United Nations peace enforcement activities by a simple vote of the UN Security Council, without the need for any further reference to Congress.

Do you not find that astonishing? The contrast with the self-assertive world-management stance of contemporary American policy could hardly be more marked. You could, I suppose, put it down to the euphoric generosity of a nation that had just won a major war. But, continues Mr Idealist, I think that would be wrong. At the end of the Second World War, the world really had evolved to the point at which the establishment of some kind of collective security mechanism, depending on the conciliar mechanisms prescribed in the United Nations Charter, had reached the realm of realistic possibility. For a brief while there were real and active efforts to create the necessary institutions. But with the intensification of mistrust between the US and the USSR these efforts came to an end. Everything that has happened to the United Nations since – from its early efforts at peace-keeping operations to its work to reduce infant mortality in Africa – has been conditioned by that Cold War. Now that the world has been released from the shackles of the Cold War, why can we not take up once again those efforts to create a real collective security system? Far better that than to wait for the long-term evolution of American hegemony – the final resolution of the contradictions in the *beikon wazai* system, the system based on 'American spirit and Japanese money', (as the Japanese wits call it in memory of the days, a century ago, when their ancestors talked of *wakon yōsai* – 'Japanese spirit and Western technology').

The Gulf War to which this jibe refers in fact provided an illustration of the concrete choices implied by the respective positions of Mr Realist and Mr Idealist. Should the measures against Iraq be United Nations-led, or should they be American-led? After having a look in Chapter 7 at the opposition between these two approaches to international action, we shall return in Chapter 9 to the alternative realist and idealist scenarios for the future. To summarize the position taken in this book in one sentence: if only Mr Idealist and Mr Realist would cooperate, then it should be possible not simply to sit back and watch what Mr Realist calls a 'natural process' but to take positive efforts to influence that evolution and bring it closer to Mr Idealist's ideals.

Before that, in the next chapters, I want to look at what one might call the pre-history of internationalist thinking. What historical truth is there in the words I put into the mouth of Mr Idealist:

> At the end of the Second World War, the world really had evolved to the point at which the establishment of some kind of collective security mechanism, depending on the conciliar mechanisms prescribed in the United Nations Charter, had reached the realm of realistic possibility.

2 The early stirrings of internationalism

ELEMENTS OF CIVIL ORDER

To be sure, the concept 'international order based on law' is not entirely clear. It might be useful to propose a rough definition, before getting on to the main business of this chapter: tracing in outline the historical development of the institutions of international order and of thinking about them.

There are three main elements involved:

1 An international law sufficiently widely recognized to exercise moral constraint on behaviour.
2 An organization which can give interpretations of that body of law, and oversee its evolution – currently, for example, the International Court of Justice or GATT panels.
3 An administrative organ which can first of all enforce the decisions of the courts, and second, prevent potential frictions and disputes from becoming court matters – or prevent open disputes from turning to violence – by offering mediation, enforcing arbitration and occasionally seeking what is known in Japan as a 'political solution' – i.e., one which sacrifices principle in favour of achieving peace by recognizing the realities of power.

Even so defined, 'an international rule-of-law order' is still an elastic concept. At least four dimensions of elasticity may be discerned:

1 The relative importance attached to the three elements listed above. Which is most important for the maintenance of civil order within Japan: the courts or the police? There is obviously a difference between civil and criminal matters, but there can hardly be any doubt as to whether a strike by the judges or a strike by the police would have more destabilizing consequences. Much the same applies internationally. A good illustration of this is in the statistics of the postwar years. From the Second World War until 1988 the International Court of Justice had exactly sixty disputes referred to it. Over the same period the Security Council discussed over one thousand.[1]

2 The second dimension is the degree to which states are prepared to accept international law or the mediation of international bodies, or alternatively seek to retain their total freedom of action in pursuit of their own interests or to promote the diffusion of their national ideology. Chinese historians speak of history as an endless succession of periods of order (*ji*) and periods of anarchy (*ran*), but truly anarchic situations are relatively rare in international relations these days. Even during world wars some of the most basic rules of international order such as those spelt out in the seventeenth century by the 'father of international' law, Grotius[2] – rules about the treatment of prisoners, about ensuring the safe return of ambassadors to their own countries, etc. – are observed. It is only cases like that of Iran after the Khomeni revolution, Albania in its former isolation, or North Korea, that one finds examples of total rejection of any international obligation, and this rejection is usually highly localized and not long-lasting.

When I wrote in the previous chapter about the 'evolution' of international order it was primarily this dimension that I had in mind – the gradual expansion of these original minimal norms of international conduct, and, with that expansion, *pari passu*, the gradual erosion of national sovereignties – of the freedom of foreign policy action.

3 The third dimension concerns the locus of the power to create and enforce international law, and in the following table this is cross-tabulated with:
4 The extent to which there is institutional development of the rule of law through the cumulation of precedent and the elucidation of jurisprudential principles.

The point of the cross-tabulation is to make what one might call a 'typology of orders'. The lines in this table have to be accepted as artificial discontinuities in what are, in effect, seamless dimensions, blurred distinctions. At exactly what point the primitive hegemonic power of ancient Rome came to be a predictable and institutionalized hegemony, and from what point it turned into a system of imperial order reinforced by 'tradition', is a matter over which historians could doubtless argue with enthusiasm for weeks, but for our purposes we can leave the delights of 'periodization' to historians, provided that we are convinced the tendencies of this transition are clear. The same applies to the transition from a primitive to an institutionalized balance of power order. If one is considering the succession of alliance treaties in nineteenth-century Europe, or the way in which in US–USSR relations, particularly after the Cuban crisis, there was an institutionalization of tension-reducing measures like the hotline and the reduction of nuclear tests, it is much less interesting for a social scientist to ask from what date was the transition than to seek to elucidate the mechanisms which underly the change – how it is linked with the interests of other countries, with questions of ideology and non-material national objectives for instance.

The agent capable of: defining rules; enforcing rules; imposing settlements of disputes	No accumulation of precedents, no development of jurisprudence; *ad hoc* settlement of conflict by power balance	Through the cumulation of precedents, the outcomes of conflict become gradually more predictable		
		The motive for accepting the arbitration of international authorities and submitting to regulation is:		
		Fear of military or other sanctions	Because submission has become customary and traditional, and the impulse to defy authority is weak	Because the regulation is perceived as applying rational (or if not rational, alterable) rules, and order itself is valued
A single great power	Primitive hegemonic order	Hegemonic order	Imperial order	
Fluctuating combination of a plurality of powers	Primitive balance of power order	Institutionalized balance of power order		
A designated plurality of powers acting according to institutionalized rules				Oligarchic rule of law order
All countries which accept the obligation to observe the rules				Democratic (or nation-cratic) rule of law order

The entries on the right hand side – 'oligarchic', 'democratic', can best be illustrated with respect to the United Nations. The present Charter gives the UN an oligarchic structure in so far as the great powers have permanent seats and vetos on the Security Council, but is a democratic or nation-cratic, one country–one vote organization as far as the General Assembly is concerned.

The argument between Mr Realist and Mr Idealist in the last Chapter can be plotted on this typology. Mr Realist's argument goes thus: hegemony inevitably develops into a more rule-bound, more predictable imperial order. Consider nineteenth-century Russia, Prussia and Japan. In all of them we see a transition from absolute monarchy to some kind of constitutional monarchy, through the creation of national parliaments, albeit with limited participation and limited powers. A hundred years later these have all grown into flourishing democracies. That evolution on a national scale can be expected on an international scale too. There is a lot to be said for a road to world order which accepts the establishment of an American hegemony as the starting point. Mr Idealist, on the other hand, says that we cannot afford to wait. Only mobilize the necessary political will and the world has already matured to the point at which it could move forward into a general rule-of-law order. The argument is one we shall come back to.

One final word about this chart. This is entirely a classification of *inter*national orders. Nowhere in it appears the possibility of a *trans*national global order. It does not chart, that is to say, the steady growth of global society and the emergence of transnational world-government organs to catalyse and foster that growth. The reason for its absence is solely in order not to complicate the chart, not at all because of any underestimation of the importance of such developments. They were the subject of a very interesting symposium held twenty years ago which examined in detail the multiple processes which could be said to add up to 'the growth of a world society', a symposium still worth reading.[3] Since then, these germs of world society – the growth of transnational corporations, the globalization of financial markets, what I called earlier the formation of international professional quasi-communities, the increasing volume of representations to the United Nations by transnational NGOs and other groups – have all become more clearly marked. Note that all these developments, while on the one hand providing glimmers of the possibility of a global, transnational social order, at the same time are factors which can serve to stimulate the growth of an international order in the present.

THE PRE-HISTORY OF WORLD ORDER

Both as history of thought and as institutional history, the movement towards an international rule-of-law order is a history of Western societies in the last three centuries. For all the reasons explained in the last chapter this is by no means unconnected with the fact that these were – at least until recently – the focal centres for the development of technology and economic organization. This is not to say that there have not been contributions from other non-Western nations over the last century. Consider the contribution to the institutionalization of third party arbitration as a means of preventing or ending disputes which Japan made in accepting Theodore Roosevelt's arbitration in the Treaty of Portsmouth (1905) – an act which won Roosevelt a Nobel prize and, because of popular outrage at the settlement, temporarily lost the Japanese government control over domestic politics.

At the beginning of this process – in the fifteenth and sixteenth centuries – those who spoke of the need for some kind of international organization all shared some kind of nostalgia for the Roman Empire – the system which until a thousand years before had succeeded in maintaining a stable imperial order in a unified Europe. This is not surprising, given that the notion of the independent nation-state – a state with a ruler who claimed the right to exercise sovereignty – and the idea of a Europe divided among such co-existing states basically developed only in the sixteenth century. Until then military conquerors who sought to establish hegemony aspired to the title of Holy Roman Emperor and, until the middle of the fifteenth century, that Holy Roman Emperor had a clear mission – the expulsion by Christian Europe of the invading Muslim Turks.

There is an interesting parallel with the way in which in Japan of the twelfth to sixteenth centuries, Japan's warring feudal lords aspired to receive from the Emperor (corresponding to the Pope) the title of Shogun 'Barbarian-Quelling Generalissimo'. There is a similarity too in the way in which the extirpation of Christianity became a legitimating element underpinning Tokugawa hegemony. One difference, however, is that whereas the peaceful stabilization of borders between fief and fief took place in the seventeenth century *because of* the hegemony of the Tokugawa family, the consolidation of frontiers – of the boundaries of sovereignty – in Europe came as a result of recognition of the impossibility of restoring European unity. Even then, the subsequent rise of nationalism and the idea that the *nation*-state was the only proper form of government increased the instability of frontiers. Franco-German wars over the possession of Alsace continued into this century and, the current dramas of Eastern Europe apart, even in a Western Europe which is seeking to move towards unity, the Austrian–Italian border is still a source of disputes.

There were a number of intellectuals – Dante[4] one of the most famous – who urged the need for some kind of international parliament with representatives from the various nations, but most of them were concerned less with the maintenance of peace than with the diffusion of their own monarch's influence or with organizing united action to beat back the Turks. Most people thought that war was an essential element in human life; Machiavelli, for instance,[5] would not accept the distinction medieval theologians made between just and unjust wars, and saw war as the natural means by which

Princes assert themselves and expand their sphere of power. That was basically also the position of Grotius, mentioned earlier as the 'father of international law', whose work was devoted to making a compilation of the emerging rules of war.

Of a markedly different colouring was a work published two years before Grotius's – the Nouveau Cynee of Crucé.[6] Crucé insisted on the urgency of creating some kind of institutional order, not to conduct wars decently but to prevent wars from arising. What is more, unlike any of his predecessors, he proposed an international organ which would embrace not only the countries of Europe but also Turkey, Ethiopia, China and Persia. Representatives should gather in Venice; they should decide matters by majority votes, and if the necessity arose they should punish countries which did not conform to the majority decision by sending an allied army against them. The Pope should be the president of the assembly and the Turkish representative the vice-president (in recognition of Constantinople's position as the second city of Rome, capital of the Eastern Empire).

In the century after Crucé the Protestant tradition gave rise to another important strain of Christian pacifism most prominently exemplified in the Quakers, and proposals for the creation of international organizations became more frequent. William Penn (of Pennsylvania) is the best-known writer in this tradition.[7] His detailed plans for international organization were highly egalitarian. Meetings should be held at a round table which had no head and no foot; there should be secret ballots so that large countries could not pressure small countries, and so on.

Penn was a Quaker and Quakers in principle rejected all forms of violence, so that Penn's book has a particular relevance to the 'peace controversy' in today's Japan. Can those who love peace actually secure it by a total abstention from violence? Or is some kind of physical coercion against those who destroy peace and destroy order always necessary? In Penn's plan the exercise of military force was not only seen as necessary – it was even to be made compulsory, provided that the decision to take such action was approved by a 75 per cent majority. How could a Quaker have arrived at such a compromise? Hinsley's[8] explanation that it reflects Penn's over-optimistic assessment of the rationality of men seems plausible. Once a system which unfailingly punishes aggression has been established, no sovereign would dare to aggress. Hence there would be no need actually to use force. Thus Penn was able to reconcile an international system for armed intervention with his Quaker pacifism.

THE RATIONAL MONARCH

Half a century after Penn, Rousseau[9] took up the question of international organization, and from Rousseau onwards the question of international organization was inextricably intertwined with questions of domestic politics, with the struggle between absolute monarchy, republicanism, and notions of democracy based on doctrines of human rights.

When Crucé was writing in the seventeenth century before the English Revolution there were few people to challenge absolute monarchy. Indeed, according to Crucé, one of the major advantages of establishing an international order would be to make internal governance easier; it would eliminate the ever-present threat to internal peace which derived from the fact that subversive elements could always count on help from their sovereign's enemies abroad.

Rousseau, Kant and those who followed them – Saint-Simon in France and Bentham in England[10] – turned this argument on its head. Bentham's starting point was his firm belief that 'there are properly no other criminals than the heads of nations; the subjects are always honest'. Only when the government of individual countries reflected the popular will would international peace be preserved. Once that happy state was achieved, the sort of international organization envisaged by Crucé and by Penn would become unnecessary. Bentham, like Kant, believed all that would be needed would be an international court to internationalize the rule of law.

When in the first half of the nineteenth century there first appeared what might be called a peace *movement*, that is to say organizations with a formal constitution (formed in 1816 in Britain, in 1828 in the United States, with the two organizations combining in a joint congress in London in 1843), it fully accepted these ideas of Bentham and of his loyal disciple James Mill.[11] These were organizations overwhelmingly dominated by Quakers – Quakers who had abandoned Penn's belief in the need for sanctions and returned to the basic Quaker principle of non-resistance towards violence. A resolution of the Universal Peace Congress roundly declared: 'The Society does *not* propose to have the International Tribunal invested with power to enforce its decision but to have the efficacy of those decisions depend solely on their justice and the honour of nations.'[12]

The *Times* jeeringly recorded its scepticism:

> We have often commented on the fanaticism of association as a distinguishing characteristic of modern times; but of all the developments of this disease which it has been our lot to handle, there is not one that can bear an instant's comparison with the vagaries and delusions of those unhappy individuals who. . . profess no less than the total abolition, throughout the terrestrial globe, of war. . . [and] all physical compulsion on the part of any civil power or authority whatsoever. . .[13]

While these debates about the possibilities of international organization were increasing in frequency and vigour there was also some development, at least on the European continent, of institutions designed to solve or forestall international disputes. When the leaders of Europe gathered in Vienna in 1815 after Napoleon's attempt to establish a French hegemony in Europe had been finally defeated, they had three principal objectives in mind. First, how to prevent France from recovering its strength and once again becoming a threat to the rest of Europe. Second, how to prevent disputes amongst the victor countries – particularly border disputes – from threatening their unity. Third – something on which Alexander I of Russia was fervently insistent and which sprang from the realization that what had turned Europe upside down was not only France's military power but the subversive ideas of the French Revolution – how could one prevent the spread of dangerous thoughts, how could one ensure that, as one aspect of collective security, monarchical governments threatened by subversion could receive organized help from their allies.

The Congress of Vienna and the treaty which resulted from it were in one sense epoch-making. Whereas, hitherto, the balance of power had been preserved by bilateral or trilateral treaties, here was acknowledged the principle of the collective responsibility of the five great powers towards Europe as a community, and here, at least in a primitive form, were plans for organizational commitments to carry out that responsibility.

They were, however, primitive. One of the most urgent matters was the settlement of boundary disputes. All current disputes were settled, but whereas it was explicitly granted that each country had the *right* to defend the frontiers so arrived at, the attempt to make equally explicit the *duty* of all powers to respect those frontiers finally failed. In the Treaty of Chaumont in the same year the statesmen of the great powers agreed to hold periodic meetings – congresses – even in times of peace, to discuss issues which could lead to dispute. But they did nothing to establish a permanent secretariat for such congresses.

There were, in fact, three such congresses in the years up to 1822, but they failed to reach agreement, particularly on plans for combating revolutionary ideologies. In particular, at the time of the Spanish war, the British were resolutely opposed to the notion of Russian troops going to Spain as part of an allied army, and did their best, as part of their strategy of resisting Russian influence, to dismantle the whole congress structure. In the event, as Canning, the British Foreign Secretary, had planned, nineteenth-century politics returned from attempts to build a collective security structure to the politics of separate alliances. Which is not to say that the visions of 1815 evaporated entirely. Even if congresses, attended by kings and prime ministers were held only twice more after 1822, conferences to discuss particular issues at the ambassadorial or foreign minister level were held no less than seventeen times, and several times very successfully defused potentially explosive situations.

At the same time it seems reasonable to say that the constraining power of these conferences – their ability to restrict the freedom of action of individual powers, held back, however much on sufferance, by the need to respect decisions of the conference – seems to have been a good deal greater in the second than in the first half of the century. Russia's policy towards

Turkey after 1856 and Britain's colonial policy in Africa after 1885 are examples.

INTERNATIONAL ORGANIZATION FOR PEACE

Parallel to this barely discernable 'evolution', there was a development of the peace movement and of the movement for the establishment of international organizations – a striking development indeed, compared with the first half of the nineteenth century. It had three main characteristics.

In the first place the movement became internationalized. Hodgson-Pratt, one of the promoters of the international movement, attempted to establish branches in Japan and China too. He did not in the end succeed, but his and others' efforts led to the convening of a Universal Peace Congress in 1889 and in every second year thereafter.

Secondly, the hitherto dominant Quaker tendency within the movement combined with a new pacifism which made socialist ideas its starting point and which urged that democratic reforms in domestic policies were an essential precondition for the creation of international organizations which could guarantee the maintenance of peace. The assumption that existing state structures were incapable of peaceable cooperation became, from the 1860s onwards, shared by the majority of those engaged in the peace movement. That movement, by and large, was a movement of people who were content to be and to be seen as anti-Establishment elements, members of a perennial opposition who clung to pure ideals. At the same time there emerged from, as it were, inside the Establishment, people who shared their concerns with international order but stood aloof from the movement activists. These gradually became more influential. Chairs of international law were established in European universities and specialist international lawyers became active in urging the need for a development of an international order.

The third important element were middle-class intellectuals of what one might call a liberal democratic caste, who believed in the possibility of the gradual reform of society through appeal to the bourgeois conscience. The International Association for Arbitration and Peace,[14] a central organization of the 1880s, a body with the declared intention of 'adjusting their proposals to considerations of practicality', was a typical expression of such a tendency. In the 1890s the Inter-Parliamentary Union with its Secretariat, the Inter-Parliamentary Bureau, was organized, and practising politicians came to take part in discussions about the international organizations which needed to be created.

The debate was lively. Was it enough gradually to institutionalize practices of third-party arbitration, or was it necessary to create an international court? If there was to be an international court would there need to be some means, including the use of armed force, for enforcing its judgements, or would its moral authority alone suffice? If there was to be some means of enforcing sanctions would this require an international organization with international civil servants or could it be left to councils of representatives of existing governments? If there was to be an international organization, should it be one which promoted certain principles and ideologies – as, on the right, Alexander I in 1815 urged united action to prevent the spread of revolutionary ideology, or, on the left, as the socialists wanted – an organization for the liberation of the working class? Or should it alternatively observe an iron law of 'non-interference in the internal affairs of states' and confine itself entirely to solving disputes between sovereign nations? By the end of the nineteenth century there was overwhelming consensus in the mainstream that, whether or not there had to be a standing international enforcement agency, an international court capable of enforcing its judgements was essential. The Quakers who continued to argue that moral authority alone would provide all the enforcement needed had by then become a minority.

Gradually these issues got on the agenda of governments and became subjects for negotiations between governments. From the 1870s onwards it became almost standard practice in international treaties to add a clause which nominated a third country ready to act as arbitrator should there be any dispute about the terms of the treaty. It became a logical extension of these practices to consider whether it was necessary to generalize and standardize the practices of arbitration and incorporate them in international law. The first attempt to do this came with the convening of the first Pan-American Conference in 1889, a Conference convened explicitly in order to create an arbitration system. The proposal to establish a permanent international court failed, but agreement was reached on procedures for creating *ad hoc* judicial committees whenever disputes broke out.

Parallel with these movements there were an increasing number of specialist international conferences to secure cooperation in particular fields – the International Postal Union, the standardization of maritime regulations, and so on. According to the Alliance for International Organisations twelve inter-governmental organizations were created in the last quarter of the nineteenth century, but twenty-one in the twenty years which followed. Meanwhile non-governmental international bodies similarly increased; 131 created in the first period and 353 in the second.[15]

That last quarter of the century was a time when what had been an apparently stable balance of power between the five great powers of Europe became a balance marked by increasing tension, largely attributable to the growing economic strength of Germany after the Franco-Prussian War. This provided further stimulus for the creation of institutions to settle international disputes. The first Hague Peace Conference which aimed to extend the Pan-American example on a world scale resulted primarily from the initiative of Nicholas II, concerned about Russia's inability to sustain the military expenditure necessary for its defence against Germany. The second Hague Conference in 1907 saw the participation from Asia of Japan, China and Thailand. It produced the Hague Convention, a codification of the rules of war which had been steadily accumulating since Grotius, and established a system of dispute resolution panels which became the origin of the present International Court of Justice.

These were indeed achievements, but too little and too late. The expectations of the promoters of these developments were dashed by their inability to prevent the outbreak of the First World War.

When, after four years of murderous bloodshed, the representatives of the victor nations came together in Versailles to sign a peace treaty, their main short-sighted preoccupation was with the 'German Problem' just as a hundred years earlier the Congress of Vienna had been preoccupied with the need to prevent the revival of French power. There was, nevertheless, thanks largely to the oratory of President Wilson, a general sense that the world had had enough of war and that it was necessary to build the foundations of a different world. The result, the League of Nations, certainly represented a leap forward from the Hague Conferences, but it too proved to be shot through with contradictions, and incapable of meeting the challenges of the next two decades. A war which cost ten million lives, while on the one hand inducing formal assent to the proposition that a new world had to be created, on the other had the effect of intensifying underlying hatreds and the desire for revenge.

The statesmen who gathered at Versailles were representatives of sovereign states who had not the least intention of permitting any genuine erosion of national sovereignty. The world was only twenty years away from the day when the United States Congress passed an amendment to the Anglo-American Arbitration Treaty which roundly declared that 'matters relating to the honour, territory, foreign policy or domestic affairs of the state shall never be submitted to arbitration'. It was a world in which, as is deeply burned into the folk memory of the Japanese people, the assembled delegates could not muster the generosity to accept the Japanese proposal for a declaration of racial equality in the treaty's preamble, entirely symbolic and lacking in concrete content though the formulation was.

What were the League's weaknesses, and why did it fail? The question is almost as complicated as the question why the Second World War occurred, but it is worth listing a number of points on which historians seem to be agreed.

1 The League's Convention was not a separate document, but embedded in the Treaty whose prime purpose was to punish a defeated Germany. The League, as an organization of the victors, never attained any moral authority *vis-à-vis* a revived Germany.
2 As was shown by the rejection of Japan's proposal to include a declaration of racial equality in the preamble, it was essentially an organization of the Western powers, and as such could exercise only a weak moral authority over – gave only a weak sense of membership in an inter-

national community to – non-Western nations, particularly Japan. (More precisely it weakened the domestic position of those Japanese liberals who sought to enter the Western club – those who, for example, accepted demands from the ILO for the reform of Japanese labour relations as a condition of entry into that organization – and strengthened the hand of the military irreconcilables and the radical nationalist diplomats like Matsuoka Yōsuke.)

3 In spite of the enormous influence of President Wilson's idealism on the formation of the League, the US Congress turned its back on the League and reverted to 'Peace in One Country' isolationism.

4 As a legal institutional structure the Convention's specification of the duties of member nations to participate in the maintenance of collective security was exceedingly ambiguous and weak. International disputes were categorized as those which centred on the interpretation of law and treaties and political disputes. The former were to be dealt with by the International Court of Justice, the latter by the Council of the League. Both the obligation to submit disputes, and the obligation to accept the judgements and mediation of the international court, and the obligation to wait three months before opening hostilities if a dispute opponent refused to accept such judgement, were all specified. But the duty of taking part in collective action for the maintenance of peace was exceedingly ill-specified. Article 16 laid down that any nation which ignored its obligations and went to war in defiance of the Convention was to be 'deemed as having made war on all members of the League' and the League could decide on collective action to punish such transgressors with boycotts, economic sanctions, or armed intervention. But in the first place, a decision on such measures required a unaminimous vote of all countries other than those directly involved in the dispute and second, in the case of armed intervention, the Council had the right only to solicit the participation of member states; it could not require it. A further weakening of enforcement powers came with the resolution of the League Assembly in 1921, which exempted countries which could expect to suffer serious losses from taking part in economic sanctions, and permitted countries simply to withdraw their ambassadors instead of breaking off diplomatic relations.

Altogether the League dealt with sixty-six international disputes. Of these twenty were passed to third party arbitration or to *ad hoc* conciliating conferences. Thirty-five, including four which had escalated to the level of armed hostilities, were brought to resolution. Critics would say that pretty much the same results could have been achieved through traditional diplomatic channels or by the mediation of neighbouring states, but that is a counter-factual which will never be proved.

The problem was the remaining eleven cases. With every repetition of failure the League lost authority and the power to meet the next challenge.

A crucial blow was its weak-kneed response to Japan's aggression in Manchuria, and Japan's withdrawal from the League in 1933 – a serious blow to the League's prestige, given that expulsion from the League was seen by the Convention as the ultimate sanction. The decisive blow came three years later when economic sanctions against Italy for its invasion of Ethiopia were under discussion, and the news leaked out that Britain and France, supposedly the active promoters of these sanctions, were holding secret talks with Italy and about to accept a compromise under which Italy would gain a half of Ethiopian territory.

If only the Americans had not turned their back on the League... *If only* the Versailles Treaty had not been so focused on taking revenge on Germany... *If only* the League had managed to act more decisively over the Manchurian Incident... One can think of all kinds of counter-factual propositions describing the turning point at which things went wrong. But the basic problem was that the delegates who gathered in Versailles had no intention of 'sacrificing' their national sovereignty. 'Sovereignty' was seen by most of them as a unitary concept – something you have or don't have. Deeply imbued with patriotism and national pride, there were few of them who were prepared to accept that any kind of arrangement for international co-existence involves some narrowing of national sovereignty – of the freedom with which representatives of the nation can act – and that the question at issue was just how much erosion of sovereignty was necessary to guarantee collective security.

By the time national delegates gathered in San Francisco to create the United Nations a quarter of a century later, that degree of rational thinking had become somewhat more common; the lesson of recent history was not entirely lost. The Second World War, unlike the first, was literally a *world* war. In the passage from Versailles to San Francisco the world's centre of gravity had moved westward, closer to Japan. It was a quarter-century which had seen not only the massacre of war, but also the Great Depression of the 1930s which demonstrated the mutual inter-dependence of the world's economies. It is not surprising that the United Nations which was then created represented an advance on the League of Nations in many respects.

3 The birth of the United Nations

VISIONS OF THE POSTWAR WORLD

July 1944. The Bretton Woods Conference which established the World Bank and the IMF was nearing its conclusion. The World Bank Committee reached an agreement on capital contributions on 21 July. Russia, which by any GNP calculation was expected to contribute $1,200 million adamantly refused to give more than $900 million, and the other delegates were forced to accept. Many of them directed cold stares at the Russian delegation.

The next day there was a plenary meeting. One of the British delegates, Lionel Robbins, noted in his diary

> this was truly dramatic. Just before it began, the Russians received permission from Moscow to raise their Bank subscription to the figure originally demanded. The secret that they had telegraphed had been well kept, and the relief, the feeling that behind all the barriers of language and discipline they [the Russians] were after all just a little susceptible to the international atmosphere, was so great that the Conference jumped to its feet and cheered to the echo.[1]

'Susceptible to the international atmosphere'. More accurately he should have said international*ist* atmosphere. It was, indeed, a time of great hopes. It was a time when, however strongly nations pressed their own interests there was, usually, enough of a sense of the possibility of building a new kind of postwar world to generate, in the end, a countervailing spirit of compromise. The war with Germany was nearly over and Japanese power in the Pacific was clearly on the ebb. The Bretton Woods Conference was going to establish international organizations which would ensure that there could never be a recurrence of the Great Depression of the 1930s when the beggar-my-neighbour policies of each government combined to worsen the world depression – a depression by no means unconnected with the rise of Hitler and of the military in Japan.

A month later at Dumbarton Oaks the plans were laid for a collective security system which would be more effective and more likely to maintain peace in order to ensure that the world did not once again repeat the history that had gradually emasculated the League and cost millions of lives. As for the exact shape those institutions should take, even Britain and America with their common Anglo-Saxon traditions and their experience as close allies in two world wars, were often at each other's throats – not surprisingly given that the one had decisively lost its position as the world's dominant empire, while the other was daily giving evidence that it had taken over that position. (For a splendid account of how this clash of national interests worked its way out in allied Far Eastern policy see Thorne's masterly history.[2]) Of a different dimension of tenseness were the relations between those two countries and the Soviet Union, the communist country which had allied with the fascist Hitler to carve up Poland. In July 1944 the military competition between the Anglo-Americans and the Russians for the prize of capturing Berlin was reaching ever-greater intensity. Yet, in spite of all this, all three countries recognized that there were common objectives which could only be achieved through compromise. There was a common recognition that, as a means both of ensuring the progress of the world economy and of maintaining peace, powerful international organizations were necessary. There was also a realistic appreciation that the establishment of such institutions meant inevitably some erosion of national sovereignties – that this was no longer a world in which claims for absolute sovereignty could any longer be sustained. In a series of meetings beginning in 1944 they, together with the much less influential Chinese, French and other allies, steadily worked on the details of those plans.

Naturally, the United States took the lead. It was not clear in 1944 that the US would emerge as the sole super power with an atomic bomb, but it was absolutely clear that America, enjoying the fruits of unprecedented economic growth thanks to the war boom, was a far more powerful nation than the Soviet Union, half of whose territory had been destroyed by invading Germans. It was taken as axiomatic that, if America was not exactly going to control the operation of the new institutions, it would at least have a dominant influence. The sacrifice of sovereignty therefore would be less for America than for anybody else, and it is not surprising that consequently the Americans undertook the work of institution building with the greatest enthusiasm. But one should not overlook the importance of what Robbins called the 'international(ist)' atmosphere. Generous humanistic philosophies come most easily to members of a leisured aristocratic class, and by the same token there were a good many Americans who were moved by a strong and genuine desire to build a better society in the interests of all mankind. When in November 1946, with the promulgation of the new constititution, the Japanese people declared that the international society in which they 'desired to occupy an honoured place' was a society 'striving for the preservation of peace, and the banishment of tyranny and slavery, oppression and intolerance, for all time from the earth', they were not just demonstrating a foolish naivety of their own about the nature of international society. Such aspirations were widespread and real.

But, of course, the outbreak and intensification of the Cold War destroyed this optimism. Within a few years the superpowers seemed on the brink of war over the control of Berlin. The World Bank and the IMF to which, on that day in 1944, the Soviet Union promised its $1,200 million ended up as half-world organizations without Russia and its communist bloc. The United Nations became an arena for confrontation between the communist and the capitalist world, between totalitarian collectivism and liberalism.

Now, between 1989 and 1991 everything changed again to subvert our established reflexes. Russia is now a country applying for membership of the World Bank and the IMF. During the Gulf War a cooperative relationship with Russia became the key to America's successful steering of its policies through the United Nations.

FROM WARTIME ALLIANCE TO THE UNITED NATIONS

There follows an attempt to summarize the history from 1944 to 1948 of the development of ideas and institutions concerning peace and collective security, and in particular plans for creating UN forces. There is one thing I ask the reader to bear in mind. After nearly half a century of stability ensured by the military balance between the superpowers, the geopolitical map of military strength has returned to what is very much the 1945 pattern – to the same overwhelming American predominance as prevailed at the time of the San Francisco meeting. At the same time, thanks to the recovery of Europe and the rise of Japan, the economic map is radically different. No longer do the two maps coincide; no longer do the distributions of power and of wealth reinforce each other in quite the same way. A central question for the future is how long this state of non-congruence between the distributions of economic and of military power can be continued.

But that the military map has returned to pretty much its 1945 shape is important. It means that the obstacles which the Cold War placed to the implementation of Chapter 7 of the Charter – 'threats to peace' – no longer exist. Now once again, surely, it is worth considering whether the plans for peace maintenance and peace enforcement activities and for the creation of a UN army which were then on the table are worthy of another closer look.

When the British, American, Russian and Chinese representatives gathered in the suburbs of Washington in 1944 for the Dumbarton Oaks dialogues on the 'postwar world order' they shared one common point of departure: what went wrong? Why did the League of Nations born in such an atmosphere of hope and joy perish in hatred and contempt before it was twenty years old? What can we learn from this experience to prevent it being repeated? There was always, of course, the attached condition: 'without too great a sacrifice of national interest and freedom of action'. But the agenda was clear, and so was agreement on its importance.

That agreement had certainly not been there three years earlier when Roosevelt and Churchill met on a warship four months before Pearl Harbor to discuss the draft of the Atlantic Charter. They were sharply divided over ideas about postwar international organization. The British draft had spoken of an 'effective international organisation [which] will afford to all states and peoples the means of dwelling in security within their own bounds and of traversing the seas and oceans without fear of lawless assault or the need of maintaining burdensome armaments'. But Roosevelt had objected. It was unwise to provoke American isolationists so far, and he himself was opposed to the idea of creating a new League of Nations immediately after the war. It would be enough if, having destroyed the military power of the Axis and assured their own overwhelming world supremacy, the British and Americans should police the world. He thought it better to wait and see how that worked out over a few years before beginning to build formal institutions.

After some traffic in telegrams between the warship and London – for his coalition cabinet contained some strongly internationalist Labour members – Churchill sought to revive the idea of an international organization in the communiqué. He argued that the arbitrary rule of Britain and America would not be acceptable; it was necessary to involve small and medium nations. The final compromise was the formula: 'since no future peace can be maintained if land, sea, or air armaments continue to be employed by nations which threaten or may threaten aggression outside of their frontiers, they believe, pending the establishment of a wider and permanent system of general security, that the disarmament of such nations is essential.'[3] (The Charter's Article 53 – the so-called 'enemy clause' notorious in Japan but almost unremarked in the rest of the world – has its distant origin in this warship debate.)

The development of ideas in the three years which intervened between that meeting and Dumbarton Oaks had been striking. What had transformed it was the beginning of the US–Japan war, neatly completing the division of the whole world into two camps. There had been a gradual reconciliation of the two contrasting views which had appeared at the time of the Atlantic Charter – the clash between those, on the one hand, who defined the agenda as being to create a universal organization better than the League and those who defined the problem as being: how can the Peace-Loving Nations which had formed an effective alliance against the aggressive Axis Powers retain their unity and prevent the re-emergence of aggressive tendencies in their enemies? By the time the officials of the British and American Foreign Offices had completed the draft for the Dumbarton Oaks dialogues the former, fundamentally stronger, League view had become the mainstream, though there were still many traces of the 'continuation of the wartime alliance' conception.

One of those was in the very name given to the organization. The words 'United Nations' first appeared in the 1 January 1942 Declaration of the twenty-six countries which had declared war on the Axis, in which they set out their war aims and justifications. There had been debate as to what the twenty-six should call themselves. The world 'Alliance' required some qualifier – the XY alliance – and it was hard to think what the XY should be, quite apart from the fact that there was potential trouble from an American Congress which had traditionally declared itself as opposed to entering into any alliances whatsoever. 'The Associated Powers' was also considered, but it sounded awkward. 'Declaration of the United Nations' was said to be Roosevelt's last minute inspiration.[4] Later, the word was used when organizations such as UNRRA for refugees were set up. At Dumbarton Oaks the Russians proposed 'world union' but the Americans objected that 'union', as in Soviet Union, sounded too much like 'federation' and raised the spectre of attempts to impose world government. They proposed that the words of which Roosevelt was still rather proud – United Nations – should be taken over directly by the new organization.[5] Japan was fortunate that it was not a literal translation of those words, but Kokusai Rengō (with Kokuren as the abbreviation corresponding to 'the UN') – literally 'international union' – which became the conventional translation.

Another remnant of the 'perpetuate the alliance' concept is to be found in the clear division within the Charter between the countries with permanent seats and veto powers within the Security Council and the rest. In the United Nations Declaration of January 1942 there were actually only four signatories – the US, Britain, the USSR and China. The other twenty-two allies had to be content with issuing a declaration of endorsement the following day. To Churchill's objection, 'Why have China in this?', the Americans who feared a separate Sino-Japanese peace and were planning to establish B29 bases in China were insistent on the importance of China. Roosevelt is said to have asked Churchill, 'What would happen if this enormous population developed in the same way as Japan had done in the last century and got hold of modern weapons?'[6]

The same four powers were present at the Dumbarton Oaks Conference – or rather dialogues. The Americans and the British met first with the Russians and then for a second phase with the Chinese: Russia not having yet declared war on Japan, it was thought indelicate to have them both at the same table. Later, after a new French government had been formed in Paris, France was added. The structure of the Security Council grew directly out of these arrangements, dividing the greater from the lesser powers.

LESSONS FROM THE LEAGUE

The draft which came out of Dumbarton Oaks became, in a slightly amended form, the Charter of the United Nations, signed in San Francisco in 1945. In what sense can it be said to have 'learned the lessons of the League to create a more effective organization'? There are, it seems to me, three salient points:

1 The principle of one nation–one vote democracy (nationocracy?) gave way to the explicitly oligarchic principle that gave the right of veto to each of the five great powers on all important aspects of collective security. It was accepted, in other words, that while the UN might succeed in mediating conflicts between the great powers, there was still no prospect for some time of an international organization capable of imposing economic or military sanctions on a great power. The realistic position was taken that a recognition of this was an essential precondition for the body's effectiveness in other lesser disputes.

2 Whereas the League could only urge member countries to adopt sanctions against aggressors, the carrying out of UN resolutions was specified as a *duty* of members. In the speech in which he opened the first UN General Assembly in London, Britain's Prime Minister Attlee pointed to this as the crucial weakness of the League: 'after the First World War there was a tendency to regard the League as something outside the ordinary range of foreign policy. Governments continued on the old lines, pursuing individual aims and following the path of power politics, not understanding that the world had passed to a new epoch.' In the new world in which the United Nations would 'assert the preeminence of right over might and the general good against selfish and national aims' things were going to be different.[7]

3 The League had been little more than a 'place' – a place for member nations to meet. By contrast, UNO – the United Nations *Organization* was to have a Secretary-General. He had a Secretariat and had also the powers to take initiatives. The United Nations constituted a responsible actor, a kind of international legal incorporated entity. This is clear at several points in the wording of the Charter. In the frequent references to 'the Organization and its Member States' and in the power granted to the Secretary-General to convene the Security Council when, in his personal judgement, there existed a 'threat to peace'. The job of coordinating cooperation among member countries in the imposition of economic sanctions responding to a threat to peace was the job of the Secretary-General and his staff, under instruction from the Security Council, and if economic sanctions failed and the resort to force became necessary, it would be member countries which would provide the armed forces, but the command structure would be part of the Organization's structure.

Prince Itō, who oversaw the drafting of Japan's Meiji Constitution, anticipated already in the 1880s that Japan's political structure would evolve over time.[8] He spoke of the possibility that as precedent succeeded precedent and began to acquire the authority of constitutional statute, there was room for Japan's system to evolve towards a British type of parliamentary democracy. Indeed, such an evolution was visible in the second and third decades of the present century. It was subsequently reversed, but it is arguable that without that early experience of cabinets responsible to the Diet, it would have been much more difficult for postwar democracy to take roots. In exactly the same way the convinced internationalists of 1945, while dissatisfied with the fact that what the actual Charter created was not much more than an alliance of the five great powers, could still hope that the UN Secretariat contained the germs of what could eventually grow into a system of world government.

There was another sense in which one might see the vision of the Charter as a vision of a future world government in embryo. Theories of the state – theories of the nature of 'government' – range from the liberal's notion of an organ which confines itself to the minimal duties of defence and the maintenance of law and order (the nightwatchman state), to the views of socialists, not to mention totalitarians, who see the state as the executive committee of a national community, responsible for the general welfare of its citizens. The functions of the United Nations as prescribed in the Charter actually come closer to the second conception, the conception of the maximal state. See the declaration of basic principles in the preamble which sets out what 'the peoples of the United Nations' have 'determined' to achieve. The first concerns collective security and the abolition of war. The second concerns guarantees of human rights; the next the urgent need to develop a system of international order; and finally: 'to promote social progress and better standards of life in a larger freedom'. The Charter also specified an organizational structure in which the first purpose would be taken care of by the Security Council, others by the Human Rights Commission, the Social and Economic Council and the International Court of Justice as part of a coordinated organization.

Internationalists were delighted with a Charter which had so clearly the basic elements for the making of an eventual government of mankind, and by the same token those who saw patriotism as the highest human ideal and looked on all talk of world government as foolish utopianism were understandably apprehensive about these declarations of 'universal human' ideals. It was to still these apprehensions that Article 2, Paragraph 7 with its clear prohibition of interference in the internal affairs of states was inserted.

The total contradiction was obvious. There can be no action to protect the lives of individual citizens which does not put into question the domestic institutions of their state. Only in one respect, in matters concerning peace and security, did the Charter escape contradiction. An exception is added to Paragraph 7 of Article 2. Interference with domestic affairs is banned, 'but this shall not be allowed to obstruct the implementation of Chapter 7 of the Charter'. The priority of conflicting principles was made clear at least in this sphere.

Chapter 7 is indeed the key to any contemporary attempts to revitalize the United Nations. In the next chapter I shall look at the origins and intentions of the Chapter 7 arrangements and at their implementation – or rather non-implementation.

4 The use of armed force

INTERNATIONALISM AND PACIFISM

The phrase in the preamble to the UN Charter, 'armed force shall not be used, save in the common interest' is a quintessential expression of the spirit of internationalism. It accepts that an international organization which seeks to deny the absoluteness of the sovereignty of individual states, to develop a sense of common humanity stronger than the ties among co-nationals, and to promote the welfare of the whole human race – a mankind interest which transcends national interests – may on occasion be compelled to use armed force. This kind of internationalism is at variance with the sort of pacifism which sees the use of military force as an absolute evil, and urges that the only way to achieve the peaceful settlement of conflict is by defusing tensions and strengthening the hatred for violence. The two strains of thought may sometimes flow together, but they are not the same. Chapter 2 described how towards the end of the nineteenth century these two streams of thought often gave rise to separate and opposed organizations.

In 1945 too there were a number of critics who were opposed to the UN Charter on pacifist grounds. Frederick Libby of the American National Council for the Prevention of War was one such. Appearing as a witness in the congressional hearings on the ratification of the Charter he claimed that an international organization which had a military alliance as its basis could never succeed. What the world needed was total disarmament and the establishment of a system of cooperation in which the use of force was impossible.[1]

However, among the fifty nations gathered in San Francisco this was decidedly a minority opinion, hardly represented at all in the debates over the proposed amendments. What Roosevelt said in his Christmas Eve fireside chat in 1943, just after his return from the Teheran Conference, had by then become the standard view: there could be no 'pious hopes' that aggressors would learn and understand 'the doctrine of purely voluntary peace'; the postwar world had to be led by the great powers acting much as policemen.[2]

There was general agreement among the other delegates that international order could not be maintained without some police force. Small village communities might manage to settle their quarrels by neighbourly intervention but there was not a single community, the size of even the smallest state, which did not have a specialist police force. How much more clearly the principle applied in international society where men and women of the sweetest disposition in their private life, once clothed in patriotism, would cheerfully murder the people of other countries in the name of serving their country.

The big questions were: under whose direction this police force should be, how it should be composed, what powers it should be given, and under what rules and under whose supervision it should operate.

DEALING WITH THREATS TO PEACE, CHAPTERS 6 AND 7

The collective security structure which the Charter envisaged can be most usefully summarized under nine points:

1 The active agent in activities to maintain, restore and enforce peace was to be the Security Council, made up of the delegates of the five permanent members and six other (after 1965, ten other) elected countries.
2 Interventions by the Security Council come in two forms. There are disputes which are dealt with in Chapter 6 and there are threats to peace dealt with in Chapter 7. It is possible for any member nation and for the Secretary-General to bring to the notice of the Security Council disputes which they deem to constitute a threat to peace. But whether they are such threats or not is decided by the Security Council itself.
3 In the case of disputes the Council may urge on the disputants certain means of mediation, or itself offer a mediation plan, but in the case of countries which threaten to breach the peace or have already broken it, sanctions may be applied against the aggressor. In the first instance it may direct members to take 'measures not involving the use of armed force' (Article 41). The words used are: the Security Council 'may call upon' member countries to take such measures, but Articles 48 and 49 make clear the obligation of all member countries to respond to the call. If the non-military measures are expected to be, or have been proved to be, inadequate, force may be resorted to.
4 In either case, the purpose of intervention is the maintenance or the restoration of peace and security. In Article 1 of the Charter there was included, as a result of a Chinese proposal, a declaration that the settlement of disputes should be 'in conformity with the principles of justice and international law', but there is no obvious recognition of this when it comes to outlining concrete measures in Chapters 6 and 7 – apart from urging maximum use of the International Court of Justice. There is no mention of law and justice, only of peace. The British and American

delegates at San Francisco explained that the Security Council was indeed to be a policeman, not a judge. There was no way policemen could do their job if they had to decide who was in the right and who was in the wrong before they intervened in a quarrel. Judicial proceedings came later.

In Chapter 14 of the Charter which deals with the International Court of Justice, member countries do indeed promise to observe the judgements of the Court and the responsibility for enforcing judgements if they do not is delegated to the Security Council.

5 If, that is, a judgement has been given, for the International Court's jurisdiction is limited. For it to take up a dispute it is necessary that all parties to the dispute should agree to its doing so. At San Francisco an overwhelming majority of the delegates wanted to include a so-called 'compulsory acceptance of jurisdiction' clause. Just as any country's citizens were required to answer charges brought against them in the Courts, so in the international sphere too the Courts should be able to act in response to the plea of a single disputant. However, the proposal fell under opposition from the US and the Soviet Union.[3] As a compromise it was stipulated that countries could make unilateral declarations that they would never refuse to respond when a case was brought against them in the ICJ, and that this declaration should have the force of a treaty. The American Congress, for all its sensitivity on national sovereignty matters – the source of the American delegates' reservations – finally passed such a declaration with some minor reservations attached in 1946. In 1985 the Reagan administration, angry at the Court's judgement against the US in the Nicaraguan affair, gave notice to the Secretary-General of its cancellation of that declaration.[4]

6 For armed intervention the Security Council would be able to call into action a military force – troops, including an air strike force in a constant state of readiness, weapons, bases, rights of passage, etc. – all of which member countries would commit themselves to providing in advance. These commitments were to be regulated by separate treaties of each member country with the Security Council, properly ratified.

7 The supervision of these measures, the preparation of structures for the use of armed force, and the strategic direction of such forces when they were used, were to be entrusted to a sub-committee of the Security Council, the Military Staff Committee, made up of the Chiefs of Staff of the five Great Powers. The command structures to put these strategic directions into operation were left to 'be worked out subsequently'.

8 The Security Council, responsible for the whole world, could delegate its functions and powers to regional (e.g. European, Latin American) bodies and there could be regional sub-committees of the Military Staff Committee.

9 When the Security Council was taking measures to resolve disputes under Chapter 6, permanent members of the Council which were interested

parties to the dispute would abstain from voting on resolutions. However, when the issue was the application of Chapter 7 to enforce sanctions against countries responsible for a 'breach of the peace' (or deciding whether or not a given dispute actually constituted a threat to peace) the permanent members were still entitled to exercise their veto power. This may be interpreted as the mutually accommodating egoism of the Great Powers or alternatively as a realistic recognition of the genuine limitations to the authority and power of any international organization.

THE MILITARY STAFF COMMITTEE

It was a Charter with many contradictions, not least those surrounding the Great Powers' veto, but these were potentially 'developmental contradictions'. The distribution of authority in legal structures and the realities of power do not always coincide. Take for example the relative positions of civil servants and politicians in Japan. Civil servants are in theory entirely subjected to the instructions of politicians, but in practice, because the bureaucrats are generally seen as being more honestly devoted to national interest than politicians thought to be perennially devoted to the pursuit of party or personal advantage, the bureaucrats have more prestige, greater authority and consequently more real power. In much the same way there was the possibility that, if the countries with the right to veto used their power to give priority to their national interests over considerations of law and justice, the Secretary-General and his staff, representing a public interest greater than the interest of individual countries, could come to acquire a greater authority. That seemed indeed to be a clear tendency, in spite of the constraints of the Cold War when Hammarskjold, an impressive personality, was Secretary-General.

However, important though the personal charisma of a Secretary-General may be, that is not enough. The possibility of real institutional evolution depends also on the quality of the staff in general and it depends also on budgets. It depends on whether the UN organization can afford to have its own independent sources of information and it depends on whether it has the capacity to evoke the sanctions which form the core of peace-keeping activities. The latter was seen to depend crucially on the character and functioning of the Military Staff Committee on which the Charter gave only outline specifications.

The idea of an international force was not new. The notorious international force which went to suppress the Boxer Rebellion in China – the occasion when Japan first received recognition as an imperial power comparable with the powers of Europe – was one example. Rather more concerned with peace-making were the forces created after the First World War in several areas of Europe where there were frontier disputes. They occupied disputed areas after the disputants' armies and police had been withdrawn and kept law and order until local plebiscites had settled where the frontiers should be. (Somewhat like UNTAG operation in Namibia, an operation to supervise the Namibian elections in which Japanese officials also took part.[5])

But that was not the sort of United Nations military operation which the Charter envisaged. It was the American delegates at Dumbarton Oaks who provided the underlying concept, and their proposal in turn owed much to French proposals at the 1932 disarmament conference. There was already in 1944 a certain amount of public debate as to whether a putative postwar international organization should have its own standing army or whether – the concept finally embodied in Chapter 7 – it should rely on *ad hoc* mobilization of military forces from member states when necessary. The debate within the American government had already been resolved; the notion of a standing army carried too great a threat to the principle of sovereignty.[6] At Dumbarton Oaks, both the Soviet Union and China suggested that there should at least be a standing air force capable of immediate action, and the British were sympathetic to the proposal, but the Americans pressed for its withdrawal, arguing *inter alia* that it was necessary to avoid provisions which could cause trouble in Congress.[7] The provision in Article 45 that, as part of the contributions they shall contract to make, 'members shall hold immediately available national air force contingents for combined international enforcement action' reflects these earlier debates.

After the ending of the first General Assembly in November 1945, that very American Congress whose isolationism the executive so feared was seized by an expansive internationalist sentiment. Thereafter it is fair to say that the driving force for implementation of Chapter 7 came from the Americans. On 20 December the United Nations Participation Act[8] passed both Houses of Congress. It contained provisions which seemed astonishing in the light of America's long tradition of isolationism and in the light of a long history of conflict between President and Congress over the right to declare war. It not only authorised the drawing up of a treaty to commit American troops to the Security Council as envisaged in the Charter; it went further to declare that 'the President shall not be deemed to require the authorization of the Congress to make available to the Security Council on its call in order to take action under Article 42 of the said Charter' the forces committed under that treaty. They agreed, in other words, that the decision whether or not American troops should be sent to shed their blood for the maintenance of world order should be left to the Security Council.

Left in effect, of course, to the American delegate armed with veto power in the Security Council. As was clear from a conversation between Secretary of State Howell and the Republican leader Vandenburg[9] a year earlier, the act would never have been passed had there not been an American veto on the Security Council. Nevertheless, it is a piece of legislation one can only read today with surprise.

Before it could enter into negotiations for the treaties governing the provision of troops, however, the Security Council had to decide a whole range of preliminary matters – details of organization, of command structures and of budgets. At a meeting in February 1946 it instructed its Military Staff Committee to report, from a military point of view, the basic principles to be applied in putting Article 43 into practice.

PLANNING FOR THE MILITARY CONTRIBUTION TREATIES

That resolution was passed at the Council's twenty-third meeting. Already the combative measures which the United States and Russia were taking to consolidate their spheres of influence in Iran and in Greece had been on the Council's agenda and antagonism between the two countries was becoming marked. It was hardly the kind of friendly atmosphere in which great powers could cooperate to plan for the development of the UN. But still, antagonisms had not crystallized to the Cold War point at which the world was divided into two opposing blocks. It is clear from the archives of the State Department and the US Delegation at the UN that the American, British and French members of the Military Staff Committee took the task they had been given seriously. In the United States a committee had been formed already, in the autumn of 1945, to consider the scale, the basis and the command structure of the forces which the United States would offer to the UN, and an American draft plan was already prepared.[10] When the Military Staff Committee began its work, the President instructed State Department officials to clear that American plan with the Senate foreign policy experts of the opposition Republican Party, before putting it to the Committee. It is not surprising that the underlying attitudes apparent in the record of these talks[11] could hardly be said to be imbued with the spirit of internationalism. The starting point was not so much 'How can we create an effective international organization?' as 'how can one increase the efficiency of the international organization without, under any conceivable circumstances, causing damage to American interests?' The Senators insisted that the Monroe Doctrine should be forever inviolable and that, in order to avoid any possibility that Russian troops might land on Latin American soil, there should be a provision that UN armed forces should be drawn from the relevant region. They were talked out of insisting on this proposal by the arguments that such a contingency could be avoided by judicious use of the veto and that the provision could backfire to exclude Americans from other areas.[12]

By the end of April 1946 the American, French, British and Chinese delegates on the Military Staff Committee had all put their countries' proposals on the table and proceeded to discuss the points of difference and search for compromise. The Soviet delegate attended every meeting, but took no part in substantive discussions. The Soviet plan promised for 3 April had not materialized by the end of June. In mid-May the American delegate to the UN wrote to the Secretary of State suggesting that 'in view of the importance of the work of the Military Staff Committee' the American Ambassador in Moscow should try to speed up the delivery of the Russian plan; he himself could get no change out of Gromyko, the Soviet delegate at the UN.[13] The answer, two weeks later, was no. In the first place, UN diplomacy should take place at the UN; and besides, there were several points of difference on the American side between the Joint Chiefs of Staff and leading senators which still had to be cleared up so that a little more delay would not be all that bad a thing.

'Speaking frankly' is a commonly used phrase, but frankness is not an all-or-nothing thing, it is a question of degree. It is probably rare for diplomats to speak with total frankness to the representatives of other nations, but reading these American archives one is impressed by the sharp difference in the levels of frankness that were attained in different bilateral relations. On a scale of zero to ten the Anglo-American relation might be set at eight, the Franco-American at around five or six. Sino-American relations are hard to judge because they were not even ostensibly on a footing of equality, but American-Soviet relations one would have to put close to zero. One interesting illustration of this is a memo written by one of three American diplomats who had had dinner with Sobolov, then Deputy Secretary-General of the UN. In the summer of 1946 a debate much more important than those going on in the Military Staff Committee was taking place in the UN's Atomic Energy Committee. The Americans had proposed the establishment of a UN organization to supervise the production of all nuclear weapons and atomic energy production. The Russians were opposed on the grounds that such an organization would inevitably be dominated by the United States, given that it was already a nuclear power continuing to make atomic bombs and in possession of high levels of technology. There could be no question that such an American-dominated organization should be allowed free inspection of Soviet installations.

At the dinner which had been planned to explore the Russian position, Sobolov, who was then formally no longer a Russian official but an official of the UN, expressed some clear and forthright opinions (for example, 'The American plan is in essence a plan for world government. The world is not yet ready for that'), but on most matters his replies were ambiguous. Even so the American diplomat who had sat for six months with his Russian colleagues on the Atomic Energy Committee noted in his diary, 'This is by far the frankest discussion with a Soviet official in which I have participated'.[14] To the average American official, Moscow was an impenetrable puzzle; it might have been the capital of Mars.

How would one rate the relations between Secretary of State Baker and the Russian Foreign Minister Shevardnadze at the time of the Gulf War? Perhaps at six or seven on the frankness scale. American and North

Korean relations apart, it is hard to find parallels to the distance which separated America and Russia in the days of Stalin.

The summer of 1946 passed without any sign of a Russian plan. Meanwhile, substantial differences of opinion had appeared among the other four. In late July there appeared on the desk of the Secretary of State a plan which a member of the British delegation had in confidence passed to Airforce General Kenney, a plan which Britain was shortly proposing to put up to the Military Staff Committee.[15] There were two main points. First, was the principle of unlimited obligation. If necessary member countries should be prepared to put their entire armed forces at the disposal of the United Nations. Secondly, it was necessary to lay the preparations for combined operations for training together, working out communication codes, standardizing vocabulary and control structures. Each country should therefore designate core forces against any future emergency and put them under training. Each of the major powers should contribute one carrier squadron, one armoured and one infantry division, four to six flights of bombers and eight to twelve of fighters and one aerial coastguard unit.

The second part of this plan (whether it was suppressed by the British Chiefs of Staff who were reported by General Kenney to be rather lukewarm about it, or whether it was dropped after meeting American opposition is not clear) was never presented. The first proposal for unlimited obligations however was presented in September and received a good deal of attention. According to one State Department official's report to the Secretary of State, General Kenney himself was strongly in favour. It was, he thought, the only way forward if the UN were ever to be effective in maintaining peace. 'The United States, as the strongest military, naval and air power, would have such a preponderant position in any total military setup, that it could only be to our interest.' In the policy paper in which the State Department set out the line to be taken in response to the British proposal, however, the instructions were to cool such enthusiasm. Given the existence of the veto it was highly improbable that the Security Council would ever appeal to the use of armed force, and certainly not against any but small countries. Hence large armies were not necessary. While the British intention to strengthen the UN is understandable, the paper noted that this was impossible without the abolition of the veto power – which Britain was not apparently proposing. If, at some future date, it seemed likely that the unanimity rule could be eliminated the question of providing large forces might then receive further consideration.[16]

Suddenly, in the middle of September, the Soviet representative began actively to participate in the debate. Instead of offering a general outline of Soviet views on the proposed treaties, he offered a suggestion that it was necessary first of all to agree on a preamble to such treaties. This was to be entitled 'the purposes of UN military activity'. This must be settled before it would be possible to discuss any other details. He offered a draft of how the preamble would go. Several passages – 'armed force shall not be used for the suppression of national liberation movements' – showed clear Russian apprehensions about the way force might be used by a UN under American dominance.[17]

The other delegates pointed out that the objectives were already prescribed in the UN Charter. To go any further in specifying them would only lead to the same sort of barren debate that occurred in San Francisco when several Latin American countries proposed including an article which would give a clear definition to 'aggression'. Surely we reached the conclusion then that it would be impossible to establish a legal and unambiguous definition, and that the attempt to do so was unproductive. In any case this committee has been charged with preparing guidelines for these proposed treaties 'from the military point of view' and this is not the place to consider political issues, etc., etc.

But the Soviet delegate would not budge. It was finally agreed to leave this question unresolved and to proceed to other matters. By the spring of next year it was apparent that even after many compromises had been reached there were still irreconcilable differences and it was decided to make a report to the Security Council which should contain statements of opposing views side by side. On the question of a preamble, agreement was actually reached. It was to say simply that armed force should be used exclusively for the purposes set out in the Charter and not for any other. The drafted guidelines were published on 30 April 1947 and put on the Agenda for the thirty-eighth meeting of the Security Council on 4 June. There was already a wide area of agreement. In the initial stages the bulk of the military forces should come from the five veto powers. Other countries would be principally asked to provide bases, rights of passage and logistic support. The forces which the treaties would place at the disposal of the UN should, until called out by the Security Council, remain under their respective national commands, and even when they were called into action, each country would be responsible for logistic supplies, and for the rotation of troops, while their commanders should be permitted to remain in touch with their own governments.

Not all the points in dispute divided the Soviet Union from the other four. While there was agreement that the Commander in Chief should be appointed by the Security Council, whether or not he should then in turn have the authority to name the three commanders of the land, naval and air forces as the US, Russia and China proposed, or whether their appointments should also become a Security Council matter as Britain and France proposed, was one such example. Another example was a clause proposed by the French and the Chinese to the effect that troops committed to the UN could, in an emergency, be employed as a matter of priority for national purposes, whereas the other three wanted to exclude the clause on the grounds that the right of self-defence was already guaranteed in article 51 and the notion of 'in an emergency' was too ambiguous to serve any purpose.

However, the most important and ultimately the fatal divisions of opinion were between the Soviet Union and the other four countries. They focused on two points. The first was the question of bases. A challenge to America's right to maintain bases in Spain had already been brought before the Security Council and Stalin in his speeches had gone out of his way to criticize the American bases in China. The Soviet Union was already showing an acute fear of 'encirclement'. This resulted in the Soviet proposal that any armed forces which had been deployed by the United Nations should, within three months of the conclusion of hostilities, withdraw to their home country, a proposal to which the Americans were adamantly opposed.

Before it got to debating this question, embodied in alternative drafts for Articles 20 and 21 of the proposed guidelines, the Security Council became mired in debate over Article 11 which led to an even more decisive confrontation, at the end of which the debate was adjourned to a later date. The issue revolved around the composition of the forces which the five powers would provide. The American draft, agreed to by Britain, China and France, spoke of a 'comparable initial overall contribution', but contributions which 'may differ widely as to the strength of the separate components, land, sea and air', given the 'differences in size and composition of national forces of each permanent member'. The Soviets, on the other hand, insisted on 'the principle of equality regarding the overall strength and the composition of these forces', with deviations only by special decisions of the Security Council. By the end of the war the United States had a strength in aircraft carriers and bombers which none of the other countries could match. The Soviet Union had powerful land forces, but was only at the beginning of its navy build-up, and it was also relatively weaker in bombers. If a UN force had to be deployed – as the American delegate stressed in his speech opening the debate 'there can be no question that the United Nations needs, first of all, a mobile force able to strike quickly at long range and to bring to bear upon any given point in the world where trouble may occur, the maximum armed force in the minimum time'. This means that the permanent members which have such forces should predominate in this mobile component, but this does not prevent contributions being 'properly balanced and rendered roughly comparable without prejudice to the interests of individual nations by arranging that those nations which make available a lesser proportion of the new mobile components could put up a larger portion of other components or other forms of assistance and facilities'.[18]

One can imagine the sort of situation the Russians had in mind. There is a war in, say, Malaysia. The initial overwhelming military force is made up of Anglo-American carriers and marines. They accomplish their objectives in a month or so, and the Soviet Union is asked to hold land forces in readiness in case they become necessary. One does not have to be a suspicious Russian delegate to guess which countries would have the greater influence on the subsequent political settlement.

Attempts to find a compromise solution were indeed made. The British delegate suggested that the Military Staff Committee should be asked to estimate the scale of the armed force which member countries considered would be necessary for peace-keeping purposes. They could then divide the estimate by five and decide whether equality of composition was a feasible principle. The debate was adjourned with a resolution asking the Military Staff Committee to produce such estimates within four days, and the meeting broke up.

Those estimates proved to differ considerably. The British and French proposals were relatively close (with the Chinese concurring with the British estimate): 1,200–1,300 planes (half of them bombers); 8–16 divisions of land forces, 120 ships, including 4–6 carrier task forces, plus the shipping necessary to land a division of marines. The American estimate was more than double; land forces were set at 20 divisions, the bomber estimate was triple that of the British and the French, and as for Naval forces they also proposed 6 carrier task forces, but 90 submarines (compared with 12 for Britain and France) and the shipping to land 6 marine divisions.[19] There was no Soviet estimate. When the Security Council met again Gromyko argued at great length, in the uncompromising manner for which he became famous, that there was no point in estimating total forces until the principle of whether there should be equality of strength and composition or only just of strength had been settled. Moreover, he said, since these estimates were simply the provisional views of a small group of officials and did not constitute formal governmental proposals, they had no justifiable place on the agenda of the Security Council.[20]

Whether one judges Gromyko as gauchely inept or just honestly realistic in making clear that his sole concern was the national interest, there was a difference at least at the rhetorical level between the Russian and, say, the British view of the matter. Two key words encapsulate that difference. The British position was: 'it seems essential to maintain, as far as possible, equality of *sacrifice* amongst the five permanent members and at the same time ensure that the Security Council is provided with armed forces from which it can select a balanced force for a specific operation.' The Soviet position was: 'the principle of equality does not permit *advantages* in the position of any permanent member.' Was peace-keeping about making 'sacrifices' for the general good of humanity, or about taking 'advantages' to further national aims? For all present it had to be some mixture of the two but there was no doubt that the mix varied.

The Polish delegate was more flexible than the Russian. He suggested that if the maximum estimate, that of the United States, were divided by five, there might be some problem with submarines, but in other respects it looked as if it would be possible for each of the five countries to provide comparable forces. But his efforts to move the debate along while supporting the Soviet stand on equal composition did not win Gromyko's approval and after three and a half hours of fruitless debate the chairman adjourned the discussion to a later date.

But that 'later date' has still to arrive. In Greece, the Americans and the Russians were already fighting by proxy in the civil war between the communist and anti-communist forces. Truman had already, three months before, announced the containment of the Soviet Union as the basis of American foreign policy. It was hard to imagine a situation in which a United Nations force could be made up of cooperating American and Russian troops. It was not surprising that hopes of arriving at agreed guidelines for such UN forces in the Security Council should have become very thin indeed. Debates within the Military Staff Committee continued in a desultory fashion, and the State Department did give consideration to bringing the matter before the UN General Assembly. But it is clear from the documents that the main concern of American diplomats was not so much to carry forward proposals for UN military forces as to make it clear to the smaller countries that these plans were being sabotaged, not by them but by the other side.

Nevertheless, proposals for the creation of UN forces still had quite strong support in American public opinion. The Senate passed a resolution in May 1948, urging that the treaties envisaged by Article 43 should be concluded as rapidly as possible. A proposal was developed within the State Department for the United States to publish its own proposed draft for such a sample treaty without waiting for a conclusion of the debates in the Military Staff Committee. It received a certain amount of support, but was quashed by a magisterial memorandum by George Kennan, the original author of containment policy:

> The Kremlin has no abstract interest in the maintenance of peace and security. The Soviet Leaders do nothing in foreign affairs which is not apt, in their opinion, to contribute to the strengthening of the Communist movement at the expense of the position of the leading members of the Western community of nations. If, therefore, in a given instance, the USSR were to choose not to exercise its veto over a proposal to use the UN forces in a security matter, this could only be because it had been decided that such a UN action would be apt to have the effect, in the last analysis, of furthering their international purposes. In any joint undertaking for the use of UN facilities in security matters, the Western powers are therefore betting against the Kremlin on the ultimate repercussions of such undertakings on the World situation.[21]

One can easily agree with his analysis. And if one were to substitute for 'the USSR' 'the United States' or 'the Western Powers', and to substitute 'the expansion of the Free World' for 'the strengthening of the Communist Movement' it would still be an accurate analysis. However, Kennan went on to say, since the implementation of Article 43 was a declared objective of American policy, and since that objective had been confirmed in the

Senate, and since American foreign policy was in principle a UN-centred policy, it might not be a bad thing for the Chiefs of Staff to continue to work on a draft treaty, and then, if something useable emerged, to check it out with the British, the French and the Canadians before bringing it back for further examination within the State Department.

Early in the following year, 1949, secret instructions were sent by the State Department to the US delegation at the UN to keep the implementation of Article 43 off the agenda.[22] In the summer of that year Dean Rusk, later Secretary of State at the time of the Vietnam War, sent a memo to the National Security Council asking for its opinion on whether or not the negotiations should be reopened. The Soviet Union was believed to have successfully experimented with an atomic bomb and the British, French and Canadians were proposing that the idea of a United Nations force should be revived. The Canadians, then holding the chairmanship of the Security Council, were particularly keen on the idea. The National Security Council's reply was discouraging, and the implementation of Article 43 had still not got on to the Security Council's agenda when the Korean War broke out in the following year.[23]

THE BALANCE BETWEEN CALCULATION AND IDEAL

What lessons – lessons of relevance to the present day – might one draw from this overview of the early debates concerning Article 43 of the Charter? The idea of giving the United Nations the effective strength to use military force for the maintenance of peace did in fact seem promising at the end of the war and the forces seeking to put it in practice were far from negligible. Can one conclude that, since the decisive obstacle was the deterioration of the international situation and the steady entrenchment of Cold War antagonism, now that the Cold War has ended, the time has come – the golden opportunity has come – to renew those efforts – this time with some chance of success?

Would that it were that simple.

There is no doubt that the ending of the Cold War provides an opportunity for action. But whether the right way to use that opportunity is to revive Chapter 7 of the Charter, in particular Article 43, is a matter of doubt. The fact that the guidelines for the proposed treaties got as far in their drafting as they did, leaving only three or four points of difference was, in the last analysis, thanks to the permanent members' veto power. It was not only that no one envisaged the possibility of UN sanctions being used against the five great powers themselves – or at least against the two superpowers. The veto also ensured that when sanctions were to be applied against a country condemned in world opinion as an aggressor, action could be prevented if those sanctions were in any sense contrary to the interests of one of those powers. But a society in which the major tax-payers approve of a policing system on condition that they are never subject to its attentions is not a healthy society, and it is not a society in which the universal rule of law and the principle of equality before the law can be fostered.

I quoted earlier a State Department official speculating on the contingency that 'if, at some future date, it seems likely that the unanimity rule could be eliminated', and indeed one is entitled to wonder whether, with the end of the Cold War, that moment has not arrived. But is that likely to be possible? Is it possible that American insistence on the veto was conditioned only by the priority given to Cold War rivalry over any other consideration of world order? And that, that rivalry now having disappeared, the United States would be prepared to consider the diminution of national sovereignty implied in the abandonment of the veto power?

There were many people in the United States who supported the idea of United Nations armed forces. There was, for example, that Senate resolution of the summer of 1948. It is hard to believe that this sprang *entirely* from the calculation that, as General Kenney pointed out, the overwhelming military strength of the United States meant that America could never be the loser from joint military operations. Hugh Thomas has said, apropos the fireside chats and radio speeches of Roosevelt and Truman, to get the American people to accept international responsibilities required – in the view of those experienced politicians – that they be given 'an idealistic explanation; Americans would not exert themselves for "spheres of interest"'.[24]

To return to the analogy of a domestic police force, what people think of the policeman depends largely on whether they identify more with the constable or with the criminal. Americans who believe themselves to be living in the world's finest model democracy find it hard to believe that their country should ever become criminalized in the eyes of the international community. By contrast (and the obvious analogy of the 1990s are the Islamic countries), the Soviet Union, imbued with a sense of its own rightness and at the same time of its minority isolation in world affairs, could only too easily foresee the possibility of finding itself in that position.

Nevertheless one should not overlook the presence of a certain 'genuine' internationalism, mixed with that American smugness. The same can be said for Britain, France and Canada: the British plan for creating a core UN force through prolonged training probably had some such inspiration. Has there ever, after all, been a country where the rule of law has been established without some element of elite smugness among the people of goodwill?

One final point. The people most likely to have that 'abstract interest in the maintenance of peace and security' which Kennan described the Soviet Union as lacking, are officials of international organizations which transcend nationalities and national interests – i.e., the Secretary-General and his staff. Reading through the archive of American internal debates on UN military operations in these years I remember seeing not one single reference to the Secretary-General, nor to the role of the UN bureaucracy. Yet the prospects for the creation of effective peace-keeping forces depend crucially on the ability of the UN to act as an independent agent, and on the leadership of the Secretary-General.

5 The enactment of Japan's Peace Constitution

THE REJECTION OF THE RIGHT OF BELLIGERENCY

On 3 February 1946, before the Military Staff Committee had had its first meeting, General MacArthur addressed a memorandum to the Japanese Government concerning revision of the Japanese Imperial Constitution. A month later, on 6 March, while the Military Staff Committee still waiting for its first proposals to be tabled, the draft for the present Constitution was published. The ninetieth session of the Lower House of the Imperial Diet drew to a close, having completed its deliberations on the draft on 20 June while in New York the other four powers were still urging the Soviet Union to provide the Military Staff Committee with the draft proposals it had promised several months earlier. The Diet had changed the brutal first draft of Article 9 'The right of belligerency is abandoned. Armed forces *must* not be maintained' to a somewhat more positive and autonomous 'desirous of peace, the Japanese people have abandoned the right of belligerency. Armed forces *shall* not be maintained'.

What connection was there between these two chains of events? On the one side a country enacting a new Constitution and abandoning both the right of belligerency and the right to maintain armed forces. On the other side moves to create a system of collective security, which would at least be the first stage towards creating a world in which the right of belligerency became unnecessary, was proceeding in an optimistic atmosphere with what many believed to be good chances of success.

Most Japanese, most of the members of the Lower House and the House of Peers who took part in the debate on Article 9 may have had a vague idea of such a connection, but only at a distinctly abstract level – the level of the preamble to that Constitution:

> We, the Japanese people, desire peace for all time and are deeply conscious of the high ideals controlling human relationships, and we have determined to preserve our security and existence, trusting in the justice and faith of the peace-loving peoples of the world. We desire to occupy an honoured place in an international society, striving for the preserva-

tion of peace and the banishment of tyranny and slavery, oppression and intolerance for all time from the earth.

The sentiment was the same as that eloquently expressed by Ashida Hitoshi (later to claim that he had amended the Constitution so as to recognize the right of self-defence) during the Diet debates. He was speaking precisely on the subject of the preamble. He spoke of the Potsdam Declaration and made the point, as a member of the Government, that it was quite wrong to criticize the draft as being simply a response to the victors' demands.

> Just look beyond the windows of this chamber and what meets our eyes. Acre after acre of scorched devastation. Think of the hundreds and thousands of corpses which lay in those ruins. Think of the orphans and widows, their cheeks never dry from their tears, who made their huts amongst the ashes. Here was the genuine cradle of the Japanese Constitution. Is that not the view of the Government? And Japan is not alone in this. Even in Britain which won the war, in the plains of the Ukraine, on the banks of the Yangtze river, everywhere the same desperate cry arises. It is in contemplating that desperation, that destruction of society itself, that we come face to face with the basic common problems which face humanity. It is this burning common desire of humanity for the abandonment of war, for the achievement of a higher culture, a higher level of living, which has brought us, a defeated country, to this point of great transition. Therein lies the essential significance of revising our Constitution.[1]

Many Japanese shared the Ashida notion that if Japan were to lead the way in renouncing war – fulfilling this common aspiration of mankind – it would thereby occupy an honoured place in international society. But there were few people thinking in concrete terms about how the UN's collective security system would in future guarantee the security of Japan.

Everybody was intent on the 'great transformation' which would wipe out the past. Historians will never agree on whether or not the idea for Article 9 came from Shidehara, but there can be no doubt from the parliamentary responses of Shidehara, the Foreign Minister, and Yoshida, the Prime Minister, to questions about Article 9's declaration that 'land, sea and air forces shall never be maintained' were given with full conviction. Indeed they defended the draft with positive enthusiasm. And doubtless that enthusiasm was fuelled by their relief at the prospect of a Japan in which fanatical young officers did not assassinate well-meaning politicians, a Japan in which there would be no more Imperial Conferences at which civilian prime ministers were overborne by arrogant generals.

Undoubtedly the decisive consideration for the Japanese Government was that, whatever anxieties they might have about the future, the only way that Japan could get back into the international community was by renouncing even the right of self-defence – because, as Yoshida said explicitly, it was widely albeit mistakenly believed that the Japanese people were 'naturally given to aggression'.[2] Even members of parliament who in thought and language were still deeply imbued by racist nationalism argued that the abandonment of the right of self-defence was an essential gesture:

> Prime-Minister Yoshida. . . argues that the right of self-defence must also be sacrificed. . . and I believe that men of understanding throughout the world will approve and admire his words. It is not the case that we have suddenly transformed ourselves into peace-loving people under the stress of defeat. We must let the world know that we are, second to none, a peace-loving race, and we must make the world understand this. . . for three thousand years this had been the great ideal of the Japanese people. I appeal to Prime Minister Yoshida, let him devote his remaining years to this cause! Let him rise up and lead us all, all eighty million people with the Emperor at our head, in this great endeavour. Therein, I believe, lies Japan's *raison d'être* in the world.[3]

It is hard to read speeches of this sort ('all eighty million people with the Emperor at our head' was a typical piece of wartime rhetoric) without reflecting on the enormous psychological gap which separates us from the Japan of fifty years ago. It is not, perhaps, surprising that the debate over Article 1, declaring that sovereignty lay with the people rather than with the Emperor, was actually fiercer than that over Article 9.

It has to be said though that the new Lower House which continued deliberating on the Constitution after fresh elections, and the House of Peers, reinforced with the addition of a number of leading scholars, contained rather fewer opportunistic, nationalistic pacifists of the type of Hayashi Hirauma, the author of the previous quotation. There were some who from a very genuinely internationalist point of view were pleased that Japan should be making a contribution to the chances of building a more peaceful world. Others held that the ideal was indeed excellent, but was it really quite necessary to go that far? Renouncing war as an instrument of policy was one thing, but renouncing the possession of armed forces and the right of belligerency was surely unnecessary, many thought, including Communist MPs. There were a number of speeches which betrayed the assumption: for victors to disarm the defeated is to be expected, and it may not be at all a bad idea to forestall the peace treaty negotiations and gain brownie points by self-disarmament, however. . . Sawada Ushimaro, in the House of Peers for instance, made his 'however' very clear.

> Surely this is going too far. Supposing the victors were to take a relatively generous attitude at the peace conference and say we could have one or two divisions. Is it wise to tie ourselves down so clearly in advance by declaring that we will maintain no forces? Armies are sometimes necessary, after all, for maintaining internal law and order.[4]

The enactment of the Peace Constitution 55

Shidehara, responding, was clearly somewhat ruffled: 'There is absolutely no connection between the Constitution and eventual negotiations over a peace treaty: and there is absolutely no connection between troops to be used for fighting foreign countries and forces for maintaining internal order about which the Constitution says nothing'.

Most of the interventions were clearly coloured by the recent experience of defeat and occupation and by the emotions they aroused. Nevertheless, there were some who looked forward from the present dismal situation and speculated as objectively as possible on what might happen under various contingencies to a future unarmed Japan after a peace treaty brought independence. It was on these occasions that the attempts of the United Nations to establish a system of collective security came up. To the Japanese at that time the United Nations itself, let alone its Military Staff Committee, was a distant and not easily comprehensible presence. A Progressive Party MP, Hara Suejirō, speaking in the Lower House debate on 26 June began with the phrase: 'According to what I understand from the foreign telegrams'.[5] In view of the failure of the League,

> in order not to make the same mistake again, the allies appear to be determined to take the lead and establish a kind of world federation... if it should be the case that there should appear over the world an imposing state power this should be able to ensure perpetual peace, in which case Japan's renunciation of war should not be a particularly worrying problem.

A week later, on 4 July, when Prime Minister Yoshida made the first detailed references to the relationship between the Constitution and the UN, he can hardly be said to have displayed more detailed knowledge than Hara. He was responding to the questions raised by Hayashi Hirauma about the rights of self-defence which were quoted earlier.

> What we have in mind is that an international peace body is being established. Once this international peace body is established, if there is any country which starts an aggressive war, this would amount to a rebellion, a revolt against the international peace body and all countries which are members of that body would be required to turn their spears against the rebel, which means that making a distinction between two types of rights of belligerency [aggressive war and defensive war] ceases to have any meaning. If aggressive wars are eliminated, then the right of belligerency and self-defence naturally ceases to exist.... According to Article 43 of the Charter of the United Nations they would have the obligation to provide armed forces and UNO itself would use armed force – the whole world would unite to overwhelm such aggressors. An ideal perhaps, and it may remain an ideal, or it may come to be a dead letter. But at any rate, as far as the United Nations Organization goes – a body created to preserve world peace, that is what it prescribes in its Charter – what

one might call its Constitution – that it will in this way maintain armed forces, that it will have special armed forces of its own, and that those who disrupt the peace, or threaten to disrupt the peace will be subject to sanctions. This Charter – when Japan becomes a member of the organization, after it receives its independence, then it will be protected by this Charter. That is the situation as I interpret it.[6]

It was certainly not with enthusiasm for the dawn of a new age that Yoshida spoke. In return for renouncing the right of self-defence which Japan had to give up anyway, it might just be – the whole thing may remain an ideal, but it might just be – that a United Nations guarantee would provide a substitute. That was as much as Yoshida knew of the matter – and basically as much as he cared. Reading his responses to the debate, his underlying attitude becomes quite clear. Quite apart from any current pressures from the Occupation headquarters, in his judgement the only way to hasten the peace treaty negotiations and create a situation favourable to Japan was by a renunciation of belligerency, including the right of self-defence. That was also a necessary condition for ridding Japan of military dominance. It was his uncompromising clarity on this issue which made him turn on the Communist leader Nosaka when the latter urged the reservation of the right of self-defence. The trouble with Nosaka, he said, was that he didn't know his history: 'most of the wars that have been fought in recent years have been fought on the pretext of self-defence.'[7] The immediate objective was to secure a peace treaty. What kind of world Japan would be living in after that nobody could predict, and it was a waste of time trying to predict it. If it were necessary to revive the right of self-defence, then they would just have to change the Constitution. Yoshida's replies on this point seem a good deal more clear and consistent than Shidehara's.

However, once Yoshida had raised the matter of the relationship between the founding of the United Nations and Japan's right of self-defence in July, it appears that a slightly wider debate took place. Somebody – presumably a newspaper commentator – had pointed out that according to Article 43 Japan would not only be protected, but it would also be required to contribute troops. How could a Japan that did not have an army fulfil its obligations? The argument gained sufficient currency for Ashida Hitoshi to go out of his way to rebut this 'formalistic argument' in a speech in the Diet; provided that Japan is seen as a genuinely peace-loving country, there would be no problem.[8]

The United Nations came up in later debates too, particularly in the form of scepticism about the value of UN security guarantees. Kita Reikichi, for instance,[9] urged that a more reliable alternative would be Swiss-style determined neutrality, while Yamazaki Iwao,[10] showing a certain prescience about post-occupation history, wondered, innocently, whether the best thing might not be to become a protectorate of the United States.

But it was only when the deliberations on the Constitution were reaching their final stages at the end of August and the beginning of September that there was any really detailed examination of the relation between Japan's future and the UN – and that in speeches which showed clear influence of internationalist thinking. They were made by two of the professors recently appointed to the House of Peers. One of them was Nambara Shigeru, later known as an outstanding President of Tokyo University. Like Hayashi Hirauma, quoted earlier, Nambara too spoke of ideals, but these were not 'ideals of the Japanese people through three thousand years of history'; they were 'ideals gradually elaborated over the centuries by the world's leading philosophers and religious leaders'.[11] The fact that 'it has fallen to the lot of the Japanese people to embody these ideals in their constitution' was indeed important and represented 'a landmark in the history of mankind'. However, he had read the UN Charter, including Article 51. Nowhere does it say that countries should renounce the right of self-defence; indeed it specifies that a country which suffers aggression has a right to defend itself until collective action can be taken to protect it.

However for Nambara the idealist, even more important was the fact, already pointed out by other members, that members of the United Nations owed an obligation to take part in collective military action.

> When Japan in the future should be permitted to join the United Nations, are we proposing to surrender this right and evade this duty? Is there not a danger that Japan will sink into that typical Oriental mood of pessimism and resignation, entrusting itself entirely to the goodwill and trust of other nations? Shall we not thereby lose sight of these great positive ideals? Should we not be ready and willing to sacrifice our blood and our sweat so that, together with other nations, we share in the work of protecting freedom and justice and establishing permanent world peace?

Shidehara, the Foreign Minister, responded by saying that the next world war, if there were one, was pretty sure to lead to the total annihilation of mankind. So there was no alternative but to give up war altogether. But he made no reference to the points about the United Nations. Yoshida, the Prime Minister, made even clearer than was his wont that in his view the new Constitution was only a 'temporary provision' and that 'the immediate and pressing objective is to retrieve national sovereignty and independence', and the whole question of Japan's membership in the United Nations should be left until that had been accomplished. Whereupon Nambara, sounding every minute more like a philosophy professor, launched into a disquisition on the essential difference between a concern for peace as a means of stabilizing the *status quo* – merely utilitarian and opportunistic safety-first-ism – and notions of peace based on justice. He did not press Yoshida on what he meant by 'provisional measure' nor return to the question of the right of self-defence or the obligation to provide troops for collective security, and so the debate ended. Professor Nambara afterwards, in the fifties, became the greatly admired leader of the pacifist left, adamantly opposed to Japan's armament. It is ironic to recall that in the 1992 debates concerning the Government's proposed law which was to permit the sending of a contingent of the Self-Defence Force to Cambodia the very phrase used by Nambara – 'shedding blood and sweat' – became a favourite phrase of those promoters of the law whom the pacifist – and like Nambara, in principle internationalist – heirs of Nambara considered dangerous nationalists.

THE PRODUCT OF INTERNATIONALIST OPTIMISM

More uncompromising logic in his attacks on the government position was shown by the legal scholar Takayanagi Kenzō. The provisions of the Japanese Constitution which aimed at the total demilitarization of Japan were perfectly appropriate for a world in which 'the use of force is permitted only as the servant of Human Reason as world policing power'.[12] But that is not what the United Nations envisages. The United Nations embodies the quite different principle that armed sovereign powers take counsel together collectively to impose sanctions on aggressors. So what exactly is the government's future intention? Is the government going, like Switzerland, to declare its adherence to permanent neutrality and refuse membership in the UN? 'To remain outside the UN would surely be the policy most consonant with our status as a country which has enacted this Constitution. Or, slightly more compromisingly, are we going to accept membership and work from inside to spread the principles of *our* Constitution? Which is it to be?'[13]

As he pressed them in turn he got various answers from different ministers. Compared with Yoshida who brushed the question aside, saying that was an issue that could be faced up to when they came to it,[14] Shidehara took him more seriously. Membership of the United Nations was certainly desirable, but when that invitation comes we shall have to make very clear the implications of our Constitution, particularly of Article 9, and enter the appropriate reservations to our candidature.[15] The Minister of State, Kanamori Tokujiro, showed his mastery of the smoke-screen:

> what attitude we shall take at that time must be thought through from a variety of angles and with a broad vision, and it seems to me that there is plenty of scope for doing so.... It is my opinion that there are a variety of paths we might take in order to achieve a suitable compromise between the two alternatives which have been posed.[16]

There are other references in the Diet debates and in the media discussions on the Constitution to the United Nations and its plans for collective security, but it is safe to say that they were anything but central to the discussion of Article 9 (and, it will be recalled, Article 9 attracted less debate than Article 1). But that is not to say that there was no connection between the passing of the Constitution and the birth of the United Nations. Had the debates on the Constitution taken place when the Cold War was fully institutionalized, and when the Military Staff Committee had already given up the prospect of a UN collective security system as lost, it is a reasonable bet that the renunciation of armaments would not have been carried so smoothly. In that sense the Peace Constitution was not simply a means of hastening the peace treaty and Japan's return to a place of honour in the international community, it was also a product of *international* optimism in the pre-Cold War period.

That, as is argued later in Chapter 8, would seem to be a good reason why, now that the Cold War has come to an end and there has been a return to a new kind of optimism, if on nothing like the 1945 scale, there is an argument for reconsidering and re-evaluating the constitution – re-evaluating it in the light of a current understanding of international society far richer than was available at the time. In 1946, for a Japan that had over many years been isolated from the rest of the world, New York was like the other side of the moon. Today when the 'increasing borderlessness of the world economy' has become a cliché of Japan's economists, we live in a different world, and one in which the concept of pacifism needs rethinking. The result of such rethinking might surely be something which Nambara suggested but did not explicitly formulate – namely a peace-promoting amendment of the Peace Constitution – an amendment which would permit Japan too, 'ready and willing to sacrifice our blood and our sweat' as he put it, to join with other nations 'in the work of protecting freedom and justice and establishing permanent world peace'.

6 From the world's United Nations to the United Nations as no man's land

THE KOREAN WAR AND THE UN ARMY

With the outbreak of the Korean War in 1950, the largest regional conflict of the postwar years, the idea of a UN military force, still barely kept alive in the desultory discussions of the Military Staff Committee, suddenly became a concrete reality. As the United Nations came to establish itself as a central locus of international diplomacy, the United States rapidly created an automatic majority in the General Assembly. It succeeded in creating a bloc of satellite nations which could generally be relied upon – and certainly when there was a clear opposition between it and the rival bloc of the Soviet Union and its satellites – to give it more than half of the votes. That was how it was able, after the Chinese Revolution of 1949, to keep the Beijing Government out of the United Nations and ensure that the right of permanent membership in the Security Council remained with the Government in Taiwan. In impotent anger, the Soviet Union declared a boycott of the United Nations.

It was this which made it possible, after the North Korean attack, for the United States, in the absence of a Soviet delegate to exercise his veto power, to use Article 42 for a series of resolutions which made the American Army a United Nations' Army, made General MacArthur the United Nations' Commander, and entrusted to the United States the mission of rolling back North Korean aggression under the UN flag. Subsequently units from other countries joined the Americans but the 'strategic direction' of operations which the Charter specified should lie with the Security Council and the Military Staff Committee was quite clearly in the hands of the American Government. When Attlee, the British Prime Minister, alarmed by reports that the Americans were considering using atomic weapons to stop the Chinese, got on a plane to cross the Atlantic, it was not to the UN headquarters in New York that he went but to Washington. It was President Truman and not the UN Secretary-General who finally forced resignation on a General MacArthur who was determined to cross the 46th Parallel and deliver a mortal blow to China. It was at this period that the idea took root in Japan – an idea still strongly held by many people – that the United Nations belongs not to mankind, but to the United States: its main significance is as an instrument of American policy in the Cold War.

There is good justification for this. Nevertheless, the North Koreans *were* aggressors. (The theories that the South had attacked first did not even seem plausible at the time, let alone in the light of subsequent evidence.) To repel aggression can undoubtedly be counted a useful step towards the establishment of a system of international order. Hence, however critical the left-wing parties in Britain and France were towards the United States and however much they charged the United States with responsibility for intensification of the Cold War and harboured sympathy for Russia, they nevertheless were not opposed to the involvement of their countries through the sending of combat units to Korea.

By the same token when, a year after the ending of the Korean War, the United States sought to build on that precedent by passing the 'Uniting for Peace Resolution' in the General Assembly, there was no strong opposition from America's critics in Europe. The purpose of this resolution which, thanks to its automatic majority, it was able to get through the General Assembly in the teeth of opposition from the Soviet Union, was to institutionalize some of the features of the previous Korean experience. In concrete terms:

1 Member countries would designate, among their own armed forces, units which could be provided in an emergency as part of a UN force.
2 Those forces would receive special training and equipment for such purposes.
3 Member countries were required to report on the measures that they had taken to these ends.
4 A fourteen-nation Collective Measures Committee was to be created to decide on matters such as future command structures – that is to say the various questions on which the Military Staff Committee had got bogged down.

All the members of this Committee were from the Western bloc; the Soviet Union declared that the whole concept was contrary to the Charter which gave 100 per cent responsibility in military matters to the Security Council, and none of its allies were willing to take part. The Committee produced three reports, but in the end did not go further than institutionalizing the precedent of the Korean War. When it was necessary to take action against aggression, a state or group of states would be designated as Executive Military Authority to do the work of the United Nations. This authority would have the responsibility for strategic planning and for negotiating contributions from other members. It would however be required to act within the policy guidelines and objectives set by resolutions of the United Nations.

62 *The argument*

The Committee had no great problems in settling some of the minor details. In order to make clear that it was the United Nations that was waging war there would, as in Korea, be UN flags, a proper UN uniform and a new system of UN military honours. But given the basic intention of appointing national agents to conduct the UN's wars, the Committee could make no contributions to the central Article 43 question of how to construct a standing UN military state of readiness.

THE YEAR 1956

It was however, astonishingly enough, not conflict between the superpowers but conflict between the US on the one hand and Britain and France on the other which led, through the Suez crisis, to the creation of UNEF, the first peace-keeping operation of the UN itself. The reports of the Collective Measures Committee proved irrelevant to this purpose and the UN found itself building up a new type of organization from scratch.[1]

1956 was a crucial year for making clear the boundaries within which the United Nations could be effective in Cold War conditions. The British and the French, seeking to inflict a mortal blow on Egypt for its nationalization of the Suez Canal, incited Israel into the second Arab–Israeli War so that they could invade on the pretext of separating the combatants and preserving an international waterway. This happened in November, the same month as the Soviet Union sent troops into Hungary to suppress the Hungarian Revolution. The Security Council received resolutions condemning the aggressors in both cases, but they were both met with vetos, in the one case from Britain and France, in the other from the Soviet Union. In the Suez case, the procedures laid down in the 'Uniting for Peace' resolution were used to override the British and French vetoes and force the British and French to withdraw from Egypt. Those resolutions – an essential part of the equation – were backed by an American threat to cut off British oil supplies, but it was important that the two countries were also offered the face-saving device of a United Nations Expeditionary Force which would perform that function of 'separating the combatants' which had been their ostensible excuse for intervening. In the case of Hungary, however, resolutions of condemnation were proffered and vetoed and that was the end of the matter: 'the lesson of 1956 was clear. The UN could act against aggression only if the two great powers were agreed or if one of them was indifferent. And only two powers counted'.[2] This was indeed the basic principle constraining the operations of the UN until, in 1990, there was only one Great Power left.

Nevertheless, however far removed from the prospects which the optimists and idealists of 1945 foresaw, the United Nations did not simply stagnate during the forty years of the Cold War. This is not the place for a detailed history of those years, but it is worth trying to summarize some of the main trends.

INTERNATIONAL DISPUTES

The greater part of the wars which have broken out since 1945 resulted from the breakup of the European empires and the birth and establishment of successor states. In situations like that of Vietnam, where the issue was whether the new successor state should be a member of the Soviet or of the American sphere of influence, the UN was unable to play any part at all and, in the case of conflicts which took place within some major power's well-established sphere of influence – in Latin America or in French West Africa for example – the tendency was for them to be left to be dealt with 'internally', under the aegis of their Great Power.

In the Congo, where conflict got beyond the power of Belgium, the former metropolitan power, to control, the United Nations undertook the formidable mission of bringing a civil war to an end and establishing a successor state. The military forces which it was able to mobilize – something close to 20,000 at the peak – were simply not commensurate with the difficulty of the situation.

Here again, Russo-American rivalry – control over Zaire's copper mines was a particularly important stake – finally led to the withdrawal of the UN troops, leaving behind them very little accomplished – but not until after personal mediation by the Secretary-General, Hammarskjold, had cost him his life. (Only recently has evidence appeared that – as was suspected at the time – the crashing of his plane was not entirely accidental; a plan hatched by groups opposed to the UN had intended to force his plane to land in order to try to persuade him to change UN policy. They had botched the operation and caused his plane to crash instead.)

Whether because it had burned its fingers in the Congo, or whether because the number of ex-colonies transiting to independence diminished, while peace-keeping and armistice-monitoring operations continued, especially in the Middle East, there was no subsequent operation which involved the formation of a UN military force capable of armed intervention on anything like the scale of the Congo until the recent instances in Cambodia and Bosnia–Herzegovina.

MEDIATION AND PEACE MAKING

Most of the dispute-resolution activities of the United Nations have taken the form of mediation for peaceful settlement. The second most common type have been situations in which the parties to the dispute have been clearly designated as offender and victim in Security Council resolutions intended to urge the offending side to amend its ways. Instances where action has been taken further – to the point of invoking Article 42 of the Charter to impose mandatory sanctions on offenders, i.e., mandatory on all UN members – were confined, until the Gulf War (during the Cold War that is), to the cases of Rhodesia and South Africa. Both were instances of racial conflict in which white people were oppressing black people, instances where the United States was moved, by consideration for its interests in sub-Saharan Africa and for the black vote at home, to overcome its normal unwillingness to cooperate with the Soviet Union.

At Versailles in 1919, Japan had the bitter experience of seeing its proposal that a Declaration of Racial Equality should be included in the preamble to the League Covenant brutally rejected. In the half century after the end of the Second World War, the confrontation of the Cold War, spreading to every area of politics and morality, seemed to create a world in which there was no basic consensus on anything. But on this one issue there *was* a firm overt consensus – a consensus in which both the superpowers concurred: all actions and deeds which seemed to condone racial discrimination had to be avoided. 'Race discrimination' in this case meant primarily discrimination between white and black. It is one of the ironies of history that the Japanese, whose delegates had campaigned for racial equality at Versailles should have been declared in South Africa to be honorary whites, and that a number of Japanese corporations should have set up dummy companies in order to evade UN trade sanctions against South Africa.

AMERICA'S LOSS OF ITS AUTOMATIC MAJORITY

The sensitivity to race issues was not unconnected with another phenomenon which transformed the UN in the 1960s – the fact that the growing number of former colonies which achieved independence came to constitute a majority of the nations represented in the General Assembly. It was at this time that there emerged the concept of a third world, distinct from the first world of the West and the second world of the Soviet bloc, a concept which acquired a certain identity and organizational form at the 1957 Bandung Conference as the group of Non-Aligned Countries – non-aligned with respect to the Cold War rivals, that is. Apart from their shared sense of resentment at the dominance of the Euro-American powers, there was not enough commonality of objectives and aspirations for the non-aligned to form a reliably unified bloc vote in the UN General Assembly, but their numerical importance effectively ended the era when the US could count on an automatic General Assembly majority on issues in which it was deeply interested.

The United States, which hitherto had valued its leadership role in the UN and given quite high priority in its foreign policy objectives to keeping the prestige which went with that leadership role, began to lose its affection for the UN and to downgrade the UN in its foreign policy objectives. American public opinion turned against the UN, one specific factor being the anger of American Jews at General Assembly resolutions which targeted Israel for special condemnation – most notably the 1977 resolution which declared Zionism to be a form of racism. (Once again, that universally potent symbol, racism.) Formerly overwhelmingly the main source of development aid, the US began tightening its purse strings (the worsening of its balance of payments contributing to this), and shifting more of its aid resources from multilateral to bilateral forms from which it could derive more direct payoff in terms of influence. It also began to delay its payments of its dues to the UN and its agencies.

It was not only that it had less and less possibility of furthering its policy aims in Latin America and the Middle East through UN diplomacy. In the all-important sphere of its relations with the Soviet Union, it was through direct bilateral negotiations, not through UN diplomacy, that steady progress was made in, for example, nuclear disarmament. It was only on issues such as Afghanistan, when the US could claim some support from third world countries, that it used the UN as a forum for diplomatic action.

AGGRESSION AND THE PRINCIPLE OF NON-INTERFERENCE IN INTERNAL AFFAIRS

The increase in the number of third world countries represented at the UN brought into new focus the question, central to the problem of creating a law-based international order: how to define the threats to peace or the actual breaches of peace which should properly call forth sanctions from international society. There had been discussion at the San Francisco conference of the definition of 'aggression', but those who wanted to include some explicit definition in the Charter lost the debate. The decision as to whether or not there had been a breach of the peace, it was argued by those who won the debate, could only be left to political negotiation, case by case, among the Great Powers – to 'world public opinion', which meant, effectively, a political (and moral) consensus among the Great Powers. It was a basic assumption of the Charter that the legitimacy of governments was established by the normal procedures of diplomacy – recognition, the exchange of ambassadors and the like – and by the procedures for granting, and revoking, membership in the UN. National sovereignty was in principle absolute, and non-interference in the internal affairs of states was a categorical imperative. Consequently sanctions were to be invoked only when – to borrow the terminology of the final resolution of the Disarmament Conference of May–June 1978 – there was a 'threat or use of force against the sovereignty, territorial integrity or political independence of any [existing] state.'

As we saw in Chapter 4, the Soviet Union had already made an issue of this in 1946 when it insisted that the work of the Military Staff Committee should begin with a statement concerning the purposes and scope of military action by the UN, its main concern being to prevent the UN from being used to suppress national liberation movements.

This was not surprising. The major European empires had not been fully liquidated. There was a widespread view that there could still be 'just wars', and that included not only defensive wars. To make the mere maintenance of the *status quo* the fundamental principle was to freeze the world's existing distribution of power and wealth. Within democratic countries it was possible to change the distribution of power and wealth through the mechanisms of institutionalized politics. But the mechanisms for doing this at an international level were, to say the least, rudimentary and hampered by the ban on interference in states' internal affairs; hence it was inevitable that in the pursuit of justice, resort would sometimes be had to armed force.

Reinforced by such arguments, a UN with a much heavier representation of ex-colonial countries showed a much greater sympathy towards 'the use of armed force in the pursuit of justice' than was evident at the time the Charter was written. The final resolution of the Disarmament Conference followed the traditional definition of culpable uses of force quoted earlier with an additional clause; 'or [the threat or use of force] against peoples under colonial or foreign domination seeking to exercise their right to self-determination'.

In fact, of course, colonialism was on the way out and, often with the help of the UN's own special organ for the purpose, the Trusteeship Council, areas of the world under 'colonial domination' steadily diminished. But that was by no means so far as the other term in that resolution – 'political domination' – was concerned.

Conflicts coming under this category which became issues at the UN can be subdivided into two types: independence movements mounted by an ethnic minority which were assisted by – or the suppression of which was assisted by – outside powers, and situations where the internal conflict derived from a political clash rather than from ethnic nationalism. One of the very first issues brought before the Security Council at the time of its birth – the Greek Civil War and the charge that Stalin, in spite of having conceded that Greece was to belong to the Western sphere of influence, was nevertheless actively aiding the communist guerillas – was of the latter type, so were the Vietnam war, and the Nicaraguan and El Salvador conflicts.

All of these were products of the Cold War, fought by proxy between the superpowers, and we may hope that with the end of the Cold War we have seen the last of them.[3] But the end of the Cold War has, by contrast, brought an explosive increase in the other type – conflicts arising from outside involvement in national independence movements. The power structure within the Soviet empire in particular, consolidated as it was by the superpower rivalry itself, had kept the lid on national aspirations which sprang to life as soon as that structure disintegrated. And while new conflicts over where borders are to be drawn break out every month in the former Soviet Union – many of them every bit as difficult of resolution as those caused by the breakup of Yugoslavia – some long-standing conflicts such as those over the Kurds' and the Karens' claims to independence still continue to smoulder – in the case of the Kurds to flare up, rather, thanks to the Gulf War.

Is it possible to discern any long-term, evolutionary trends in the UN's handling of these matters? The Cold War factor is of such overwhelming importance that it is difficult to be sure, but one might hazard the following generalizations:

a   The principle of non-interference is no longer the iron rule it once was, but that is not to say the power of the UN itself to intervene in such conflicts has increased.
b   Namibia was, after all, brought to peaceful UN-supervised elections. It is hard to say what will be the outcome in Cambodia, but at least the Paris accords were signed and a UN operation mounted. In Yugoslavia, despite their obvious sympathy for the Serbs, the Russians refrained from vetoing sanctions against them. These examples suggest that in both great and small powers there has been an increase in the number of diplomats and officials who are capable of transcending to some degree their own national interest and seeking to judge the rights and wrongs of conflicts by objective criteria. Khrushchev is famous for the phrase, 'There are neutral countries, but there are no neutral men.' I believe – I would like to believe – that slowly this is becoming less true.
c   And as to what counts as justice and even-handedness, in spite of the rise of Muslim fundamentalism and its frontal challenge to the dominant Western scale of ethical values, would it not be true to say that there is a long-run tendency for the creation of a judgemental consensus to become easier? Consider, for example, the fact that even many of those outside the United States who were highly critical of that country's motives in the Gulf War nevertheless recognized that Iraq's invasion of Kuwait was something to which the international community was obliged forcefully to react.

THE POWERS OF THE SECRETARY-GENERAL

It is not clear that one can call it an evolutionary trend, but one aspect of the United Nations which was at first unclear but has subsequently become gradually clarified through actual UN practice – and the importance of which has also gradually become clarified – is the role of the Secretary-General. As already noted, the League had been conceived as nothing more than a council of the representatives of sovereign states. The UN was not much different, in that there was a clear avoidance of any provisions which smacked of the creation of an embryo 'world government'. But it did go just one step further in giving to the Secretary-General the 'right' to put on the agenda of the Security Council any situation (situation, not conflict) which he thought constituted a threat to peace. (There was a proposal at San Francisco to amend 'right' to 'duty', but it was defeated.) However, the powers of initiative of the Secretary-General and his direct staff working on Security Council affairs have turned out to be a good deal broader.

This was particularly the case during the eight years (1953–61) when the most impressive of postwar Secretaries-General, Hammarskjold, occupied the post. On several occasions he was able to transcend the role of Security Council emissary and positively seize the initiative to act as mediator, in his unique capacity as a person who by virtue of his office could transcend the interests of any single nation. In the Thai–Cambodia dispute of 1959, when the two parties were about to appeal to the Security Council, he persuaded them not to exacerbate the dispute by doing so, but instead to accept the mediation of his own personal envoy. Already in 1955 he had established the 'Beijing precedent'. A US military plane had force-landed in China having lost its way. The crew were taken prisoner and not allowed to return. The Security Council passed a resolution urging their release and asking the Secretary-General to go to Beijing to negotiate. He went only after making clear to the Council his disagreement with the wording of the Resolution's criticism of China, and extracting the understanding that he had a free hand to negotiate a settlement which the Council could either approve or disown, but only after the event.

The Secretary-General's scope for initiative and his effectiveness depend on his, and perhaps eventually her, personality and also on the general prestige of the UN. It has not been a story of steady expansion. Even so, in 1982, at the time of the Falkland crisis, when America's plainly evidenced antipathy to the UN had brought it to a low point, the Secretary-General was very close indeed to getting a settlement which would have avoided war. In the mid-1980s an expert on the UN wrote as follows:[4]

> there can be little doubt that the only important winner in the intra-institutional struggle has been the Secretary-General. The General Assembly can make more noise. Security Council can still act when there is unanimity of the permanent members. But to the limited extent that the UN is now having any salutary effect on the real world beyond its own compound, it is primarily because of the functions being performed by the Secretary-General.

In the post-Cold War world of the present, the intra-institutional struggle is rather less important than the extra-institutional struggle for influence – as exemplified for instance in the fact that the job of brokering the peace process in the Middle East – what one would imagine to be an ideal role for the Secretary-General – has fallen not to him, but to the American Secretary of State.

INTERNATIONAL LAW AND THE LAW-ABIDING SPIRIT

There are a number of Japanese proverbs which convey the notion that justice has precious little to do with the way the world works. 'You win and you are the state; lose and you are the rebels'; 'Money talks, even for the judgements of Heaven.' And not surprisingly, for that is the way most societies in human history have been. And the way modern societies still are, some might say – pointing, for instance, to the fact that former Prime Minister Tanaka, for all the court proceedings against him for bribery, still has not gone to jail. But in fact modern Japan is vastly different from the Japan of the Edo period, 150 years ago – far closer to being a 'rule of law' society. It has become a society in which everyone can, and most people in fact do, expect that if they have a strong enough case they can get an impartial hearing in the courts of law, even against the most powerful in the land.

But international society is very different: it is still in its Edo period phase, where most disputes are settled not by principles of justice interpreted in courts of law, but by relative power; through compromises worked out by 'political' negotiation. The so-called 'Northern territories' question is a case in point. Japan, instead of appealing to the International Court of Justice, has continued to seek a 'political' solution, using various means to persuade the Russians to make concessions – highly unlikely though such concessions might be, given the nature of Russian domestic politics. (Though that did not prevent the Japanese delegation at the Munich G7 summit in 1992 from expending enormous diplomatic capital in order to get a reference to the territorial dispute inserted in the summit communiqué – an expression of hope for a solution in accord with 'justice and international law'.)

But in fact the world has moved on from its 'Edo period'; the International Court of Justice may not be very much used, but there are signs of an evolution, both in its capacity to deliver unbiased judgements, and in the extent to which there is a general expectation of it giving such judgements. If the Japanese Foreign Office refrains from referring the territorial dispute with Russia to the Court because it fears it would lose the case, one can understand its position; but if the reason is fear that the Court will not judge fairly, they are probably wrong. Daniel Moynihan has written about the 1979 incident when Iranian 'students' took hostage the members of the American embassy in Teheran.[5]

> The most elemental rule of international law, the immunity of envoys, was thus challenged. The response of the United States was wholly tactical. Emissaries were sent, intermediaries sought out. There was no lack of energy in the face of an extraordinary international event which immediately became a domestic crisis, but the State Department turned every which way save toward law.

On 20 November, some sixteen days after the embassy had been seized, this senator went to the floor to ask why we had not gone to the Court:

> I suppose there will be those who ask, what can the International Court of Justice do? I can answer with, I think, some precision. The International Court of Justice can say what is law and which party has violated it. The United States Government has put too much of its hopes and efforts into the rule of law to ignore the institution of the Court at this moment.

Almost as an afterthought we thereupon did so. Within the executive branch there was no confidence in the Court. Surely a Soviet judge would assert that we had provoked the students; a South American judge would require more submissions; an African judge would wish to conduct a parallel inquiry into human rights violations in South Africa. The Iranians wouldn't respond. Etc. Yet, two weeks later, December 15, 1979, a unanimous court handed down its provisional order which clearly established that the rights of the United States were being violated, that the government of Iran was obliged to restore the embassy to United States control and release the hostages. In the manner of such rulings, it was further ordered that neither party take any action to exacerbate the situation, pending a final judgement.

On April 24, 1980, one month before the Court issued its final judgement, the United States launched a rescue operation that failed. The world had then to endure a televised display of the charred remains of eight American servicemen. Had the United States awaited the final ruling of the Court, delivered on May 24, 1980, we could then have proceeded to a much more public and far more punitive mode and without the risk of the kind of failure we had encountered.

[The operation was highly sophisticated, but essentially risky and the probability of failure high.]

> This was in fact a weak policy. A strong policy would have awaited the decision of the Court, hurrying it a bit if necessary. Inevitably, unquestionably, the decision would be handed down in our favor. It was. By thirteen votes to two, the Court held 'that the Islamic Republic of Iran, by the conduct which the Court has set out in this Judgement, has violated in several respects, and is still violating, obligations owed by it to the United States of America under international convention in force beween the two countries, as well as under long-established rules of general international law.' (The dissenting judges were Syrian and Soviet. The Soviet judge had a certain argument. The United States had clear treaty rights, but the 'military invasion of the territory of Iran' deprived it of them.) In any event, a unanimous Court stated that Iran 'must immediately terminate the unlawful

detention' of the hostages, return the Embassy and Consulates, and such like measures.

Here is the moment of truth for international law. Who will enforce it? The same question arises with respect to domestic law, and the same answer is to be given. The political system enforces it.

[The probable scenario: the US goes to the Security Council; economic sanctions are decreed and if they have no effect, military sanctions are taken.]

Quite possibly some or all of the hostages would have died. Vastly greater numbers died to put in place the principles we would now be defending. . . .

The irony is that the Carter administration genuinely believed in the United Nations. But knew nothing about it. I attest that the principals involved with the hostage rescue had barely heard of the Court and did not at all appreciate our rights under Article 94. Had they done, Jimmy Carter might well have been re-elected. Instead, at noon on January 20, 1981, Republican senators on the West Front of the Capitol stood fiddling with transistor radios, catching the news that Iran had released the hostages the moment Ronald Reagan became president.

I have quoted this at great length because Moynihan's testimony on behalf of the ICJ bears the greater force in that it comes from one who was the US Ambassador to the UN at a time when America was seeking to combat the growing strength of the third world in that organization.[6] More – is the burden of his remarks – than one might reasonably think, the ICJ has matured; its judgements are not all that much influenced by political bias. In this respect at least, the postwar history of the UN has been a history not of stagnation or of backsliding, but of progress.

HUMAN RIGHTS

I have argued that there were signs at least of movement towards a greater international consensus in judging whether particular actions of states constitute aggression and what counts as justified use of force, but perhaps the most persuasive support for an optimistic belief in progress can be found in the field of human rights.

One can crudely summarize the opposing positions on the role of human rights issues in international relations as follows: on the one hand, the total insistence on the absoluteness of national sovereignty which forbids any interference in a country's internal affairs whether it be by other countries or by international organizations. Not quite the same logic, but a similar non-interventionist conclusion follows from a different argument, namely that, of course it is bad to permit oppressive government and the abuse of human rights, but the consequences of wars between states would be far worse. And if it is the case that the only feasible basis for effective international organization to prevent war is to recognize the absolute sovereignty of member states and their freedom from interference in their internal governance, then so be it; the human rights abuses are a cost that has to be borne. One might call the first the principled and the second the instrumentalist version of the non-intervention argument.

Opposed to that is the – to use the Chinese phrase – 'all men are brothers' appeal to common humanity, the claim that we are human beings first and Japanese or Italians or Scots second. If fellow human beings are being abused, it should not affect our desire to do something about it whether the abuse is taking place in our own country or in Latin America or at the North Pole. We all aspire to live not just in a country, but in a world, in which people are not tortured and ill-treated. Hence interference across frontiers is perfectly justified.

In actual fact there are few people, probably, who do not feel slightly more emotional involvement when they read about, say, a child abuse case in their own country than when they read about a similar case in a distant part of the world; but nevertheless, from the Anti-Slavery League onwards, there have been not a few people who have actually devoted their lives to attempts to change other countries' maltreatment of their citizens; and many many more people who would firmly endorse the 'common humanity overrides nationality' principle *qua* principle.

The UN Charter sits contradictorily between the two polar arguments. On the one hand it endorses (Article 2.7) the non-intervention principle, and on the other (Article 1.3) it declares one of the major purposes of the Organization to be further international cooperation designed to ensure that individual rights and basic human freedoms are guaranteed irrespective of race, sex, language or religion. Perhaps 'compromise' is a better word than 'contradiction'. Among those who signed the Charter there were undoubtedly many dyed-in-the-wool 'absolute sovereigntists', but there were also many who were drawn to the 'common humanity' position and were persuaded to accept the principle of non-intervention, only on instrumental grounds.

But the starting point is less important for present purposes than what has happened since, and here, I think, one can see clear evidence of a shift in the balance of opinion towards the 'common humanity' end of the spectrum.

From the beginning, the UN's Economic and Social Council set up a Commission on Human Rights which for twenty years did little except produce reports on promoting respect for human rights and getting countries to report on 'the present situation with respect to human rights' in their own country. As for taking up particular instances of human rights abuse and seeking remedies, there were far too many delegates conscious of their own country's vulnerability to criticism; the 'people in glass houses...' principle always operated to prevent effective probing.

Between 1966 and 1971, however, a series of resolutions began to change things. South African apartheid was the catalyst. The growing number of African members states, keen to use the human rights issue as a means of mobilizing international pressure on South Africa, made possible the creation by the Sub-Commission on Prevention of Discrimination and Protection of Minorities of a new procedure for investigating and exposing abuses of human rights. Once these procedures were established, the efforts of the Soviet Union – which had supported their introduction when they were aimed at South Africa – to limit them to racial issues were unsuccessful and they came to be frequently applied to cases of purely political oppression.

The main elements of this new departure were, to summarize briefly: i) the committee could receive representations concerning abuse of human rights not only from official government delegates, but also from individuals, NGOs and other bodies concerned with human rights issues; ii) if the representations made to the Commission 'appear to reveal a consistent pattern of gross and reliably attested violations of human rights and fundamental freedoms', several further steps were possible – immediate report to a plenary session of the Human Rights Committee, confidential negotiations with the government concerned to bring about a correction of the abuses, the despatch of an investigatory mission with the consent of the country concerned, or if such a mission were refused entry, the appointment of a special investigatory team to make what investigations it could in the teeth of that opposition – all of which could result in sending a report to the plenary session of the Human Rights Committee criticizing the offending country.

The procedure was certainly complex and cumbersome. From a working group of the Sub-Commission on Prevention of Discrimination and Protection of Minorities, to a sub-committee of the Human Rights Commission, to the Commission itself and then on to the Economic and Social Council; every stage offered opportunities for strangulation and suppression – a process in which political considerations played a far greater role than questions of the adequacy or otherwise of the evidence. Nevertheless, to take one example, anger against the brutality of the repression in Chile after the fall of the Allende regime was sufficiently widespread that many countries normally dedicated to anti-communism voted for a motion of censure in the General Assembly. It was, in fact, from this time onwards that human rights activity began to become brisker and (in spite of the subequent reversal when Reagan came to power) the Carter Human Rights Diplomacy gave a boost to these institutional developments after 1976.

Only in the two Southern African cases has the UN carried human rights protection to the point of imposing sanctions, but one should not underestimate the effects of condemnatory resolutions in the General Assembly. Recall the consternation in Japan when the situation of Koreans resident in Japan was taken up in the Human Rights Commission. It may well be that Japanese are more sensitive to outside opinion than most peoples, but even the most evil dictators can be surprisingly thin-skinned unless, like fanatical Islamic fundamentalists, they have wholly turned their back on the outside world and its opinions, which they condemn as embodiments of wickedness.

The above summary relates only to activities in the UN, but it should not be forgotten that regional organizations have also played a role. Especially important since the Carter days has been the Organization of American States whose human rights activities have been a major influence on developments at the UN. And in Europe, the 1975 Helsinki Declaration not only promoted dialogue between East and West but made sure that human rights were firmly on the agenda of that dialogue. Just how great was the contribution of this 'Helsinki process' to the democratization of Eastern Europe and the Soviet Union will always remain a matter for argument rather than accurate measurement, but that it made a considerable contribution can hardly be disputed. An American scholar remarks that it is easy to be cynical, but one needs an historical perspective. It took seventy-six years from the time America's founding fathers won a revolution in the name of man's unalienable rights before the slaves were emancipated. The distance the UN has travelled since

> its first steps in the field offers one ground for optimism about its future course. Another is the effort so many governments have made to restrain the organization's forward progress and to evade its primitive machinery of enforcement. By their acts they have acknowledged the influence the idea of human rights has acquired over the minds of their subjects. Hypocrisy continues to offer credible evidence of the possibility of virtue.[7]

THIRD WORLD DEVELOPMENT

The area of concern which has come to overshadow the UN's original dominant concern with peace and collective security – especially in the various specialist organizations of 'the UN family' is, of course, the question of third world development, of foreign aid, the North–South problem – the phraseology varies, but the phenomenon addressed, the distribution of the world's wealth and income, remains the same. It is the sole concern of the UNDP – a dependent part of the UN itself – and a dominant concern of some of its specialized agencies; the ILO and the WHO which have existed since the days of the League of Nations, and those, like UNESCO, UNIDO or UNCTAD to which the UN itself has given birth. If one includes those dealing with development within the economic and social divisions of the UN itself, some ninety per cent of the total staff of the UN family are engaged in development work.

Can one, in this field as in the field of human rights, find evidence of 'progressive evolution'? It is hard to say yes. From the early 1950s through to the end of the 1960s, the Development Decade, as the UN General Assembly dubbed it, indeed, up to the oil crisis of 1973, there was a steady expansion of aid activity. One after another, ex-colonies became independent, became UN members and prepared their plans to transform themselves into modern states. Given that bilateral assistance often carried a faint whiff of 'neo-colonialism', the role of the multilateral agencies in providing guidance, technical and capital assistance, acquired increasing importance. It was a time of great optimism. Penicillin and public health would have a dramatic effect on death rates; a national system of elementary schools would abolish illiteracy; new universities would train efficient civil servants and, in two or three generations, one could expect the poorest African ex-colony to become a prosperous modern state. Such was the vision which permeated not only the speeches of politicians, but even the writings of expert social scientists.

The current mood of disillusionment is vastly different. There are many reasons for the change, but one important one is the shift in attitudes and policies of the United States. America's loss of its automatic majority in the UN General Assembly, with the accession of large numbers of ex-colonies, was closely followed by the turbulence in the world economy set off by the oil crisis. And the oil crisis, an example of the third world defying the West, was one factor in the rise of a new ideology of confrontation, led by left-wing governments and intellectuals of Latin America, and leading intellectuals of the Arab world – an ideology of confrontation *vis-à-vis* the developed countries, and especially *vis-à-vis* the US. 'A New World Economic Order' was their slogan. Its precise policy content was often hard to define, but the tone of anger and confrontation – a long, long way from the gratitude thought proper in humble aid recipients – was impossible to mistake. The rich countries reacted with a similarly adversarial stance. It was around this time that the phrase 'third world development' began to give way to 'the North–South problem' with its zero-sum implications. The confrontation was at its most acute in UNESCO, where the developing countries demanded a 'New World Information Order' which the developed countries dismissed as a device for curbing Western press reporting of third-world corruption and bad government. The split reached the point at which the United States demonstratively left the organization, followed by Britain and several other countries.

The New Information Order was not the sole reason for their protests. The UNESCO bureaucracy had always had a reputation for inefficiency, waste and frequent corruption but, the protesters charged, under the regime of its Senegalese Director, M'Bow, these defects were multiplied. UNESCO was only the extreme example; the impression was widespread that the UN agencies in charge of development were prone to the worst type of bureaucratic behaviour – preoccupation with turf wars to the exclusion of a concern for getting the job done; pursuit of personal gain rather than organizational objectives; favouritism and appointment of low-quality officials. And this provided a second reason for the disillusionment over development which set in in the 1970s.

A major source of the problem is the national quota system of staffing, with each member country having a presumptive 'right' to a number of staff posts roughly equivalent to its dues contribution. Each agency sets its own recruitment standards and is not obliged to take incompetent individuals. But, since in most cases candidates are proposed by governments, the agency is in luck if it turns out that a government proposes someone who is a) able and b) actually interested in doing a good job of work, rather than in enjoying the perks and privileges of an international civil servant. At the agency's annual meeting the Director-General has to handle an assembly of many scores of delegates. However dedicated he is to maximizing his agency's contribution to making the world a better place, he has to get his budget and activity plan voted. He has to negotiate with delegates who are said to be planning amendments that would cut out one of his favourite projects. 'Right,' he might be told, 'we'll go along with that. By the way, I hear, incidentally, that such and such a Director is leaving and you're looking for a replacement. As a matter of fact, we've got a splendid chap in our Ministry of Agriculture who. . . .' Hard to refuse, and if it subsequently turns out that the splendid chap in the Ministry of Agriculture is the delegate's cousin, nobody is particularly surprised. For an official in a poor African country, life in Rome or Geneva or Vienna on a UN salary is a close approximation to heaven.

There are differences among the agencies. Those which require specialized technical knowledge from most of their staff – like the FAO – are better able to insist on objective criteria for recruitment and are less subject to inefficiency and 'privatization' than a UNESCO where mastery of dubious rhetoric and the deployment of fuzzy concepts are an essential part of the stock-in-trade. But none of the agencies escapes this kind of criticism. From Japan's point of view it is unfortunate that WHO, which hitherto had a very good reputation, is widely reported to have declined sharply in both efficiency and morale since a Japanese, Dr Hiroshi Nakajima, took over as Director-General.

The third reason for disilluionment is that it needed only a decade or so of experience to show that the optimistic hopes entertained earlier were, indeed, naive. Some countries showed healthy growth, some did worse than stagnate, and the amount of aid they received seemed to have nothing to do with it. It was especially over the prospects for Africa that the disillusion was most intense. The most optimistic of development experts expect that it will be decades before countries like Ghana and Tanzania see anything like the economic growth of a Korea, and many of them are, in their hearts, long-term pessimists who see differences in economic performance as probably reflecting differences in natural talents – though the charge of racism which such a statement would give rise to prevents them from ever saying so openly.

All of which means that the question of the unequal global distribution of the world's wealth and income has become far more acute than ever before. It is no longer possible to take the simple view that with a little capital assistance and a little technical assistance – to help people in the poor countries to help themselves – the problem would be solved. So what is to be done? If one were to take as starting point the possibility of that 'sense of common humanity' which came up in the foregoing discussion of human rights, the answer is clear: the 'development question' becomes transformed into the 'welfare question'. One is led, that is to say, to the idea that just as within individual countries, welfare schemes tax people who have ability or luck to give a basic income to those who cannot or will not help themselves, so a world welfare system might arrange the same kind of income transfers on a global scale. As yet, however, the world has not even got to the point at which such ideas are seriously discussed.

Not as yet. But can one expect such discussions in the near or distant future?

I said at the beginning of this section that there was little sign of 'progressive evolution' in the development field. That is true. But if one asks about the field of North–South relations, rather than development, and if one asks, not about 'theoretical assertions of common humanity' but about an 'underlying sense of common humanity', perhaps it *is* possible to discern some faint signs that it is on the increase.

In the first place, it is surely not accidental that the two of the UN's agencies which have the reputation of being the least subject to corruption and inefficiency are those most directly concerned with individual welfare, the children's agency UNICEF and the refugee agency UNHCR. Their clear and direct humanitarian purpose acts on those involved with them as a sort of prophylactic against their corruption.

At the same time, compared with forty years ago, the volume of emergency aid – for famines, for earthquakes and typhoon disasters – channelled through the UN, through direct government contributions, or through private charities, has vastly increased, and so has the effectiveness of such aid.

All of which is not unconnected with the fact that it is relatively recently we have all had television sets, and that their screens have come to show us the actuality of skeletal children on the point of dehydrated death.

STAGNATION, PROGRESSIVE EVOLUTION, REGRESSION

How should one evaluate all these various trends? There can be no doubt that in many respects the high hopes which many people entertained in 1945, the idealism and the optimism, have been betrayed. By the criteria implicit in the objectives of internationalist thinkers and activists since the nineteenth century – the erosion of national sovereignties, an increasing consensus on the values shared by all mankind and an accompanying increase in the extent to which international organizations intervene into disputes in order to assert and affirm those values – by those criteria, the forty-five-year history of the UN was from some points of view a history of at best stagnation, at worst regression, with the UN itself becoming the arena for prosecution of the Cold War. Yet, in other respects – in the field of human rights, in movement towards a consensus on what constitutes aggression, in the evolving role of the Secretary-General – there are elements of what, given those criteria, can reasonably be described as progress.

But there are few people in academic circles who are prepared to agree with that judgement. Fashions change quickly in the study of international relations. The dominant centre from which the fashions spread out to the rest of the world is of course the United States, or, if Britain also deserves acknowledgement for playing a minor role, the Anglo-Saxon countries. For a quick check on the fashions of the postwar period, just look along the shelves in the international relations section of any library. In the 1950s and the early part of the 1960s there are large numbers of books on the United Nations. The large majority endorsed, albeit with many qualifications, the assumption that movement towards internationalist ideals constituted progress and that the UN was a not inconsiderable step towards that progress.

But after the Congo debacle, the end of America's automatic majority in the General Assembly and the beginning of disillusionment with the effectiveness of foreign aid, the academic community changed too. Kissingerian realism – foreign policy is the application of power in the national interest; peace is achieved by the constant, ingenious and *ad hoc* maintenance of a power balance – became the ruling assumption. The study of international organization and international law became something for a minority of idealist softies who did not appreciate the realities of the world. Books on these latter subjects become remarkably rare after 1970. Strategic studies became the core of the new realist IR field. It appears that the majority of Japan's leading professors of international relations – those whose names appear most frequently in the media – received their training in American graduate schools where this hard-nosed realism prevailed.

Consequently, a majority of them would be inclined to ignore, or indeed, deny that it is possible to see signs of what I have called progressive evolution in the UN even during the Cold War years. An example of what I take to be a common approach among Japanese scholars is the following passage from a discussion recorded in *Sekai* magazine.[8] The speaker is Professor Terumasa Nakanishi of Shizuoka University.

> My view is that there is one clear lesson from the Gulf War. Chapter 7, including the article which authorizes the use of force, ought to be entirely cut out from the UN Charter. The UN should concentrate on peaceful efforts to sustain peace as a body which has no means of coercion available. . . .
>
> On the one hand there was the Anglo-Saxon, American sense of justice;

but on the other hand the different Arab position; there was a Japanese point of view. Given the present situation as regards a sense of international justice, is it reasonable to expect a single transnational organization to be effective in the management of an international order and dealing with problems of security?

Basically, order in international society has to be preserved by political adjustments. One can say that this simply means maintaining a balance of power and interest, but if you ask me which is the better – that or a collective action approach, still under experiment and liable to be politically misused – then I have to say that I go for the conservative notion of international order.

If you want the UN to be a body which deploys armed force, then you need a fair degree of cultural consensus – consensus about justice. We have to face up to the fact that we just don't have an international society of that sort.

Professor Nakanishi's argument is clear and logically watertight. But his 'conservative notion' that gives pride of place to power and interests assumes a view of international society as something eternally unchanging. It is a view that ignores the possibility that the various institutions which maintain the international order are constantly adapting to secular evolutionary change, taking advantage of those trends of change and progressively being strengthened as a result. It likewise precludes the possibility of preaching that we should all try to help that process along.

This is the realism dominant in the academic international relations community, compounded of contempt for the UN, contempt for the notion of 'international public opinion', an emphasis on the legitimacy of the pursuit of national interest as the objective of, and the deployment of national power and national prestige as the only methods of, diplomacy.

Professor Nakanishi is, of course, quite right to argue that for the UN to be able effectively to deploy armed force there needs to be a cultural consensus, a consensus concerning ideas of justice, and that such a consensus does not exist. The question is whether, as compared with earlier periods – as compared, say, with forty years ago – we are now closer to having such a consensus, and whether there is reason to believe that we shall become closer in future.

I believe that the answer to those questions is yes. On the day that I am writing this the letter which follows, a comment on the UN intervention in Somalia by a British lawyer, appeared in the correspondence columns of the *Independent* newspaper. It makes a fitting end to this chapter.[9]

No doubt one should be cautious in defining a principle that permits troops of one state to enter the territory of another. But discussion of the doctrine of humanitarian intervention [needs a proper view of] the history of the doctrine.

In international law, a right of unilateral humanitarian intervention was largely developed in the 19th century. Both then, and among those leading jurists who have claimed that this right survived the creation of the United Nations, it was carefully restricted to apply only in extreme cases of exceptional humanitarian need.

[It is not] accurate to stigmatise the doctrine by suggesting that it is claimed as a 'Western' prerogative. When Indian troops entered East Pakistan in 1971 to halt the widespread rape and slaughter of East Bengalis by the Pakistan army, or when Tanzanian forces invaded Uganda in 1979 to assist Ugandan exiles seeking to overthrow Idi Amin who had inflicted mass atrocities on the Ugandan people, these interventions were not rejected as 'unwelcome' by the affected populations.

It is now recognised that human rights are not purely a domestic matter for independent states. A unilateral right of intervention is clearly open to abuse, and its exercise invites careful scrutiny. But it would be a still more cynical world that denied even the UN any right to intervene to prevent widespread atrocities and extreme human suffering.

The resolution authorising the dispatch of troops to Somalia was supported by all 15 members of the Security Council, including China, which had hitherto consistently opposed a doctrine of humanitarian intervention. The need today is not to sacrifice that doctrine on the altar of a rigid concept of state sovereignty, but to develop the principles whereby a right of collective intervention on humanitarian grounds is defined and controlled within the framework of the UN and regional organizations.

In short, this lawyer is saying, the convergence of values and ideas of justice which Professor Nakanishi denies has indeed been taking place, it is possible to take the process further, and the UN is the appropriate forum for that to happen. I agree.

7 The revival of the UN

From 1947, and especially after the Berlin blockade of 1949 and the Korean War of 1950, right up to the late eighties, the central peace-or-war question was whether the Cold War would ever become hot. In Vietnam and Afghanistan, in Ethiopia and in Angola, many hundreds of thousands of lives were lost in wars fought by proxies of the Cold War principals, but even these were on a different scale from the third – and nuclear – world war which the world seemed to be staring in the face at the time of the Cuban Missile Crisis of 1962.

These were dangerous times, but one can still read in them evidence that the 'force of reason' was at work, small step followed by slightly bigger step, to constrain and contain aggressive adventurism in the Cold War principals.

The Eastern European revolutions, the collapse of the Berlin Wall and the dismantling of the Soviet Union all happened so quickly that we are apt to forget all the small measures taken between the Cuban Missile Crisis and 1989 which served to reduce the possibility of a Russo-American war. Such, for instance, was the hotline which was already in place and played an important role during the Cuban crisis itself, and a number of other measures which likewise sought to reduce the possibility of an accidental war resulting from a misunderstanding of the other side's intentions. Such also were the successive SALT talks which tried to halt the tendency of overkill capacity steadily to increase. And of especially great importance was the Helsinki declaration and the subsequent Helsinki process, starting off from human rights issues and proceeding to a variety of confidence-building measures.

But nearly all these developments took place outside the framework of the UN. I say 'nearly' because there were exceptions; in the 1973 Israeli–Egyptian war, for example, the UN played an indispensable mediating role. Since the whole war lasted only 34 days, it is not as well remembered, but some would argue that the two superpowers came even closer to the brink of war than during the Cuban crisis. Twenty thousand Egyptian troops were encircled by the Israelis; the Russians, judging that they could not allow the destruction of the Egyptian army, had begun mobilizing, and the American air forces were mobilized in response. It looked as if

American and Russian soldiers were going to confront each other on the battlefield. At that point:

> After some backstage consultation, the non-aligned members of the Security Council tabled a resolution designed to bring about a ceasefire and the deployment of UN peacekeeping forces to separate the combatants and to create the peaceful conditions in which negotiations could be resumed. The superpowers had been provided with the ladder down which to climb from their dangerously exposed positions, and the crisis passed. It is awe-inspiring to contemplate what the outcome might have been if the superpowers had not had the UN alternative to bilateral action, or if they had not been in the mood to make use of the UN machinery when the chips were down.[1]

Whether the UN could have performed that function a decade later is questionable. The early 1980s saw the UN at the nadir of its fortunes. The people who ran foreign policy under the Reagan administration took the view that there was no place in the serious business of negotiations between grown-up superpowers for the barbarous, backward and powerless third-world nations whose infantile representatives were incapable of anything except emotional speeches in the General Assembly. Other leading nations like Britain, France or Japan did not show such open contempt for the UN, but were much more interested in developing the annual G7 Summit meetings as a central forum for world decision making.

When the Nicaraguan government took the United States to the International Court of Justice over the CIA's mining of Nicaraguan harbours, the Reagan government responded by giving formal notice of abrogation of its original agreement, under Article 36 of the founding statute, to accept the Court's jurisdiction in any dispute referred to it by other parties. It also refused to pay a portion of its dues to the UN, and withdrew from UNESCO. It was generally agreed that the M'Bow regime had brought the organization into deep trouble – blatant favouritism in appointments, a deeper concern with protecting third-world rulers from press criticism than with promoting freedom of expression. But it was the Americans, with the British and others following, who led the move to give up hopes of reform from within and simply to withdraw.

In spite of having the UN on its own soil, indifference or downright hostility dominated American attitudes towards the UN. And, although the presence of a vocal pro-Israeli Jewish lobby which missed no opportunity to denigrate the UN gave a special edge to American attitudes, those attitudes were by no means confined to America. In spite of Geneva being the home of many UN agencies, and a favourite site for peace conferences, when the Swiss government decided to abandon its traditional policy of permanent neutrality and seek membership in the UN, the proposal, put to a national referendum, was defeated three to one.

The mood spread to academic circles. Among American students of international relations, and among the Japanese and British scholars who had been brainwashed in their graduate schools, an interest in research on the UN all but disappeared. The general assumption ruled that you had to be pretty naive, or else pretty maverick, to take seriously what were, after all, empty rituals with minimal impact on real power relations.

NEW DEVELOPMENTS

In that Anglophone academic world – that cultural community which is steadily increasing its hegemony in world culture – it took some time for the realization to grow that in the late 1980s the role of the UN – particularly in its central functions of peace-maintenance and dispute resolution – was changing. But changed it was indeed. To list four important developments between 1987 and 1990:

1 A Security Council resolution of 1987 finally brought an end to the Iran–Iraq war. Desultory discussions in the Security Council ever since the war began in 1980 had led to precisely nothing, but in January 1987 Pérez de Cuéllar was able to call a Foreign Minister-level Council and secure the backing of both superpowers for a negotiating effort which, eight months later, led to a stable cease-fire.[2]

2 In 1988, four separate agreements signed in Geneva finally brought an end to the eight-year war between the Russian-puppet government of Afghanistan and guerrilla opponents fortified with an unlimited supply of American arms via Pakistan. The complex arrangements – the formality of a treaty between the Khabul government and Pakistan with the two superpowers as guarantors, and in particular the delicate negotiations on the relative timing of, and means of monitoring, the withdrawal of Soviet troops and the cutting off of arms supplies from Pakistan – owed a great deal to the tireless negotiations of the UN Secretary-General and his staff. The UN demonstrated that it had a role to play even in the resolution of a conflict in which both the superpowers had invested considerable resources and prestige.

3 The final conclusion, in December 1988, of the two agreements regulating the independence of Namibia and the withdrawal of Cuban troops from Angola, is generally counted as an American diplomatic success, but here again the UN played an essential role. The 1978 UN resolution setting out the conditions for Namibian independence, and the long negotiations which led up to it were the work of the UN, and it was the UN which provided the formula which allowed Russia to climb down from its intransigent opposition to any linking of a Namibian solution to the withdrawal of Cuban troops from Angola. Had the agreements not been signed in the presence of the Secretary-General and had there not been the promise of

a UN election supervision force to oversee subsequent elections, there would have been no prospect of agreement.[3]

4 Likewise, the Cambodian peace negotiations, in which eventually Japan played an important role, really began to get seriously under way in 1988–9.

THE RUSSIAN CHANGE OF DIRECTION

There were several reasons for this revitalization of the UN, but overwhelmingly the most decisive was the change in the attitudes of the Soviet Union.

The Russians had never shared the view of the American right wing that the UN was either a white elephant or a 'dangerous place'. The UN had considerable priority in Russian foreign policy – but never, ever, as an organization which embodied the hopes of mankind for the building of a peaceful world order. It was seen, rather, as an important arena for the pursuit of Russian interests, and of something considered indistinguishable from those interests, the spread of communism which embodied the 'hopes of mankind' in a far more important way than the UN. Its primary concern was to take advantage of any issue on which enough third-world countries could be mobilized to form an anti-American majority in the UN General Assembly. They took the UN seriously – but as an arena in which they could prosecute the Cold War through full exploitation of the principle that the enemy of my friend is my enemy, and the enemy of my enemy is my friend.

But as Gorbachev began to consolidate his power, that began to change. Though clearly afraid of giving grounds to his conservative domestic critics for accusations of 'weakness' *vis-à-vis* the US, he began to show signs of support for the UN which went beyond tactical exploitation. The Russians took positions on various issues which seemed to be dictated not simply by a concern to score off the US, but by some, what can only be called moral, judgement concerning what was just and fair, and by some honest assessment of what might lead to a peaceful settlement of disputes. And in that context the criteria of 'just' and 'fair' and 'honest' were not derived from communist ideology, but from the universalistic principles dominant in Western civilization.

The fact that the Soviet Union expended considerable efforts working cooperatively to bring about the Iran–Iraq settlement, the Angolan and Namibian settlements – and, indeed the Afghanistan settlement in which it was a principal actor – and often in doing so put its great power prestige at risk, was a product of this change of Russian attitude. And without that change none of these settlements would have been possible. The same applied to the election for the Director-Generalship of UNESCO. The fact that the Russians abandoned the large group of third-world countries which had supported the M'Bow regime and joined the 'Western camp' in supporting their candidate was crucial in providing the opportunity for the restructuring of UNESCO.

THE BACKGROUND TO RUSSIA'S U-TURN

It will be obvious that the change in Russia's UN policy proceeded in parallel with, and was intimately related to, the thawing of the Cold War tension between the superpowers. The former was much less commonly discussed than the latter, both at the time and since, but was equally epoch-making.

What brought it about?

The predominant American view, particularly the view of right-wing Americans, is that the change represented a reward for the determination with which America pursued its Cold War strategy, particularly its policy of constantly reinforced armed strength, Star Wars included. The Soviet economy was simply unable to bear the minimum burden of military expenditure necessary to maintain a military balance with the US. The innate appeal of democracy, plus the clear demonstration of the inability of a planned Soviet economy to deliver the same economic growth rates as free-market capitalism, provide a full and sufficient explanation.

That this is an exceedingly important part of the explanation is clear. It is reasonable to expect those who are conscious of their own weakness to be much more keen on the building up of a system of law and order – a system of order which will protect them from exploitation by hegemons – than those who have confidence in their own strength. And in that light perfectly understandable that a weakened Soviet Union should come to re-evaluate the UN as the only approach to world order on offer.

But that is surely not the only factor. Consider the growth of the educational system. When Khrushchev came to power in the 1950s only a third of the Russian population had been to secondary school. By the time of Gorbachev's accession to power, two-thirds. University graduates had increased from two to nine per cent of the population. And this diffusion of education had not simply subjected larger segments of the population to the study of dreary ritualistic dialectical materialism – a bit like the prewar Japanese schools and their diet of 'national essence' texts like the *Kokutai no Hongi* – it had also nurtured a wide acquaintance with the culture of Tolstoy and Pushkin and Dostoevsky, the rich, philosophically and ethically sophisticated culture which until the revolution had been the exclusive possession of a tiny middle and upper class. Conscience, the values of reason, truth and consistency of principle – and the tendency to 'judge matters objectively on their merits' – were strengthened in Russian society. The moral sentiments which led to the anti-Vietnam War movement in the United States had their counterpart in opposition to the Afghanistan war in the Soviet Union.

Very probably another factor of importance was the failure of Russian aid policies towards the third world – policies which were closely tied to its earlier strategy of using the UN as an arena for mobilizing opposition to the US. It was, of course, very much a matter of using aid to buy political support against the US, but the strategy was also informed by the belief that third world countries in the Soviet bloc, thanks to Soviet techniques of economic planning, would grow faster than than those in the American free-market bloc. Instead Guinea, Mozambique, Somalia, Ethiopia, Angola – even North Korea which shared the same cultural preconditions as the growth miracle South, and even favourite son Cuba, turned out to be problem children. Some abandoned the Russian bloc; those which remained consituted an ever more burdensome drain on Russian resources. Russia lost not only faith in its domestic economic policies, but also faith in its ability to write prescriptions for economic growth elsewhere.

DISPUTE SETTLEMENT AND COLLECTIVE SECURITY: NEW DEPARTURES

The change in the UN policy of the Soviet Union first became apparent in its actions. Its adoption in the summer of 1987 of a policy of full cooperation in efforts to end the Iran–Iraq war was widely noted, but generally interpreted as simply one aspect of its move towards peaceful cooperation with the United States. From September, however, the change in UN policy was spelt out and given concrete form in proposals for the reconstruction of the United Nations. An article which appeared in a Moscow journal under Gorbachev's name (the author is reputed to have been the international organization expert, Vladimir Petrowski), called for a fundamental restructuring of, and expansion of the role of, the UN. The organization should, said the article, take more positive initiatives on environmental issues and on the restructuring of third world debt; the powers of the International Court of Justice and of the International Atomic Energy Agency should be expanded; there was need for a new agency to deal with international terrorism, and in various ways the role of the UN in the maintenance of peace should be strengthened.[4]

It was on the last point that the most emphasis was placed and that the discussion was most detailed. As concrete measures, the article proposed:

- the establishment of a new agency for the management of peace-keeping operations – an agency which should have the capability of collecting accurate intelligence on areas where conflict had occurred or was likely to occur;
- when that agency was established, resumption of the work abandoned in 1947 – the implementation of Article 43 concerning the commitment of member states' forces to the UN;

- extending the competence of the Secretary-General to take independent initiatives to prevent disputes;
- holding annually (preferably when the General Assembly was in session) a Foreign Minister-level meeting of the Security Council devoted not to the consideration of particular disputes but to a survey of the world situation and the exchange of views on situations which might pose danger to peace;
- convening other sessions of the Security Council not always in New York, but sometimes in areas where there were dangerous tensions and sometimes in the capitals of other states.

In the following month the Russians paid up all their back dues to the UN – including special levies to support peace-keeping operations to which hitherto they had declared themselves to be opposed in principle. It was also announced that whereas, hitherto Russian nationals had been permitted to take jobs in the UN bureaucracy only on fixed-term contracts, henceforth they could accept ordinary career positions.[5] (I recall a long argument over dinner in Rome many years ago with a Russian UN official with whom I was working on a report on land reform. Was Nureyev in deserting the Bolshoi simply exercising his basic human right to live and work wherever he pleased or, as my Russian friend insisted, was he a despicable 'defector'? He accepted it as perfectly sensible that Russians like himself should be rotated into UN posts on short-term contracts to prevent their 'going UN native' and losing their Russianness. He owed his secondment to the UN from the Russian Academy to the fact that his specialty was American labour history and he needed a spell in the US to collect material.)

The climax of this series of events was Gorbachev's speech to the UN in December 1988.[6] What attracted most attention was his announcement – on the first anniversary of the signing of the INF Treaty – of the unilateral reduction of land forces in Eastern Europe by half a million men and the withdrawal of six tank divisions from Eastern Germany, but it was also, more broadly, an occasion for exposition of the new 'UN-centred foreign policy' philosophy. Much of it was couched in abstract language but it went a good way beyond the regular rhetorical statements of praise for the UN traditionally produced by Russian foreign ministers. It was necessary to create a United Nations capable of sustaining a world order adequate to the internationalization of the world economy and the 'maturing of the social consciousness of mankind'. There was, in fact, a clear basis for this in fundamental human values, and to root the new international order in such values was, in effect, 'to de-ideologize relations among states'.

> We are not abandoning our convictions, our philosophy, or traditions, nor do we urge anyone to abandon theirs.
> But neither do we have any intention to be hemmed in by our values. That would result in intellectual impoverishment, for it would mean

rejecting a powerful source of development – the exchange of everything original that each nation has independently created. . .[7]

It is couched in abstract language, but there is, nevertheless, an important point being made. The theorists of international hegemony, who love to talk about the Pax Americana and the possibility of it giving way to a Pax Japonica, frequently argue in the following terms. What made the Pax Britannica viable was not just Britain's economic and military strength; an integral part of the story was the sense of Britain's mission to civilize the world. Likewise, the postwar Pax Americana is unthinkable without the American sense of a mission to spread democracy. Japan can never be a similar hegemon unless, out of its own traditions, it can evolve a similarly universal 'mission'.

Nonsense, Gorbachev, and through him Soviet intellectuals, were saying, it is precisely these 'missions' that are the cause of war. We can do without that kind of pax. World order now can be built and should be built on universal values; and there is in fact already something of a consensus as to what those value principles should be – sufficiently, at least, to run a reasonably efficient international organization.

US–USSR RELATIONS AND RUSSIA'S UN POLICY

Was this new Gorbachev line, and the conversion of the Soviet Union to such a positive view of the UN, simply a device adopted by the losers in the Cold War to make their peace with the Americans on the best terms possible? Was it just a face-saving device which enabled the Russians, as they moved from confrontation to cooperation, to claim that they were doing so in the name of 'universal human values'? Or was it for real? Or was it a sort of hybrid product; half deriving from the personal value preferences of Russian foreign office officials, half from a calculation that, if Russia had indeed to bow to American supremacy in a single-superpower world, it was in Russia's national interest, as well as in the interests of world peace, for Russia to try to seize the moral high ground by arguing for a less hegemonic, more conciliar form of world order – a Pax UNica, rather than a Pax Americana?

In terms of an historical analogy, were the Russians behaving in a manner analogous to the Mori and the Shimazu families after the battle of Sekigahara, when they accepted the supremacy of the Tokugawa and accepted their status as *tozama* lords? Or were they acting more like the four rebellious clans two centuries later who challenged Tokugawa hegemony in the name of a superior value system – the restoration of imperial rule?

As a total amateur in the interpretation of Russian foreign policy, I can only guess, but there is some evidence that, whatever priority may have been attached to UN policy, it was not adopted for purely tactical reasons, without any element of conviction involved.

In the first place, Gorbachev's speech showed some discrimination in its judgements. On the one hand he warmly praised America's cooperative attitude in helping to find a solution to the Afghanistan problem; on the other he was harsh in his criticism of America's refusal to grant a visa to Yasser Arafat.

That too could be explained tactically – the Soviet Union still needed to strengthen its influence with Arab governments. That must certainly have been an important consideration. But perhaps a more suggestive indication of Russian UN policy was its attitude at the beginning of the Gulf crisis in 1990.

In Japan, there is a general tendency to accept without question that cooperation with the UN meant nothing more or less than cooperation with the American-led Multinational Force. But that is by no means axiomatic. The Gulf crisis offered in a clear form the choice between a world order based on American leadership, and a world order maintained by a more conciliar structure centring on the United Nations. And the former alternative was the one chosen. The war was fought by a multinational force under US command, legitimized by UN resolutions which granted the United States a wide freedom of discretionary action; a war which began at a time chosen by the United States, and which was ended by the United States at the moment when it decided that the legitimate objectives – as the United State interpreted them – had been achieved.

That was certainly, in my personal opinion, a much better outcome than if the world had simply stood by with arms folded and allowed Iraq to swallow Kuwait. But there was a more constructive, if more difficult, alternative, namely, as is specified in Article 47 of the UN Charter, to form a United Nations command under the Security Council's Military Staff Committee, a command which would control, under the 'strategic direction' of the Military Staff Committee, what, though multinational in composition, would be a United Nations force. This would of course be the pattern specified in the UN Charter which, as we saw in Chapter 4, was the pattern which the negotiations of the early postwar period, before the intensification of the Cold War, sought to create.

That was indeed the line which the Soviet Union sought to follow at the beginning of the Gulf crisis. Within twenty-four hours of the Iraq invasion during the night of 1–2 August, the Security Council passed a resolution demanding immediate withdrawal, and it met again on 6 August to impose the sanction of a total trade embargo – a sanction which the United States and the EC had already unilaterally imposed two days earlier, and which Japan also decreed at almost the same moment as the Security Council was due to meet. The question was; how could the embargo be enforced against sanctions-busters? The United States had been the first to react militarily to the Iraqi invasion. Invoking Article 51, and the right of a threatened Saudi Arabia to fight in self-defence, it had already responded to Saudi requests by sending military forces there and by summoning aircraft carriers from both the Atlantic and Pacific fleets. Within the United Nations there was disagreement about the legitimacy of using warships to enforce the blockade simply on the basis of the sanctions resolution, which had invoked Article 41, but made no mention of the 'use of force' provisions of Article 42.

The position of the Soviet Union was an important element in this debate. On 3 August the Foreign Minister Shevardnaze and Secretary of State Baker had met at Moscow airport. Afterwards Shevardnaze said that 'The USSR has no plans to use force at present, and I understand the US has no plans', while Baker, asked about the use of force said that 'nothing can be ruled out'.[8] On 7 August they held a further half-hour telephone conversation which the *New York Times* reported under the headline 'US and Soviets as Allies. First time since 1945'. Sources close to the Bush administration were, it said, contemplating a request to the Soviet Union to take part in the enforcement of the blockade.[9] On the same day, Yusin, the Washington correspondent of *Izvestia* was quoted as saying that, 'If it is done under a UN flag, the Soviet Union might participate. But it is my personal feeling, based on some informal conversations, that they would only do it under a UN flag.'[10] This was confirmed when, on 9 August, the Russian government issued a statement in Moscow urging that the United Nations should act through a multinational combined fleet, and proposed the revival of the Security Council's Military Staff Committee. The French were reported to support the Russian position, and a resolution was said to be being prepared which would call for the use of military forces to enforce the trade embargo in accordance with Article 42 of the Charter.[11] After, on 11 and 12 August, the United States and Britian announced that their fleets had been given orders to stop Iraqi tankers, even if this meant the use of force (the Article 42 word 'blockade' was consciously avoided),[12] the *New York Times* reported that 'the United States is largely isolated. Russia, Canada, China and Finland are arguing that a new resolution invoking Article 42 is a prerequisite for any resort to force.'[13]

At this point the United States changed its mind, and on 14 August called the other four permanent members of the Security Council to a meeting to consider 'what role the Military Staff Committee might play in the implementation of Resolution 661' – the resolution which imposed the trade embargo. 'The United States Navy remains of the opinion that it already has full authority to enforce the blockade, in spite of the criticism other countries have directed at its stance, but according to State Department sources, its position in the matter has become more flexible.' 'The invocation of Article 42 and Article 43 [concerning the placing of national forces under UN command, i.e., the policy proposed by the Russians] and the creation of a combined UN fleet was one option being considered', reporters were told, and the other four permanent members were said to be of the view that there was no reason to resort to the use of force until it was properly ascertained that the embargo was not being respected.[14]

This was not the first time that the Soviet Union had proposed the creation of a combined fleet flying the UN flag. In December 1987, the first year of the new era of US–USSR cooperation, when the two countries were discussing means of bringing the Iran–Iraq war to an end, the Russians suggested a ban on all arms exports to Iraq, with the embargo to be enforced by a UN fleet made up of the two countries' navies.[15] It was said that the idea was rejected by the US navy as a clever spying device to gain knowledge of the latest American weapons, electronic devices and communications systems. The same reaction appears to have been evoked the second time.

There is no doubt that the technical problems of suddenly creating a combined fleet, given the complexities of modern technology, would have been enormous. Equally daunting would have been the task of reviving the Military Staff Committee, and creating the kind of organization under it which would be genuinely capable of exercising strategic command over such a fleet. Whether it was because these practical considerations blunted the force of the Russian proposal, or for other reasons, at the end of the negotiations which stretched over eleven days from 14 August, the Russians gave in. It is clear that the Americans had not the least intention of letting American armed forces' freedom of action be circumscribed by the possibility of a Russian or Chinese veto. It is not clear from contemporary newspaper reports how far those eleven days of negotiations concentrated on the control issue, and how far they revolved around the other point at issue – whether a resolution to use force was already necessary, or whether the Security Council should wait until there was clear evidence that the embargo was being broken. An American spokesman who enumerated these two issues to a reporter was, however, very clear about the American position. The US believes it already has the right to act. But a 'UN umbrella' would be advisable. 'The US was willing to go to some lengths in meeting Soviet concerns.'[16]

Britain supported the American position. France was more critical of the idea of an American-led operation, but on the other hand had no long tradition of pro-UN policy to incline it towards the counter-proposal of a UN-controlled operation. China, primarily concerned with recovering the ground lost by the international outcry over Tienanmen, had no particular reason to make an enemy of the Americans simply over the question of control of a Middle East operation.

And, ultimately, a Russia badly in need of Western funds for the reconstruction of its economy was in a like position. The US, France and Russia fnally agreed the text of a resolution on 23 August.[17] The Russians argued for two more days, got two face-saving amendments before they agreed, and Resolution 665, invoking Article 42, was passed on 25 August.[18] The first concession was to recognize – albeit in an exceedingly ambiguous form – the role of the Military Staff Committee. States were requested 'to coordinate their actions in pursuit of the above paragraphs of this resolution using as appropriate mechanisms of the Military Staff Committee' (but they were only asked to submit reports of their actions with the *ad hoc* committee set up at the beginning of August to coordinate sanctions). The second was to substitute for the original phrase 'the minimum necessary use of force', the alternative 'measures which the situation makes necessary'.

JAPANESE PERCEPTIONS OF THE CHANGE IN RUSSIAN POLICY

How far was the development of Russian UN policy over these years known in Japan, and how was it interpreted? Having read only a tiny fraction of the many hundreds of books and many thousands of magazine articles about Russia published in Japan in these years, I am in no position to give an opinion. Fortunately, however, a good friend at Princeton *has* read this literature and has recently published a splendid analysis of Japanese attitudes towards Russia.[19] It appears that neither the minority represented by Wada Haruki of Tokyo Univesity – those sometimes branded as 'pro-Soviet' ('Japanese faces but Russian in spirit'), nor the so-called mainstream, known to be close to the Foreign Office line (Itō Kenichi, Kimura Hiroshi, Sase Masamori), nor those like the former diplomat Hogen Shinsaku, considered as rather 'right-wing' even by the Foreign Office, have paid much attention to Russian UN policy. At any rate, in Rozman's 330 pages of analysis of the internal debates it never appears as a topic. It seems that the Japanese reader just was not kept informed.[20]

The left-leaning group, quite naturally, were mostly concerned to follow and explain the internal developments in Russia; what perestroika and glasnost really meant. But what about the mainstream group, made up of specialist students precisely of international relations? Why was it that, in their lengthy discussions of Russian policy towards the US, towards Japan, towards the Middle East, towards China, they rarely touched on Russia's policy towards the UN? My own guess, after reading Rozman's analysis, is that there were several factors involved.

1. As children of the Cold War, who had grown up with the Cold War, they clung to the one fixed point in their universe – the Japanese–American security alliance. The very thought of the possibility that a 'UN-centred foreign policy' might one day come to mean, not 'a policy of cooperation with the US', but 'siding with Russia in opposition to the US' was impossible for them to contemplate. Hence they tended to pass over Russia's UN policy in silence.
2. Dulles' policy of the 1950s with regard to Japan's claims to the Northern Islands – encourage the Japanese to inflate the importance of the issue to maximum, thereby strengthening Japan's commitment to the alliance against Russia – has succeeded too well. The Japanese public at large, and the mainstream Soviet experts, have become so preoccupied with the issue that everything that happens in Russia tends to be interpreted

solely in relation to the effect it might have on Japan's chances of getting the islands back. Thence another reason for not paying much attention to Russia's activities at the UN which might seem to have little bearing on the matter.
3 Quite a number of Japan's Russian experts seem willing at the drop of a hat to break into disquisitions on the essential nature of the Russian national character – 'basically a hunter culture', etc. – but there is little evidence that they are readers of Tolstoy and Pushkin, much less of their twentieth-century inheritors, Mandelstam or Akhmatova.

THE SOVIET UNION GIVES WAY TO RUSSIA

The Soviet Union has disintegrated and Gorbachev has given way to Yeltsin. Russian foreign policy is clearly an extension of that of the Soviet Union, but how smooth has the transition been, how much discontinuity – particularly as regards policy towards the UN? It is hard for a non-expert to judge, but it seems that the discontinuities are not great. The Foreign Minister, Khozylev, belongs to the 'internationalist' wing of foreign policy experts, and has acquired a reputation for a frankness which goes beyond mere ritualism. At the December 1992 meeting of the Council on Security and Cooperation in Europe, he startled everyone with an astonishing speech delivered apparently with great seriousness. The Western countries, he declared, had no object but to weaken Russia. The sanctions against their fellow-Slavs, the Serbs, were outrageous. Hitherto Russia had cooperated with America and the rest of Europe, but that era was at an end. Universal consternation and shock. Forty-five minutes later Khozylev asked for the floor again and explained that he simply wanted to offer an example of what would happen if the rightist nationalists ever gained power in Russia, and to underline the need for cooperation from other countries to prevent that happening. The ploy evoked much criticism and even anger,[21] but the lapse from solemn international-meeting decorum which aroused that anger seems to me, on the contrary, sign of a real and open seriousness. Imagine what might have happened if, in the 1930s, Shidehara addressing the League of Nations had used the same ploy to warn the world about the Japanese army and the Matsuokas who would follow him as their spokesman.

Nevertheless, Russia's weakness is plainly apparent. That the government has to give full priority to domestic problems is clear. In terms of economic cooperation, and as a source of hard aid cash, Germany plays the biggest role, but sympathetic cooperation from the US is also essential. There is not much chance that Russia will seek to play a role as proponent of a UN-led international order in contradistinction to a US-led order at the risk of trouble in its relations with the US. Indeed, it is strengthening its global cooperation with the United States; on the day that this is written

Russia joined the US, Britain and Canada in delivering an ultimatum to the Iraqis to withdraw their anti-aircraft platoons from the Shiite air exclusion zone or be bombed.

So if the Russians are in no position to become champions of the concept of a UN-based world order, who might be? It has to be a country which, economically, is not *dependent* on the United States. A country which can withstand a certain degree of friction with the United States, or is already accustomed to friction with the United States. It needs to be a country in which, however it might at the moment be unfocused, there is a fair quotient of vague idealism, and a fair number of people who would be attracted by the prospect of their country being seen as a 'champion of the universal values of mankind'.

Might Japan be such a country?

8 Japan's international role and the Constitution

A DISCLAIMER

As someone who is not a Japanese citizen, I have no right to declare that this or that should be Japan's foreign policy. (And, in a country like Japan where, until very recently, it was actually illegal for non-citizens to become tenured staff at national universities, there must be many Japanese who would think so.) On the other hand, there *are* many Japanese who have for years been willingly accepting the 'guidance' of Americans, and while I would not be so arrogant as to suggest that what I am offering is guidance, I can claim to have some reasonable grounds for expressing my opinions. They are that for forty years I have been visiting and for various periods living in Japan, and have acquired a lot of Japanese friends. That has given me some basis for 'If I were a Japanese, I would. . .' sort of statements. I have also acquired a certain affection for Japanese society (for 'Japan', I'm not so sure.) In general, moreover, I do not attach much importance to nationality; I have a much stronger sense of belonging to an international community of university intellectuals than I do to the British nation, a stronger occupational identity than sense of patriotism. Whether that is justification or not, what follows is a personal expression of my views about what I would like to see Japan doing.

THE MEANING OF A 'UN-CENTRED FOREIGN POLICY'

There is nothing new in suggesting that Japan should follow a 'UN-centred foreign policy'. One will find the phrase repeated in every annual edition of the government's *White Paper on Foreign Policy*. But those words can mean several different things.

1 Faithfully to conform to all Japan's obligations as a member of the UN, and to respond positively to proposals for new UN initiatives.
2 To seek to strengthen the UN and other international agencies, and to expand the sphere of their competence, and not to be deterred from

any moves in that direction by the consideration that they would lead to an erosion of the national sovereignty of Japan as of other countries.
3 Not only to consider favourably such proposals when they originate elsewhere, but also to be constantly seeking opportunities for creating such initiatives – in other words to give the strengthening of the UN a high priority in Japan's foreign policy.

When the Japanese Ministry of Foreign Affairs says 'UN-centred policy' I think they have level 1 in mind. What I want to argue for is level 3.

THE PURPOSES OF FOREIGN POLICY

Absurd, many people will say. The purpose of foreign policy is to further the national interest. Depending on the definition of 'national interest' I can agree with that. The first problem of such definition is the time horizon to be adopted. Is one to interpret 'interest' in the short term, or is one thinking of the interests of those who will be living in one's country in one's grandchildren's generation? The second question is what one counts as an interest. As I have already argued in my preface, it seems to me useful to think of interest in three different dimensions; aiming to give one's country greater security, greater economic prosperity, and greater dignity – in sum, the triple goals of safety, profit and pride.

Nobody much questions the first two. The third is perhaps more controversial. In spite of the fact that the preamble to the Japanese constitution talks of Japan seeking a 'place of honour in the comity of nations', diplomats, officials, politicians and scholars are all likely to deny that 'the pursuit of dignity' has much importance. But its importance in practice seems to me undeniable. Consider the currently rising tide of sentiment described in Japan as *'kembei-shiso'* – dislike of America. This is not a reaction to the prospect of economic damage from American trade policy. The response to American 'Japan-bashing' is surely a feeling that the Japanese people are not being treated with proper respect; that America has hitherto tended to treat Japan as a satellite country.

In discussions of foreign policy in general, the pursuit of dignity tends either to be underestimated, or – as in the theory behind Kissinger's Vietnam policy – to be treated simply as a means to security or economic objectives. (If the US lost in Vietnam it would lose prestige; would be less admired and less trusted. Consequently the instruments through which it secures greater security and economic advantage – namely its promises and its threats of economic or military sanctions – would become less effective.) As to why the pursuit of dignity should be generally undervalued in discussions of foreign policy, it partly has to do, surely, with a general psychological rule that 'one loses face by showing oneself over-concerned about saving face'. But there is probably another psychological mechanism involved. In any society, the people in secure elite positions are not very preoccupied with questions of dignity. They can afford not to be; anyone who does not show them respect can be easily dismissed as rude fellows of no consequence.

The same thing applies in the society of nations. Top nations do not have to worry very much about their prestige. The fact that international relations as a university discipline very largely developed in the top nations of Britain and America may explain why the pursuit of dignity is not treated with the importance it deserves.

I think it fairly clearly demonstrable that Japanese diplomats and politicians, and the Japanese people in general, are by no means so indifferent to matters of national dignity. About ten years ago, when it seemed that the Iran–Iraq war was likely to go on for ever, the possibility emerged that Japan might act as mediator and bring about a cease-fire. It was a distinctly low-probability possibility which was hardly reported in the Western press. But in Japan, for two or three days running, it was top news which merited front-page headlines. And that interest is only to be explained by the boost to Japan's international standing in general which pulling off such a coup seemed to promise.

There may be people who would explain the particular importance of the pursuit of dignity for Japanese foreign policy in terms of Japanese national character – *bushidō*, 'shame culture', the importance of 'face', would be the sort of terms employed. A far more convincing explanation is provided by the 'sociological law' already mentioned. In a very stable traditional society, it is not only the elite who are not much bothered about their dignity ranking. The lower classes do not waste their time seeking social prestige which is in any case going to be denied them; enough that they seek to be respected for behaving in a manner appropriate to the position in life to which it has pleased God to call them. But as societies become more fluid and mobile, that changes. The various dimensions by which men are ranked – their power, their family origins, their achievements, their charm or personal effectiveness – cease to correlate as highly as they did. Many people become more aware of relative rankings, more sensitive to them; the sensitivity of the *nouveau riche* – the man of wealth but of low birth and low breeding – is the classic stereotype of this phenomenon.

The ones who have this sensitivity most markedly are likely to be both those who are upwardly and those who are downwardly mobile. When the Japanese were poor and Japan had little economic power while the United States was affluent and dominated the world economy, the Japanese accepted their younger-brother role, even if the elder brother did behave with a certain arrogance. In all the recent frictions and the spread of 'Ame-phobia' there is surely an element, not only of the frustrations of an upwardly mobile Japan, which sees itself as not receiving the respect appropriate to a country as economically powerful as it is, but also the frustrations of a United States made ever more aware of the increasing limitations on its power and prestige.

A UN-CENTRED FOREIGN POLICY AND THE DIMENSIONS OF DIGNITY

Nobody now makes fun of the Rockefellers. When the *nouveau riche* create foundations and devote themselves and their money to social causes, dignity can accrue – especially if their good works seem to be guided by clear criteria founded in principled belief. My argument, applying much the same principle to international society, can be summarized as follows:

1 There is a strong desire among the Japanese public for an advancement in national dignity to become, along with security and economic advantage, a major objective of Japan's foreign policy – probably stronger than among the publics of any other major country.
2 It would be a good thing if those in charge of Japan's foreign policy would explicitly acknowledge that fact.
3 There are, by and large, two ways of pursuing such an objective which one might roughly call the Israeli and the Swedish. The Israeli method is to get oneself respected for the strength and single-mindedness with which one pursues one's own objectives (of security and economic advantage), rejecting compromise and resorting when necessary to force. The Swedish method is a bit more like the Rockefeller formula. Be clear about the criteria and the principles of justice under which one acts, but base those criteria not solely on the pursuit of national interest, but also on some clear conception of the interests of humanity, of international society as a whole.
4 There are many people in Japan for whom the Israeli formula is the ideal choice. One only has to look at the pronouncements of Ishihara Shintarō MP, author of *The Japan That Can Say 'No'*, to be sure of that. And indeed, over the Northern Islands issue (by, for example, trying to force Russian concessions by economic sanctions, rather than refer the matter to the International Court of Justice), the Israeli formula is, in a very soft sort of way, being followed. But are there many people who really believe that if Japan were to increase its armed strength, and acquire nuclear weapons that somehow Russia could be made to disgorge those islands? Even members of the Patriotic Party who put all those posters on the Tokyo telephone poles which talk about 'the day when we take back our islands'? The world has, after all, become a slightly more civilized place; there are growing limits to what you can achieve by the exercise of force.
5 The choice of the Swedish formula would seem more reasonable. It is not necessarily the formula of weakness. It can display great strength depend-

ing on, first, the clarity of the underlying beliefs about what is 'in the general world interest', and second, the firmness and consistency with which those beliefs inform policy.
6 Since Japanese advocates of the Israeli formula are so active and so well-known outside Japan, if Japan were to opt for the Swedish formula, quite determined high-profile expressions of policy would be required to convince the world of that fact.
7 The most effective means of doing that would be full adoption of what I called a 'level 3 UN-centred foreign policy'. That is to say that there should be a vigorous national debate, not only within the foreign policy community but more widely, over the sort of UN the world needs; what sort of institutional reforms would make it more effective, whether the Charter needs to be revised; how to reform the UN's financing. And, as a result of that debate, the forceful presentation of such proposals to the world at large.

On 8 December 1941, the writer Itō Sei noted in his diary: 'It's something in our fate: there is no way we can come to feel that we are first-class citizens of the world, except by going to war with the first-class white nations.'[1] It is already half a century since that attempt to apply the Israeli formula ended in failure, and in that half century the world has changed, changed in such a way that now the alternative Swedish formula – cooperation not only with the 'first-class white nations', but also with other nations which are neither white nor first-class, in positive efforts to build a better world order – has become a viable alternative.

The whole purpose of this book is to try, now that the Japanese people have come to feel themselves 'first-class citizens of the world', to bring that alternative to their attention.

REQUIREMENTS FOR THE ROLE OF REFORMER

If Japanese diplomacy were to concentrate on a 'diplomatic movement' to reform and strengthen the UN what might be the conditions for success? (Note in passing that I used the term 'diplomatic movement', not the more familiar 'diplomatic offensive'. The latter term – like Clausewitz' famous dictum that war is the pursuit of national diplomatic objectives by other means – belongs to that whole set of accepted ideas based on the premise that foreign policy is solely about the pursuit of national interest. I use 'movement' as one uses it in discussing internal politics – as in 'women's liberation movement' – that is to say, activity directed towards some conception of social improvement and not likely to lead on to civil warfare. Hence, in this case, efforts to improve international society which transcend – at least in any narrow definition thereof – considerations of national interest.)

What, in that case, might be the conditions for mounting a successful 'movement'?

THE LEGITIMACY OF THE USE OF FORCE BY THE UN

The first is to have some clear conception of the role of armed force in the effort to create a world without war, or genocide or abuse of human rights. As was recounted in Chapter 2, until the middle of the nineteenth century, the view that any international organization created should very deliberately eschew the use of force – a view springing from Quaker origins – was a very powerful strain in the internationalist movement. And it still had a tiny minority of advocates, as Chapter 3 recorded, at the time of the San Francisco Conference. Their ideal template for world order was not the model of the modern nation-state which uses physical force, but only through accountable specialists – police. It was, rather, the social control system of, say, a Japanese village in the Edo period, where order is preserved not by specialist police but by a village consensus on minimum norms of conduct and *murahachibu*: ostracization – economic sanctions and withdrawal of social respect – for those who offended against that consensus.

But it is precisely because the mechanisms of consensus and ostracization begin to break down as soon as village communities in which everybody knows everybody else give way to urban agglomerations of anonymous migrants, that police forces are created in modern nation-states. Oversimple analogies are always dangerous, but it is clear that the modern nation-state is a better analogy for the international society of states than is the medieval village. By the end of the nineteenth century the internationalist movement had been almost wholly converted to the view that any effective international organization would have to be able to apply, not only economic sanctions, but if necessary armed force as well. Chapter 7 of the UN Charter was the latest product of that strain of thought.

There are people in Japan – Professor Nakanishi quoted at the end of Chapter 6, for instance – who would argue that, however dominant that view might be, it is still mistaken. Chapter 7 of the UN Charter does much more harm than good. There are some among those in Japan who would describe themselves as *heiwa-shugisha* – members of the peace movement – who are explicit in holding that view – though I suspect not many.

And it is a long way from being a dominant view in Japan. I imagine that while there might be many reservations about the exact provisions of Chapter 7 of the Charter, there would be little opposition to the idea in principle that an effective UN must be one which can deploy armed force.

That is to say, I imagine there would be little opposition in principle to the idea that members of the UN should accept it as reasonable, indeed as a duty, to send troops, sometimes at the risk of their being killed, not to further some national interest but – as to Yugoslavia, Somalia, Angola, Cambodia – to stop some human beings from doing unacceptably evil things to other human beings. But whether Japan's views on the rules which should govern such interventions would carry much weight would depend on whether the acceptance of that principle is followed by the rider: 'And Japan, as one participant in the international system, is prepared to co-operate fully in such peace-keeping, peace-making, peace-enforcing activities', or whether by the rider: 'However, Japan is in a special position.'

As someone who thinks that the first is the only reasonable position to take, I have tried to listen carefully to the arguments of those who would advocate the alternative. I may not have fully understood, but it seems to me that there are several strains in their argument which I shall try to summarize – I hope without caricature.

VARIOUS ANTI-ESTABLISHMENT POSITIONS

i) It may be true that in the short run, world order requires force-deploying policemen, but in the long run we must look forward to an order such as that just characterized as that of the medieval village, an order which does not depend on the use of force. It is precisely the belief in the long-run possibility of such an order that is enshrined in Article 9 of the Japanese Constitution. Whatever the historical background which was responsible, the appearance of a country with such a clause in its constitution, represents a precious landmark in human history. Keeping that faith alive is to make a contribution to mankind of far greater importance than sending several hundreds or even several thousands of soldiers to die in Cambodia or Somalia. What Japan should do, therefore, is to make Article 9 a reality by completely disbanding the Self-Defence Forces, so that Japan *has* no soldiers to send on peace-keeping missions, thereby demonstrating to the world that Japan takes its Constitution seriously, considers it not as a shackling restriction on its freedom of action, but as a source of real national pride.

ii) The heart of the second view may perhaps be found in Yosano Akiko's famous poem at the time of the Russo-Japanese war – 'Please, brother, don't get killed' – or in the slogan of the postwar women's movement; 'never again shall we send our sons to war'. It seems to be based on the assumption that the sufferings of the Japanese people in the last war greatly exceeded that of other participants, and that Japan therefore has a right to a special dispensation. What greatly reinforces this idea is the 'we common people are always duped' assumption. Akiko's brother, and the youth who went to die in the Great East Asian War, gave up their lives in the belief that they were dying for a noble cause, but in fact they were only instruments of imperialism. What's so different this time when a Japanese government talks about 'obligations to humanity' and the need to take part in PKO expeditions?

102 *The argument*

iii) In principle there is no doubt that Japan should play a full part in UN peace-keeping operations, but there are special circumstances in Japan's case. Civil society is still weak in Japan. Its power to resist the military is not to be taken for granted. Give the army the chance to take part in UN peace-keeping operations, the chance to play an honoured role in Japanese society, and you can never be sure how it will end – it could well lead to the revival of Japanese militarism and the collapse of democracy. That being in the nature of the Japanese people, the best contribution Japan can make to world peace is to prevent that possibility from becoming reality. That is far more important than any contributions Japan might make to peace-keeping.

iv) Once you recognize that Japan has a duty to play a full part in peace-keeping operations, you immediately raise the question of amending the Japanese Constitution; start messing with the Constitution and in no time you could be back with a Fascist Japan.

Of those four arguments, only the first seems to me to have its own logic and to be worthy of respect. I think it is mistaken, but that is a value judgement, not a question of reason and consistency. But how many people in Japan actually take that view? In a Japan in which even the Social Democratic Party's leader has proclaimed the nonsense formula that 'the Self-Defence Forces are unconstitutional but legal', how many people are seriously arguing that Article 9's 'Land, sea and air forces shall not be maintained' should be taken seriously? Of the other three arguments, none seems to me compelling. They all ignore the evolution of Japanese society. Just across the water, in South Korea, we have seen an army *junta* which for years held the country in an iron grip, finally forced to give way to democratic processes. The difference between today's Japan and the Japan over which the army seized control in the 1930s simply cannot be ignored. It is not just that the Meiji Constitution which gave the military command formal parity with the civilian government has long since disappeared. The army command in those days was a genuine elite. For the peasantry and the lower middle classes, for perhaps eighty per cent of the population, to have a son pass the stiff entrance examination for a free education in an officer's training school was a keenly sought honour. The modern officer corps, recruited from the graduates of the Defence University, is of a very different calibre, both in terms of the 'social ranking' the Defence University has in *hensachi* terms (the level of academic ability needed to pass its entrance exams), and in terms consequently of the sense of eliteness, the basis for elite self-confidence, which their career gives them. It may well be that if there were a revision of the Constitution those conservatives who want the Emperor defined, not as a 'symbol' but as the 'head' of state would have their way. But does anybody really believe in the likelihood of the Emperor being deified again? In a Japan in which the present Emperor's accession speech was much commented on both for its simple non-awesome language and for the phrase about 'pledging, with all my fellow-citizens, to uphold the Constitution'? I can see the possibility of Japan becoming a really unpleasant society. I would not rule out the possibility that it becomes a more disagreeable society than the United States – given the growth of inequality and the gradually strengthening hereditary transmission of class differences. But the likelihood of a return to something like the military-fascist world of the 1930s seems to me to come in the 'hell freezing over' category.

Ask a Japanese diplomat why arguments like the four enumerated should have such wide currency, in spite of their apparent lack of foundation, and if he is uncharacteristically frank, he will say, 'because the people who believe them are idiots'. But it is more complicated than that. The people who believe them are on the whole good, decent people. In the first decade or two after the war, in the period of the so-called 'reverse course', when the right-wing movement to amend the Constitution was at its height, the postwar democratic system was genuinely under threat. Many people devoted a great deal of time and energy to combating these tendencies and 'Defend the Constitution' or 'Defend the Peace Constitution' were the great rallying cries, rallying cries which became the heart and core of their political beliefs, something which they cannot bring themselves to abandon, however much circumstances may change. And that is why the very left-wing intellectuals in Japan who are most firmly opposed to chauvinistic nationalism, most conscious of their membership in a common humanity, most sympathetic to the internationalist initiatives, should be the people most deeply opposed to Japan's participation in UN peace-keeping activities.

And that stance is reinforced by one other, highly relevant set of arguments:

- Protection of the Constitution is a categorical imperative.
- The conservative, or rather, reactionary forces which are seeking to change the Constitution – those represented in the Liberal Democratic Party – are consequently the categorical enemy.
- For forty years those groups have been giving full and obedient cooperation to the United States in its efforts to exert global domination. The eagerness of the United States to see Japan set itself free of the constraints the Constitution imposes on military cooperation with the US is clear.
- The Gulf War provided an excellent opportunity for the US to pursue this ambition. It is a matter of common knowledge that the PKO Participation Law had its origin in pressure exerted on the Japanese government through personal contacts between Ambassador Armacost and Ozawa Jirō, then Secretary-General of the LDP.
- Consequently, actual Japanese plans for participating in UN peacekeeping have nothing to do with a spirit of internationalism; they are simply an expression of a pliant and subservient Japanese government's complicity in American designs to dominate the globe.

THE VARIOUS STRANDS OF THE ESTABLISHMENT POSITION

While the interpretation just quoted of the sources of Japan's policy during the Gulf War is probably correct, to put everything down to 'conservative or reactionary forces subservient to the United States' is a much too crude over-simplification. The support for the PKO Participation Law came from a variety of separate and distinguishable strains of belief and calculation, which might be roughly classified as follows.

v) For all the problems involved, Japan just has to maintain a cooperative relationship with the US. Why? The answers would vary. Because it's a wonderful country. Because Japan needs American support in international organizations; otherwise it would find itself isolated. Because, with North Korea and China both having nuclear bombs, the 'nuclear umbrella' has not lost its meaning. Because America is our biggest market and we have to stop protectionism. Because we owe the Americans a debt for the way they aided Japan's recovery and its return to international society. For whatever reason, cooperation with the US is important, and it was therefore sensible to bow to American pressure and pass that law. Thereafter, two variants:

v.i) Because of the principle of not sending armed forces to fight overseas, it was necessary to circumscribe the conditions for taking part in peace-keeping operations very narrowly. Which actually was fortunate; we were able to show our sincerity by doing the best we could within constitutional limits, and at the same time minimize the danger that young Japanese would be killed with serious domestic political repercussions.

v.ii) All that nonsense about the Japanese PKO forces not having any but small arms for personal defence, etc. may have been necessary but was entirely regrettable; we really have to overcome these constitutional limitations – even if the only way of doing so is the way adopted hitherto – gradually creating *faits accomplis* by tiny shifts in the 'interpretation' of the Constitution.

vi) Talk of 'Japan's international contribution' derives from nothing but a naive idealistic sort of internationalism, betraying a faith in the possibility of world order. But this remains, and will remain a world in which the only thing really respected is power. A great economic power which is not also a great military power is not worthy to be called a great power. What Japan has to do as soon as possible is not just to revise its constitution, but to arm itself, if necessary with nuclear weapons, to a level commensurate with its real strength. And given the superior quality of the Japanese people this would be a good thing for the world too. However, given that revision of the constitution is at the moment politically not feasible, there is no real alternative to measures like the PKO Act which gradually erode the constitutional constraints a little bit at a time. It also has the advantage of allowing Japanese soldiers the experience of active service abroad.

vii) It may well be true that the PKO Participation Act would never have seen the light of day except for American pressure, but taking part in peace-keeping activities has, in fact, much greater significance outside than inside the sphere of US–Japan relations. America is not the only country which expects Japan, with its present economic strength, to make a commensurate contribution to the world. So also do the countries of Europe. Unless we do so, our opinions will carry little weight, either in international organizations or in bilateral diplomacy. That being said, given that view vi) above is unfortunately the view of quite a lot of people in Japan, and known to be so, what we must at all costs avoid is to give the impression that Japan wants to become a great military power. That would work greatly to our disadvantage. The sensible thing, then, is to avoid revision of the Constitution, and to continue to do what we can by gradual enlargements of its interpretation.

Of these three 'Establishment' arguments, the last is the one with which I find it easiest to sympathize and to engage in debate. But the point I wish to stress here is all three of these arguments, *and* all four of the anti-Establishment arguments, *have two basic assumptions in common* – assumptions which I would question. They are:

1 Japan's foreign policy agenda is set by others. Foreign policy is about deciding how to respond to the expectations and pressures directed towards it by others. In other words there is not a trace of any sense that Japan might be faced with the opportunity of playing a constructive role in securing mankind's future by taking part in the building of world order.
2 Revision of the Constitution means, in effect, revising or eliminating Article 9 – i.e., 'abandoning the Peace Constitution'.

On the first point I have already made my view clear in choosing the title for this book – *A Japan That Can Say 'Let's Do This'* (*'Kō shiyō' to ieru Nihon*), and not just *'Can Say 'No'* as in the title of the book by Morita and Ishihara. But the more interesting assumption is the second. It seems to me by no means obvious that revising the Constitution has to mean 'abandoning the Peace Constitution'. It ought not to be impossible to revise the Constitution in a manner which meets current needs and aspirations, and yet actually *strengthens* claims to the title 'Peace Constitution' – and to do so in a manner which is feasible given public opinion and the alignment of political forces in Japan.

REINFORCING THE PEACE CONSTITUTION

Presumptuous though it may seem, the best way to make clear what I mean is to offer a concrete example of a possible revised text – with apologies if the Japanese hardly has the sonority appropriate for a Constitution.

The present text of Article 9 is as follows:

> Aspiring sincerely to an international peace based on justice and order, the Japanese people forever renounce war as a sovereign right of the nation and the threat or use of force as a means of settling international disputes.
>
> In order to accomplish the aim of the preceding paragraph, land, sea and air forces, as well as other war potential, will never be maintained. The right of belligerency of the state will not be recognized.

There is no reason to change the first clause.[2] The second could be replaced by something like the following:

> In order to make clear the resolution with which they make that declaration, the Japanese people hereby declare that their military forces and means of warfare on land, sea and air shall be used only for the following purposes;
> i) defence against any who should invade, with hostile intent, the internationally recognized borders of Japan,
> ii) disaster relief within and outside Japan,
> iii) participation in UN peace-keeping activities, and operations to restore peace conducted under the control of the United Nations in accordance with Article 47 of the Charter.[3]

'Operations to restore peace' refers to the use of military force to repel or reverse the effects of aggression utilizing Article 43 of the Charter – as in the Gulf War. 'In accordance with Article 47' would exclude participation e.g. in the multinational force which fought the Gulf War under American control, and limit operations to those under a command appointed by and answerable to the UN itself. It is an arrangement which has never yet been activated, but reference to it in the Japanese Constitution might give it new life.

I find it extraordinary that so few people in Japan are bothered by the fact that their country has an army, a navy and an air force equipped with the latest weapons, and spends one per cent of GNP on defence, and yet still has a Constitution which says that 'Land, sea and air forces and other war potential, will never be maintained'.

Throughout the slow evolution of these military forces – starting with the Police Reserve created for 'the preservation of internal order' (which the Constitution did not rule out), going on to their transformation into the Self-Defence Forces, the drawing of those forces into joint strategic planning with the US, the development of sea-lane defence plans, the steady escalation of firepower – at every step of this approach to 'normal' military capabilities, the government has made promises. Thus far, and no further; agree to this and we will guarantee not to seek any further enlargement of the military or its freedom of action. And then, at each stage, the process of promise-erosion begins again. It is hardly a history the Japanese people can look back on with pride. I wonder how many newspaper readers could read the daily reports of the Diet committee examination of the PKO Participation Act – the convoluted explanations of the officials of the Diet Legal Office, the bland assurances that 'provided the Self-Defence Forces are not walking about all the time with their pistols loaded', there should be no 'problem of illegality under the existing Self-Defence Forces Law and the current interpretation of the Constitution' – I wonder how many Japanese could read these exchanges without a sense of shame or disgust.

That 'current interpretation of the Constitution' – now so much taken for granted that it is hardly discussed in Japan – is the nub of the problem.

See the text above. The current interpretation, quite simply, is the following. Although the article says that Japan will never maintain armed forces, that is no reason for not having an army for self-defence. One influential argument is that the opening phrase of the second paragraph, 'In order to accomplish the purposes of the preceding paragraph', alters the meaning of the 'land, sea and air forces' which follows. It comes to mean 'land, sea and air forces maintained *for the purpose* of settling international disputes by armed force, and therefore does not ban defence forces. Nor does 'the right of belligerency', which is renounced, include the right of self-defence.

There was a famous occasion during the Diet debates on the Constitution – 28 June 1946, to be precise – when the Communist Party leader, Nosaka Sanzō, protested (and he was one of the very few who did) against Article 9. All countries must have the right of self-defence, he argued, and Article 9 should be rewritten to make that clear. Prime Minister Yoshida answered him in the following terms.

> The argument seems to be that wars which spring from the legitimate right of nation-states to self-defence are justifiable wars, but I think that this is a dangerous argument. [Applause] It is well-known that most wars in recent times have been prosecuted in the name of the right of self-defence. Consequently, to recognise that there is a legitimate right to self-defence would simply be to invite war; to make war more likely.[4]

It is hard to read this exchange between arch-conservative and arch-communist in today's Japan and keep a straight face. I recall an occasion, in 1953 or 1954, when Ashida Hitoshi came to give a lecture at the Royal Institute of International Affairs which explained the 'current interpretation' of the Constitution. He boasted with great pride – quite unaware of the impression of petty, sly deviousness he was leaving on his audience – of how he had inserted the phrase 'In order to accomplish the purposes of the preceding paragraph' precisely in order to preserve the right of self-defence.

Ashida began saying that the phrase in question had that effect from the end of 1946 onwards, but it was some time later that he began claiming he had imparted that intention at the time to the secret sub-committee which was formed to guide the Diet proceedings on the Constitution, thereby hoping, obviously, to lend 'intention of the legislators at the time' weight to what was on the face of it a tenuous argument. Some plausibility came to attach to this story when, after Ashida's death, his 'diary entry' for the day of the relevant sub-committee meeting was published in the daily newspaper *Tokyo Shimbun*. This 'diary', however, turned out to have been written by a reporter and the *Tokyo Shimbun* had to issue an apology.

The historian Furuseki,[5] who has analysed these events, shows quite clearly the origin of this controversial phrase. It was inserted at the same time as the opening phrase: 'The Japanese people', and was meant to draw the two clauses together by referring back to 'the pursuit of peace' as the 'purpose' for the renunciation of arms. In the original Government draft, neither phrase had appeared. It had begun with the bald phrase 'War as an expression of national sovereignty', and looked, it was thought by those who proposed the additions, simply like the normal process of the victors disarming the defeated. Something was needed, they argued, to show that this was indeed the intention, willingly embraced, of the Japanese people. It was in the same spirit that the words in the original draft: 'land, sea and air forces *must* not be maintained' was changed to '*shall* not be maintained'.

Ashida himself, during the committee session at which the amendment was made, said that the phrase about the pursuit of peace ought properly to come at the beginning of each paragraph, but they had substituted 'In order to accomplish the purposes. . .' to avoid repetition.[6] And, twenty days later, he was explaining the change to the Committee in the following terms:

> The reason why we put the phrase 'Aspiring sincerely to an international peace based on justice and order' at the beginning of the first paragraph, and 'In order to accomplish the purposes. . .' at the beginning of the second, was to emphasize that our motives in making this renunciation of war, and abolition of armed forces sprang overhelmingly from our desire for world peace and harmony among mankind.[7]

Shidehara, the Foreign Minister, also went on record as follows, in answer to a question as to the scale of armament which might be permitted (given the abolition of the army) to a police force for the purposes of maintaining domestic order:

> The purpose of Article 9 is quite clear in the phrase 'Aspiring sincerely to an international peace based on justice and order', and the question of

the maintenance of internal order does not enter into the matter. And in the second paragraph where we say 'In order to accomplish the purposes of the preceding paragraph' we 'shall not maintain military force', that does not mean that we cannot have a strong police force. It means that we cannot maintain armed forces capable of fighting wars with foreign countries. . . . We are saying that *in order to accomplish our purpose* of seeking international peace we are deciding not to have an army. . . What is clear is just that we are not going to have an army which can engage in war with other countries.[8] [My italics]

There is a certain irony in the fact that at the time, the only people known to have perceived it as a possibility that the phrase 'in order to accomplish. . .' might be used to justify a self-defence force were a few officials of the Legal Drafting Bureau and a former member of that bureau, Minister of State Tokujirō Kanamori.[9] Kanamori himself, four years later, wrote about Ashida who was then openly giving this interpretation, that it was a typical 'barrack-room lawyer's argument'.[10]

As, indeed, it is. So is the subsequent argument, taking off from this interpretation, that the 'self-defence capability' of Japan's Self-Defence Forces does not come in the category of 'land, sea and air forces and other war potential' How did such barrack-room lawyer-type arguments gain respectability? How is it that a country which in its most authoritative basic law has declared unconditionally that, as an expression of its sincere desire for international peace based on justice and order, it will not have an army, has now come to have a very considerable army? Why is it that over the years fewer and fewer people have been heard to denounce this development as an act of gross violation of the Constitution which casts doubt on Japan's claim to be a country based on the rule of law? Why do fewer and fewer people seem moved to question whether any foreigner will believe in Article 9's declaration of the Japanese people's sincere devotion to peace, if they do not even show a devotion to basic honesty?

The simple answer lies, I think, in the – caution shall we call it? or cowardice? – of the Japanese legal profession. Take first, the judges. There was, in 1973, the famous Naganuma judgement in the Sapporo District Court, which declared the Self-Defence Forces' existence to be unconstitutional. But it could not be expected that such a naive judicial declaration would survive. It was finally overturned in the Sapporo High Court three years later.[11]

As for the Supreme Court, it had already ruled, in the case arising from the Sunagawa Incident of 1953, that the US–Japan Security Treaty was a matter 'of a highly political character, touching on matters of grave concern for' the sovereignty of the nation, and that 'unless there was any clear *prima facie* contravention of the Constitution' it should be considered to 'lie outside the range of the Court's jurisdiction'. Given that it was nowhere specified in the Constitution that Japan should not allow American bases on

Japanese soil, that was a perfectly reasonable judgement. But when the Naganuma case finally came to it on appeal, it extended that Sunagawa judgement, arising from American bases and the Treaty, to matters arising from the Self-Defence Forces Law. It declared that this was a political matter which did not carry the justiciability implied in the Court's right to pronounce on the constitutionality of legislation. Hence, one cannot say whether the Court would consider the Self-Defence Forces Law to be just as clearly not a contravention of the Constitution as the US–Japan Treaty, because it has studiously avoided having to make a judgement on the matter. Its first evasive action came in 1952 when the constitutionality of the law establishing the National Police Reserve (the precursor of the Self-Defence Forces) was questioned. Then it ruled that it could only take up the question of constitutionality if there was any question of particular individuals being deprived of their constitutionally guaranteed rights – by, for instance, a conscription law or a secrets act. The justice argument came in later.[12]

So much for the judges. What about legal scholars? Listen to one of the most prominent of their number.

> As for the Constitution's character as a document promoting peace, and the interpretation of Article 9, this requires a rigorous and impartial judgement integrating all its various aspects with the highest level of objective rationality and scientific investigation, since it must go back to fundamentals in examining in a multidimensional, multifaceted manner, the three basic principles of Peace, Human Rights and Democracy; the relation of law and politics; and of domestic with international political aspects, not only subjecting the actual wording of Article 9 and the logic thereof to rigorous analysis, but also – *a propos* the equation of 'self-defence capability' with the existing Self-Defence Forces – conducting the most exhaustive examination not simply of the concept itself but also of the objective character of those Forces' actual mission, composition, armament, training and state of mind.[13]

What a wasted talent! If Professor Fukase were only a Bureau Chief in some Ministry his mastery of the convoluted evasive phrase, of the truth-concealing verbal smoke-screen could get him on the 'Today in the Diet' television programme every night. To be able to wrap up the core phrase 'the actual wording of Article 9' with such impressive parcelling shows a high level of art. But it makes zero contribution to improving public understanding of the issue or improving the state of health of Japanese politics.

It is notable how uncomfortable many Japanese become when they are asked how the Self-Defence Forces square with the Constitution. Surely, for most people, a revision of the Constitution which recognized the existence of the Self-Defence Forces would bring only relief: good riddance to a nagging sense of discomfort. And if it were accomplished after a lively internal debate and a national referendum, the act of revision itself could have a salutary enlivening effect on Japanese democracy. What is more, if it were in a form which embodied a realistic and genuine concern for international peace appropriate to the world we currently live in, it could be, for many Japanese, not just good riddance to a nagging problem, but a source of genuine national pride.

SUBSEQUENT NOTE

It appears that the parallel debate in Germany over the revision of the Basic Law – its Constitution – has already got well beyond the question of whether or not there should be revision. The debate now focuses on how the international mission of the armed forces should be defined. The SPD wants to restrict international involvement (as I suggested above) to peace-keeping and peace-enforcement activities which are directly under UN control, and thereby seek both to strengthen the UN and to prevent the German army being involved, in its old role as US ally, in wars which are basically fought in pursuit of American interests. Chancellor Kohl is reported to want the sort of revision which would allow Germany to take part, e.g. in the sort of multinational force organized at the time of the Gulf War.[14]

9 A UN-centred foreign policy and bilateral relations

The transformation of the 1945-model 'Victor Nations UN' into a genuinely global twenty-first-century model UN is the great task of the 1990s. If Japan were to make the accomplishment of this task its number-one foreign policy goal, it would, I am trying to suggest, not only be applauded by foreigners like myself; it would also give a great deal of satisfaction to its own people. For a Japan in whose newspapers and magazines the phrase 'international contribution' occurs so frequently, what better contribution could there be? That, in brief, is the message of this book.

But there is an obvious question which such a thesis is likely to evoke: what would be the costs to Japan of becoming advocate and champion of the UN?

No one could accuse Japan of being indifferent to the UN hitherto. It has paid its dues promptly; it has willingly sent Ministers to meetings where Ministers' presence was requested, and in some things it has taken effective initiatives. For example the Group of 18 – the panel of 'wise men' which was set up to make the UN more effective and did contribute to the administrative rationalization of the UN system – was established on the initiative of Japan in 1985. On Cambodia, Japan took the initiative several times in the course of the long, drawn-out informal negotiations which resulted in the creation of the ten-nation committee, and the UN's Cambodia involvement would probably have proved impossible if Japan had not offered to carry the bulk of the cost. The creation of the UN register of international arms shipments – the first tentative step towards international control of the arms trade – was proposed, with British support, by Japan. It was also Japan's initiative to create a trust fund as a means of bringing some stability into the financing of UN peace-keeping operations.

They were modest initiatives, but not by any means to be underestimated. They were, however, in a sense 'costless' initiatives. Japan could make them without necessarily incurring the hostility of, or using up its credit with, other nations. To go further and to make proposals which require sacrifices on the part of other nations, might well be at the cost of incurring their hostility. And insofar as proposals to strengthen the UN are likely to imply some erosion of the sovereignty of individual states, such circumstances are likely to be far from unusual.

At the beginning of Chapter 8, I suggested as the strongest, third-level definition of a 'UN-centred foreign policy' 'giving UN diplomacy priority over bilateral diplomacy'. What, in effect, would be the effect of giving that degree of priority to the strengthening of the UN on those friendly bilateral relations which it is in Japan's national interest to maintain? Clearly the crucial question here is the effect on US–Japan relations.

US–JAPAN RELATIONS

Chapter 7 ended with the suggestion that we face a choice between a 'UN-based world order' and a 'world order based on American hegemony', and left the impression that these were contrasting and incompatible alternatives. If that is really the case, then a switch from a foreign policy based on friendship with the US to a UN-centred foreign policy would indeed require Japan to make a 180-degree change of direction. One could well imagine that it would lead to a deterioration of a relationship already fraught with trade frictions, and provide ideal material for a renewed onslaught by Japan-bashers in the United States.

But does that necessarily have to be the case? Before accepting too readily the 'conflicting alternatives' view, one needs to look a little more closely at what, concretely, 'strengthening the United Nations' is likely to mean in the near future, and that means taking up again the dialogue between Mr Realist and Mr Idealist which was left unresolved at the end of the first chapter.

ROADS TO GLOBAL INTEGRATION

Let us begin with one major assumption. People who have studied the problem of nuclear proliferation suggest that within ten years into the next century the number of countries which possess, or could at short notice produce, nuclear weapons will exceed twenty, and the number capable of producing mass-destruction chemical or biological weapons will probably be double that number. Already, on the grounds that Iraq was guilty of aggression, the UN has ordered Iraq to destroy all its nuclear, chemical and biological weapons, and is supervising compliance with that order. One can well imagine that, through repetition of such incidents, there will emerge a single organization claiming a monopoly of the production, possession and use of weapons of mass destruction – in some sense a world government. Indeed, it is plausible to argue that unless there is some such development, the continued existence of mankind may well be at risk. My first assumption then is the optimistic one that such a development *will* take place, an assumption that draws reinforcement from the hunt for nuclear weapons in Iraq – a modern version of Hideyoshi's 'sword hunt' at the end of the sixteenth century – which has already taken place.

My second assumption is that one can actually learn something from 'the lessons of history'. In order to write the possible scenarios which might lead the world eventually to some kind of world government which has monopoly control over the weapons of mass destruction, it can actually be useful to look at the historical patterns of unification and pacification – the ways in which states have come to establish a similar monopoly of the means of violence – within individual states. The same 'human nature' is involved, and nowadays, however much talk of the 'global village' is rhetorical hype, the world has undoubtedly shrunk. Boston is much closer to Osaka today than ever it was to Virginia in the days of the founding fathers, or than Osaka was to Tokyo when Ieyasu was establishing his monopoly of violence in Japan.

What historical patterns do we see? The ones Mr Realist sees and generalizes from are examples of the appearance of a hegemon, the establishment, by force of arms, of an absolute monarchy. The ones Mr Idealist sees are like the Japanese feudal lords after the Meiji Restoration, voluntarily surrendering their feudal titles – the acceptance of a unified state through rational, conciliar discussion.

It is obviously, however, not just a matter of two contrasting alternatives. The hegemon's former opponents, the defeated barons, are generally by no means powerless; they are capable of exercising all kinds of constraints on the monarch's power. They can create their own councils which can set terms to define what is and what is not 'legitimate' in the exercise of that power. The history of Britain, from the Magna Carta to the end of the seventeenth century is in effect a history of the frictional struggles arising from that process. As the barons steadily lost their independent power, the state organs in which they were represented, along with the dignitaries of the Church – the Privy Council and the House of Lords – became gradually institutionalized, to the point at which the king could only act legitimately if he acted with their approval. Legitimacy, in other words, became as important as armed force for the maintenance of monarchical power and national unity.[1]

One might call that the 'intermediate pattern' to set beside the 'hegemonic pattern' and the 'conciliar pattern' of movement towards unity. How might this 'patterning' help in thinking about the United Nations? As we saw at the end of Chapter 7, at the time of the Gulf crisis there was a difference of opinion between the US and Russia as to whether operations against Iraq should be set in train by reviving the Military Staff Committee and establishing a command structure directly under UN control, or, as the Americans without much difficulty succeeded in insisting, by creating a multinational force under American direction. If one leaves aside all considerations of oil and other particular national interests and simplifies the problem simply into one of dealing with aggression, then this may be seen

Foreign policy and bilateral relations 115

as a straightforward clash between the hegemonic recipe and the concilar recipe.

Post-Gulf War America was bursting with confidence. Many Americans saw their country as undisputed world leader; the United Nations was of no consequence. Americans were the only people with an adequately keen sense of justice and an adequate appreciation of the rule of law; hence the responsibility for the maintenance of world order had to be America's. Nor was this merely man-in-the-street prejudice. Those were the lines of thinking clearly apparent in the Defence Planning Guidance document, which was leaked from the Pentagon and made top news in March 1992.[2] The *New York Times* correspondent to whom the document was leaked commented that the world it envisages is 'a world dominated by one superpower, whose position can be perpetuated by constructive behavior and sufficient military might to deter any nation or group of nations from challenging U.S. primacy.' As for where those challenges might come from, apart from a Russia, still capable of turning the American continent into an inferno, the most obvious sources are Germany and Japan. One thing that might become necessary is to use military force to prevent an Iraq or a North Korea from acquiring nuclear weapons. Otherwise Germany and Japan might resort to nuclear armament as a means of defence against these countries, and once nuclear-armed, those countries could eventually emerge as rivals to challenge the US. The US has also (the reporter is quoting from the document) to 'sufficiently account for the interests of the advanced industrial nations [pre-eminently Germany and Japan] to discourage them from challenging our leadership or seeking to overturn the established political and economic order'.

It is noticeable that the document assigns no role whatever to the UN or to other institutionalized forms of collective security. There may be, it says, occasions for joint military action with other nations; 'but we would expect these coalitions to be ad hoc assemblies, often not lasting beyond the crisis to be confronted, and in many cases carrying no general agreement over the objectives to be accomplished'.

The document does not look forward to any eventual establishment of world government; it seems to envisage a stable state of US hegemony of indefinite duration, but there can be no doubt as to how sharply this thinking on the part of the Pentagon hawks (henceforth 'the Pentahawk view') contrasts with the 'conciliar recipe' for establishing world order. Should such views become dominant in the United States, then there is no doubt that if Japan were to press for a strengthening of the United Nations in such a way as to restrain the freedom of manoeuvre even of the remaining superpower, it would inevitably meet with considerable hostility from the United States.

It does not, however, seem likely[3] that the Pentahawk view will actually come to dominate in US policy. At the time of the Gulf crisis, as already recorded, while America quickly brushed off Russian suggestions for a

116 *The argument*

UN command, nevertheless, though it started out by declaring that it intended to use its warships to enforce the blockade of Iraq and did not feel obliged to await an authorizing UN resolution before it did so, it began to backtrack when it saw the US becoming isolated. At that point, US delegates at the UN started working flat out to get the resolution agreed. And from that point on, as the situation worked steadily towards the Gulf War denouement, at every stage the US was scrupulously careful to get the support of legitimating resolutions for its actions.

What one saw, in fact, was an example of the 'intermediate pattern' – something between the 'conciliar pattern' which the Russians advocated, and the 'hegemonic pattern' of the post-Gulf War Pentahawk view. And one should not be surprised. Whatever might have been the case with the Saudis, had the US not armed itself with UN legitimacy, it might not have been able to count on the cash contribution it got from Germany, and it is rather unlikely that Ozawa Jirō, the Secretary-General of the LDP, would have succeeded in raising the thirteen-billion-dollar subsidy which it paid to the US.[4]

The fact remains that no other country had the military capability of dislodging the Iraqi army from Kuwait – remains to provide an uncontrovertible factual basis for the Pentahawk view. But the US no longer has the *economic* capability – or, perhaps one should say, no longer has the political capability to mobilize the economic resources – necessary to deploy that armed strength in any part of the world. That is equally part of the reality, and the basis for writing an 'intermediate pattern' scenario for the long, long path towards some kind of world federal government.

But what would that mean in practice? At the beginning of the Gulf crisis President Bush made a much quoted speech about 'world order'. It was long on rhetoric, but hardly a policy framework. What the Gulf War was about, he said, is 'more than one small country; it is a big idea; a new world order.... new ways of working with other nations... peaceful settlement of disputes, solidarity against aggression, reduced and controlled arsenals and just treatment of all peoples.'[5]

What part, exactly, the United States is going to play in the construction of this new world order was not specified. Nor was it, later, when Bush gave his farewell speech at West Point on the same theme. This lacked the overwhelming confidence of the earlier speech, but had all its ambiguities. The US was to be a world leader, but not a world policeman. Instancing his decision to send troops to Somalia, he declared that armed intervention was something that could only be considered case-by-case. The cooperation of other countries was important; it was equally important to seek some sharing of the cost...

There was, in short, no Bush doctrine. What there was, as the *New York Times* reporter who broke the news of the Pentahawk document quoted earlier suggested, was a rather easily defined set of basic assumptions. They may be summarized as follows:

1 The US should cooperate with the UN, and abstain from any use of the veto, except in cases where the majority view posed a very high level of threat to American interests.
2 Where the majority view coincides with US interests – or could with some effort be made to coincide – action through the UN should have the highest priority; UN blessing is always desirable for any despatch of US troops abroad.
3 To play the leader role in this way is the best way of ensuring that the UN follows policies aligned to American interests.
4 It is also the best way of minimizing the costs. 'Mercenaries for mankind' may not be a very appealing concept, but the US did in fact make a profit from the Gulf War.
5 Apart from the pursuit of national interests, it is also sometimes appropriate to act in response to moral feelings on the part of the American public – of outrage (Iraq) or of compassion (Somalia). (Depending on one's definition, satisfying the public's moral feelings may also be seen as a 'national interest'. It certainly helps in winning presidential elections. In the case of lame-duck Bush's decision to send troops to Somalia, 'place in history' considerations doubtless also came into play.)
6 But the US should never allow its freedom of action to be circumscribed by the UN. American interests may sometimes require that America takes decisive military action unilaterally, without waiting for UN sanction, and even, if need be, in the face of hostility from 'world opinion' as the UN reflects it.
7 And there is no question of making the strengthening of the UN a foreign policy objective, even though there is no cause to seek to weaken it either. Bush's farewell speech at West Point on the theme of the role of the American armed forces in the world used the word 'leadership' eight times in the course of its thirty minutes. There were only two references to the UN, one being about how 'it was we who galvanized the UN into action at the time of the Gulf War'.

This, what might be called the Bush–Baker line, is significantly different from the 1980–1987 Reagan policy of hostility to the UN – and from the Pentahawk line noted earlier which is closer to the latter. As this is written, ten days before the inauguration of a new President, it seems that the Bush–Baker line is widely accepted in the Washington civilian establishment, and will be continued by Clinton and Christopher.[6]

If that is indeed the case, there should be room for evolution along the lines of the 'intermediate pattern' – for, that is to say, a strengthening over time of America's willingness to work within the framework of the UN system, a weakening over time in the will to take military action which ignores, or flies in the face of, majority opinion in the UN, a diminished frequency with which it does so, until one reaches a situation in which it becomes more or less unthinkable that it should do so.

What can other countries do to help the US along such a path of possible evolution? The answer in a word: to raise the cost to the US – the prestige cost – of doing otherwise. In concrete terms:

1 To respond to what America does in the way of exercising its leadership role in the UN, or to what America does outside the UN framework which might become UN matters – e.g. its invasion of Panama in 1989 – not in a way primarily determined by ties of alliance or coincidence or non-coincidence of interest, but determined instead by considerations of 'international law and justice' – i.e., judging rights and wrongs rather than costs and benefits.
2 Not to forget that the response to every crisis creates precedents. When considering, in the case of Bosnia, for instance, whether to impose sanctions on Serbia as an aggressor, it should always be borne in mind by those involved in discussion on the Security Council and elsewhere, that the decision will affect the accepted definition of 'aggression', and the obligations the UN should assume in dealing with it, and the effect this would have on situations which are occurring, or are likely to occur, in other parts of the world.

If other nations were consistently to respond to US policy in such a manner, it might have a considerable effect on US policy. If it were the case that the use or the threat of military force overseas by the US was confined to cases where it was acting for the United Nations, and that the decisions of the UN were based on principles which were genuinely part of the basis of a 'world order', every such action would bring rewards to the US in the form of enhanced prestige. And as the principles of that 'order' became recognized as such and reinforced with repeated invocation, so the loss of prestige involved in unilateral action outside the UN framework – action which contravenes those principles – becomes greater. And the higher probability of losing an acquired position of high prestige makes such action more unlikely.

This scenario for taming American power – for making a 'good citizen out of the US problem child' by moral and other pressure from other nations – makes one big assumption. That assumption may be put in terms of the contrast made in the last chapter; i.e., between the Israeli recipe for gaining international respect by a show of strength, and the Swedish 'good neighbour, model citizen' recipe. The assumption is that the world becomes increasingly the sort of place in which the Swedish recipe cuts more ice than the Israeli one. If that assumption is mistaken, then the arguments above largely fall to the ground.

And so also does the most obvious basis for hoping that the human race might survive to have a long-term future.

AN EXAMPLE OF THE INTERMEDIATE PATTERN

The Gulf crisis provides an illustration of what might happen. It made clear to the United States that, provided it acted according to resolutions of the Security Council which embodied basic principles of world order (such as that aggression must not go unpunished) it could expect economic and other forms of support and an enhancement of its prestige. (That need to keep within the compass of UN authorization seems to have played a part in Bush's decision to end the war as soon as the objective of liberating Kuwait had been achieved and not pursue it until Saddam Hussein was overthrown.) Again when, in his last week in office in January 1993, Bush ordered the American bombing of Iraq which no UN resolution could be interpreted to authorize, there were sufficiently strong voices of protest from America's allies that the US was forced to backtrack. It is reasonable to expect that as these experiences are repeated – international applause when acting to execute UN resolutions; fierce criticism when breaking loose from them – the US propensity to use its hegemonic military supremacy and its ability to convince itself of its own righteousness in unilateral action will diminish. And the effectiveness of UN resolutions in binding the actions even of great powers will increase. That is what one means by 'institutional evolution'.

Another example: the Security Council ordered the removal of nuclear weapon-making facilities from Iraq and the IAEA sent inspectors to Iraq to accomplish the task. However, only the US and Russia had spy satellites capable of identifying the relevant sites, and where evasive shifting might be taking place; the IAEA had none of its own. It had to rely for its intelligence on the Pentagon. Hence it is not surprising that the inspection team contained a number of Americans, or that, when the Iraqis tried to stop some of the documents which had been seized from being taken away and the inspection team was holed up for several days in a car park, it was to the Pentagon that they were reported to be transmitting the said documents via fax and a satellite phone line. It is not surprising that there was a chorus of protest from Arab countries, complaining that anything revealed to the Pentagon was equally available to the Israelis; the UN was revealed as a mere instrument through which superpower US and its Israeli running dog pursued their own interests.

This was a good illustration of the ambiguities, of the two steps forward, one step back nature, of the intermediate pattern. On the one hand it gave the Arab countries every grounds for doubting the UN's objectivity, and thereby lowered the prestige of the UN. On the other it created a precedent for direct action in the name of the international community to prevent the proliferation of nuclear weapons. And one might hope that, given the justice of the criticism that the IAEA was too dependent on the Americans, it might have hastened the day when the IAEA gets its own spy satellite and intelligence-gathering capability.

The argument

The case of Somalia has many significant aspects. There were two clear elements in the situation at the end of 1992. The first was famine – the harrowing pictures shown on television of thousands close to death from starvation. The second was the collapse of the Somali state, the transformation of the Somali territory into an open arena for anarchic conflict between heavily armed rival factions. The famine was in large measure a function of the lack of order; relief supplies from the Red Cross and other voluntary agencies would be hijacked by armed gangs before they reached the starving.

What could an international agency which, unlike the voluntary bodies, can deploy armed force do about such a situation? The first thing it can do is to send soldiers to protect those who are engaged in relief work to make sure that supplies get to their proper destination. As the cumulative effect of harrowing television pictures built up, and media commentators increasingly called for action, President Bush, responding to that public opinion (with an eye, some would say, in his last month in office, on the rating he would get from historians) decided to take action – after consultation with, though not at the initiating request of, the UN Secretary-General. He sent 30,000 troops with the mission to escort food convoys; which job they were expected to have accomplished within two or three months after which they would return home.

But the problem of establishing civil order was not one to be accomplished in two or three months. The Secretary-General began urging on the Americans that the only long-term solution to the problem lay in the disarming of the rival factions and the establishment of a structure capable of effectively exercising state authority and maintaining law and order. What the response will eventually be remains to be seen.

What Boutros Boutros-Ghali is in effect advocating is a step towards world federal government. Consider the analogy of India which has a federal constitution. Provisions in that constitution permit – indeed require – the central government, whenever in any Indian state there is a breakdown and paralysis of effective government, to declare 'presidential rule' and to assume state authority until some kind of stable order can be rebuilt. They are provisions which have been resorted to several times. It is something like that on a world scale which Boutros-Ghali is advocating; open interference in the domestic affairs of countries where state authority has collapsed – in many ways an extension of the functions of election supervision which the UN has already exercised on several occasions.

If this is in fact the way it turns out, then – another example of 'combined pattern evolution' – action taken by the American government without any conscious intention of strengthening international organization will have proved in effect to have advanced internationalist principles.

To return to the original point – what effect would it have on US–Japan relations if Japan were to adopt a UN-centred foreign policy? – one might summarize the answer as follows. It could increase the contribution that the US might make to the strengthening of world order. If consistent skill is deployed – that is to say, if the other nations of the world do in fact make it their long-term goal to create some kind of conciliar world order distinct from US hegemony – and if they were to judge America's actions by their conformity to that long-term objective, giving full recognition to and showing full respect for America's contributions – there is no reason why a shift to a UN-centred policy should necessarily mean a worsening of US–Japan relations.

It would also have the advantage that Japan would no longer be the object of jibes that it acts as little more than a satellite of the United States.

To give one concrete example: if Japan had consistently followed a UN-centred – or, more accurately, an international organization-centred – policy, it would not have accepted the American call in 1990 to enter into the talks which became known as the Structural Impediment Initiative. If the intention was not just to do something to appease the US Congress, but also to strengthen the world trading system, a more appropriate response might have been on the following lines. The general question of how far the internal domestic institutions of a country – its tax system, its distribution of income, the business ties between its firms, its *keiretsu* and so on – ought to be changed in order to increase its propensity to import goods from abroad – how far they have an obligation to do so – is not just a matter for Japan and for the US. It is a matter of the institutional underpinnings of the world economic system. The Large Retail Stores Law, for instance, which the US says Japan ought to change, has its parallels in France and in Italy. These are not, then, primarily matters for bilateral negotiations. They should be discussed in the GATT framework, as matters that concern all participants in the world trading system. That would have been a perfectly reasonable response. If that *had* been Japan's response, it would not only have had the same cooling-off perspective-widening effect as the intervention of relatives can have in marital quarrels; it would also, by posing clearly the general question of principle – just *how far* do countries have to sacrifice sovereignty to run a full free trade system – have contributed to the strengthening of the system of international cooperation, and of international organizations.

RELATIONS WITH RUSSIA

Two or three years ago, when the strengthening of the UN system actually had a high place in the long-term policy objectives of the USSR, countries with the same objective ought frequently to have found themselves in alliance with Russia and clearly at variance with the US. With the transition from the age of Gorbachev and Shevardnadze to that of Yeltsin, however, the UN has once again become, for the Russians, primarily an arena for the pursuit of long-term advantage. What Russia should do in that arena has become a matter of fierce internal debate. At present, the line followed by the Foreign Minister, Khozylev, the line much criticized as 'playing lackey to the US', still prevails, but there is always the possibility, strengthened by the sympathies with Serb nationalism evoked by events in Yugoslavia, that it will give way to policies rooted in racialist nationalism – anti-Western, anti-Semitic and pro-Arab – and that forces favouring such a course could emerge victorious from a future election. Russia's attitude towards the UN being, thus, unpredictable, it is difficult to make general predictions about the effect on relations with Russia of Japan's adopting a UN-centred foreign policy.

But the link between Russo-Japan relations and UN policy is clear in one basic sense, however. At present those relations are poisoned by the question of Japan's territorial claim to the four northern islands – a hangover of the Cold War politics of the 1950s. It is quite extraordinary that even today, in 1993, the two countries should be the only major powers who mutually restrict the travel of the other country's diplomats.

Whatever the rights and wrongs of Japan's claims, whatever the truth about the role of John Foster Dulles in the process by which the claim to those islands became the number one priority of Japan's Russian policy – one could almost, at times, say the *only* concern – it is hard to see anything healthy in the fact that Russo-Japanese relations are deadlocked in a state of near-paralysis.[7]

There seems not the slightest prospect that Yeltsin, engaged in a struggle with nationalist conservative forces on so many other issues, will make the concessions Japan asks for on this one – however much he may want to start a flow of Japanese aid. And any successor to Yeltsin is likely, if that is possible, to be even less disposed to concede. And, on the other side, it is probably politically impossible for Japan to lower the priority it gives to the Northern Islands issue. But there is, surely, a way out of the present cul-de-sac. Japan can appeal to the International Court of Justice. There would surely be many advantages.

On the Russian side there are good grounds for refusing to countenance any concession on the Northern Islands on the grounds that with so many of Russia's frontiers disputed one way and another, to make any concession in one area simply opens a Pandora's box. But the Northern Islands issue is in an important respect different from all the others. The others involve claims based on the presence of ethnic minorities, now or historically. The dispute with Japan is the only one which, being a dispute about the interpretation of treaties, is admirably suited for the ICJ's adjudication. Hence there is a good chance that the Russians could be persuaded to accept the Court's jurisdiction.

Second, with luck the Court could take two or three years in its deliberations. In the meanwhile the issue would be frozen as a diplomatic issue, and Russo-Japanese relations could evolve in a more natural direction meanwhile. Very probably, if more friendly relations developed and more Japanese firms started investing in the USSR, even if, on the question of ultimate sovereignty, the final verdict went against Japan, the likelihood would be that, in the matter of fishing rights and other substantive issues, Japan and Russia could reach agreements which were favourable to Japan.

And third, of course, it would be a clear demonstration of Japan's commitment to a peaceful international order.

RELATIONS WITH ASIA

It seems a worthy idea that, just as efforts are being made in Europe to strengthen the CSCE – the Conference on Security and Cooperation in Europe – there is a need for something like a CSCA in Asia to substitute for the individual bilateral alliances between Asian countries and the US as the chief means of ensuring security and the peaceful settlement of disputes in an area of the world full of situations of potential danger, including disputes over borders. It is an idea worth support, even if the European example is hardly encouraging, the efforts to develop the CSCE being seriously hampered by the inertial presence of that product of the Cold War, NATO.

The speech made by Prime Minister Miyazawa during his tour of South-East Asia in January 1991 – sometimes spoken of as announcing a 'Miyazawa doctrine' – may or may not have foreshadowed the intention to push for precisely such a development. One would certainly like to see it as a symptom of the emergence of a Japan which *does* take initiatives. The time is surely coming when Japanese policy towards Asia need no longer be dominated by the careful avoidance of anything which might be interpreted as a sign of the re-emergence of a 'militarily self-assertive Japan'. A decisive step in that direction would, of course, be accomplished if there were to be a revision of the Japanese Constitution along the peace-declaration lines suggested in the last chapter.

One proviso should be added. Regional collective security organizations can indeed be very beneficial, as Chapter 8 of the UN Charter clearly recognizes. But, as that chapter insists, the coordination of such regional efforts with the global organization of security based on the Security Council is essential. If nations are increasingly becoming 'borderless', so too are regions.

RELATIONS WITH CHINA IN PARTICULAR

In Asia, prediction of the effect on bilateral relations of Japan adopting a UN-centred foreign policy is most difficult in the case of China.

Think of what would happen on the following, not unreasonable, assumption: viz., over the next quarter century Europe and North America have growth rates of 2 per cent, Japan of 3.5 per cent, and China of 10 per cent. If one takes China's per capita income as at present one-twentieth of that of Japan,[8] this would mean that, given the difference in population size, China's total GNP would exceed Japan's in something like eleven years' time.

The trade frictions which could result from these differential growth rates – especially if China, as is likely, developed strength in the high-tech industries and began to follow Japan in challenging the position of the US in European and Latin American markets – could be portentous. It would not be altogether surprising if 'Japan-bashing' gave way to the perception that the West faced a more general threat – a new form of the 'Yellow Peril'. And the result might be to force Japan and China into a sort of defensive alliance.

To be sure, there will be trade troubles enough between Japan and China themselves. But consider the frictions which arose between Japan and Taiwan or Japan and Korea during their period of rapid growth. In spite of the fact that relations with Korea were skewed by bitter memories of the colonial period, and characterized by continuous mutual recrimination, economic cooperation has continued steadily. The annual meeting of the Korean and Japanese artificial fibre industry associations, for example, seem to be conducted a good deal less acrimoniously than the automobile industry talks between Japan and the United States.

Cultural factors are by no means to be ignored, either. On central political issues, the post-Confucian states do seem to have different assumptions and different sensibilities from the states of Mediterranean cultural origin. Consider the differences between Japanese and American approaches to China after Tienanmen; or the coolness of Japan towards the attempts by Hong Kong's governor, Chris Patten, to press hard for greater democracy in Hong Kong in a last effort to assert British prestige. There are subtle but clear differences between Japan and the Anglo-Saxon countries on the whole complex of issues involving the relationship of authority and order to democracy. It is not hard to imagine Chinese and Japanese businessmen shaking their heads over something at a party and telling each other that, 'You can't expect Westerners to understand that, though, can you?'

What I am trying to suggest is that it is not impossible to imagine that a China–Japan versus US–Europe confrontation might in twenty years' time become the main centre of tension, the main fault line of world politics. It is not mere sensation-mongering to say that it is a scenario to be considered – and I would suggest that one of the best ways of preventing it happening is for Japan to adopt a UN-centred foreign policy. Japan and China are not simply engaged in a bilateral relationship involving their respective national interests. They are also, as members of various international bodies, severally involved, along with the representatives of other segments of the human race, in dealing with common global problems. In GATT, WHO, the UN itself, Japan might on occasion, for reasons of national interest or for reasons of principle, find itself in alignment with China; on other occasions aligned with, say, France or the US and in opposition to China. These interactions with China in international bodies contain an element missing in bilateral relations – a shared consciousness of having, as equal members of the international community, equal responsibilities for, and an equal interest in, maintaining a system of international order. It is in this sense that, the more priority is given to a 'UN-centred foreign policy' which emphasizes the importance of these multilateral relations, the better the chance that the alarming 'Japan–China versus Europe–America' scenario described above can be avoided.

I have dwelt at length in this chapter on the meaning of a 'UN-centred foreign policy', and how its advantages might outweigh its disadvantages. In all this, there was an underlying assumption – namely that, through the efforts of Japan and other countries, the UN might evolve into a more effective body, more capable of responding to the aspirations of mankind. What this might mean in terms of specific institutional developments is the subject of the next and final chapter.

10 The restructuring and strengthening of the UN
A survey of the issues

If Japan were to make it a major object of foreign policy to seek to take positive initiatives to strengthen the UN, what sort of initiatives might it take?

Not being a specialist on international affairs I can hardly speak with confidence about 'what ought to be done'. But a certain amount of reading in recent years has given me some idea of what the main issues and options are. In this chapter I shall try to set them out as clearly and as simply as I can. Some of the suggestions may seem pretty outlandish. They include suggestions for the revision, in some cases fundamental revision, of the UN Charter. But this is not, perhaps, so outlandish after all. As Japan's Foreign Minister, Mr Watanabe, said in his General Assembly speech in 1992, the call for charter revisions is growing in strength, and with the fiftieth anniversary of the Charter in prospect for 1995 it is likely to grow even stronger.

THE SECURITY COUNCIL

The League Convention was a part of the Versailles Peace Treaty. Although that mistake was avoided this time, the UN Charter bears clear traces of being a 'victors' charter'. To take the most obvious example, Article 53 – well-known in Japan as the 'enemy country article' – specifically authorizes an exception to the rule that regional security organizations should not take armed peace-enforcing action without the approval of the Security Council: it may be permitted in the case of former 'enemy states', 'renewing their aggressive policies'. The English name for the organization itself – United Nations – was a carry-over of the name of the wartime alliance against Germany and Japan. (Who was responsible for rendering it into Japanese as *Kokusai Rengō* – literally more like 'International Confederation' – I do not know, but it was a wise choice.)

Much more important a wartime legacy was the building into the structure of the Security Council of permanent seats for the five leading allied powers, and awarding them each the right to veto its decisions.

It hardly seems wise for Japan to react to this situation as it has done hitherto – basically it seems to be saying: we are now a great and powerful country and we want to be admitted to the club. Suppose instead that Japan were to say: we would rather not just be admitted to the club in a way which endorses its present unreasonable structure. If, however, the Security Council were to be revised thus and thus, then both Japan and other countries would be able to play a much more constructive role. Such an initiative would doubtless arouse the hostility of Britain and France which cling to their UN seats the more firmly precisely because of the decline of their relative position in the world, but it would certainly earn more general respect. And no one would be able to challenge either the logic of such a position or Japan's right to say it, given that Japan's contribution of twelve and a half per cent of the UN budget is greater than that of Britain, France and China put together. (Germany's at nine per cent also exceeds that of any of those three veto powers.)[1]

The question is, what to propose for the 'thus and thus' – what concrete measures to advocate. Certain starting points seem obvious.

1 Differential voting rights are obviously unavoidable. The more a country possesses the wealth and power, the deployment of which is necessary for the effective functioning and development of the UN, the more important is its cooperation, and there is probably no better way of securing that cooperation than by giving it greater voting influence on decisions.
2 It appears that many matters are today decided by informal discussions among the five veto powers. The procedure works because few are involved. The need for a sort of 'inner cabinet' to work out draft resolutions is clear and such an inner group should not be too big.
3 When the UN was founded it was generally believed that for any of the Big Five themselves to be made the object of sanctions by the others, would either lead to a new world war or to the breakup of the UN itself. The right of veto was the institutional recognition of that reality. But that argument is far weaker today, now that the major likely cause of a third world war – the ideological and geopolitical competition between the US and Russia – has come to an end, and now that – partly thanks to the UN itself over its half-century of history – the restraining effects of 'international opinion' on the behaviour of states is a good deal stronger than it was.

Given the above, one might think of the problem as one of getting the right balance on three different dimensions.

a) The composition of the Security Council; a replacement for the notion of 'permanent member'. One needs some arrangement which allows flexible change over time, reflecting changes in the power balance and changes in 'international opinion' – for example three or four seats for 'major powers' elected for ten years at a time and re-electable; and several two-to-three year seats for 'middle-range powers'. The criteria for categorizing countries into their respective 'major', 'middle-range', 'lesser' constituencies could be multiple. Financial contributions to the UN would be one, but so would population. (If it is 'mankind's UN', one has to listen to the countries which have a large share of mankind.) Perhaps there should be regional constituencies as at present. There is a lot to be said also for performance criteria – the willingness to contribute to the UN and its work, as evidenced in prompt payment of assessed contributions, provision of troops and funds for peace-keeping, the proportion of foreign aid channelled through multilateral agencies, etc. Such criteria could usefully encourage countries to 'earn brownie points' in ways that strengthen the UN system.

b) One might also think of institutionalizing a kind of inner five-or-six-country cabinet or 'standing committee' of the Security Council. A Japanese diplomat's analysis of the present situation in the Security Council is suggestive.[2] At present, resolutions are mostly drafted in informal meetings of the five permanent members, and thereafter it is as much as Japan or any of the other ten members can do to effect minor amendments. Moreover, of those five members one can observe 'a generally shared outlook and value system on the part of the four – US, UK, France and Russia'. China tends to play a passive onlooker role, and on many issues, out of weakness, abstains. But in one thing it is consistent – in challenging anything which smacks of 'intervention in countries' internal affairs'. Given the tendency for the other powers to be increasingly willing to contemplate such interventions, it may, he suggests, be only a matter of time before China uses the right of veto which has been in abeyance for (as of then) over three years.

The long history of thinking about the need for international organization – about the creation of a 'government of mankind' – is indeed a product of the 'generally shared value system of US, UK, France and Russia', that is to say of the cultural traditions which had their origins in the Mediterranean basin. Can one expect nations representing a different – a Confucian or an Islamic – cultural tradition to converge towards that value system – at least that part of it relevant to ideals of an international order based on the rule of law? What inhibits such convergence at the moment – as seen in China's rejection of all 'internal interference' – is not, it seems to me, primarily a difference in *culture* in itself. When Confucian scholars spoke of 'peace and plenty under Heaven' they did not mean anything very different from the Christians' 'peace on earth'. The problem lies, rather, in the fact that for several centuries it is white-skinned peoples of Mediterranean Christian culture who have dominated over and frequently colonized peoples of Confucian and Islamic culture, and that it is still those same nations which quite frequently act as if they were masters of the earth, putting pressure on others in ways seen as oppressive. That is the reason why the concrete interpretations of 'human rights', 'justice', 'rule of law' as defined by those white-skinned nations are not likely to be accepted without resistance – because they are seen sometimes as arguments justifying their superior attitudes. But, as argued at the end of Chapter 6, apropos the argument of Professor Nakanishi, actual convergence in the values themselves seems to me not impossible – a view supported not just by appeal to arguments about 'common humanity', but by the evidence of the evolution in the years since the war of inernational activity in support of the protection of human rights. To conclude, therefore, what started as a discussion of a possible 'inner cabinet' of the Security Council, it would need to have, in its membership, representatives from the Confucian and Islamic culture areas.

c) One could think of various kinds of substitute for the present (almost unrestricted) veto power. For example, certain countries might have the right of veto over a particular resolution, but with provisions for reconsideration of the matter, this time with majority voting provisions (an eighty per cent majority, say) if, after a certain period of time, no compromise could be found. There might also be formal rules to preclude from voting on resolutions critical of, or imposing sanctions on, certain countries, those countries themselves and countries which are in military alliance with them.

One other thought. In most national parliaments there is a rule that before a member speaks on a certain policy issue, he is required, at the beginning of his speech, to declare any personal interest he might have in the questions at issue. Might one look forward to the day when speeches in the Security Council begin with a declaration of the national interest reasons delegates might have for favouring one or the other party to a dispute? It is unlikely that the practice could be legislated from nothing. It would require certain countries which were agreed on its desirability to agree to adopt it, thus eventually, one hopes, shaming the others to conform.

DISPUTE PREVENTION

Soon after the Gulf War, Brian Urquhart, reflecting on forty years' involvement with the management of peace-keeping operations in the UN, wrote the following:[3]

> If the word 'security' is to acquire real significance, the UN must find a way to keep a continuing systematic watch on destabilizing developments all over the world, socio-economic as well as political and military. Special attention must be given to dangerous buildups of armaments beyond what Mr Shevardnadze has called 'criteria of defence sufficiency' and to potential threats, especially to the weaker nations.

What would this mean in practical terms? One possibility is to enlarge and strengthen the *role of the Secretary-General*. Article 99 of the Charter already authorizes the Secretary-General to bring to the attention of the Security Council situations which seem to pose a threat to peace. As the Soviet delegate Petrowski pointed out in his 1988 proposals for strengthening the UN,[4] it requires only a slight expansion of the interpretation of that article to give the Secretary-General the right to summon a special meeting of the Council when he thinks necessary, or to hold periodic meetings, at which the Secretary-General gives his assessment – if necessary a confidential assessment – of situations likely to lead to conflict. Even more important is to strengthen the capacity of the Secretary-General, or his personal representatives, to intervene to offer mediation and conciliation. As noted in Chapter 7, it was, in fact, recognized in Hammarskjold's time that it can be more effective for someone who can claim to be 'the world's' Secretary-General to mediate with a free hand, rather than to force him to operate within the limits of SC resolutions known to have been steered through by particular countries which may have particular axes to grind. In the present Secretary-General's plan for strengthening the UN, his *Agenda for Peace*, he is is careful to emphasize:[5] 'the good offices of the Secretary-General may at times be employed most effectively when exercised independently of the deliberative bodies [The Security Council and the General Assembly].' He is careful, though, to make clear that this is not a mere expression of power lust, acknowledging that the mediator's effectiveness is enhanced by 'strong and evident support from the Council, the General Assembly and the relevant Member States acting in their national capacity'.

As Boutros-Ghali emphasizes in that same *Agenda for Peace* (published in June 1992, in response to a resolution of the Prime Ministerial-level Security Council in January asking for his proposals) the UN's 'fact-finding capability' is all-important.[6] The proposals in that document include:

i) establishing structures and procedures so that, at the request of a country which considers itself endangered, a fact-finding mission can be immediately despatched;
ii) the need for all countries to respond promptly to the Secretary-General's requests for information;
iii) provisions for the Secretary-General to send observers to gather information on his own initiative;
iv) the more frequent use by the General Assembly and the Security Council of their right to call for fact-finding missions;
v) occasionally convening the Security Council in areas where tension is running high.

He points out that both the despatch of fact-finding missions and a local meeting of the Security Council could in themselves have an effect in reversing the build-up of tension.

Agenda for Peace does not go quite that far, but some would urge that the UN should have its own permanent intelligence-gathering capability. At a Kyoto meeting in the summer of 1991, the former Chief Scientist of the British Ministry of Defence urged that only if the UN had its own spy satellites would it be freed from dependence on the information supplied by particular countries, information possibly slanted to serve those countries' own interest. If the UN had its own means of judging whether troop movements betrayed aggressive intentions, general confidence in the objectivity of those judgements would be greatly enhanced.

PEACE-MAKING, PEACE-ENFORCING, PEACE-KEEPING

Peace-keeping, as is well known in Japan where recent debates have made PKO a universally known term, has hitherto chiefly involved the sending of lightly armed troops after a cease-fire in a conflict situation – and sending them with the concurrence of all the involved parties – to monitor the observance of the terms of a conflict settlement. They may patrol and police disarmed neutral zones, provide aid to victims of war, or supervise elections, but in principle it is not their role to intervene by force of arms.

This is no longer enough, said Boutros Boutros-Ghali in his *Agenda for Peace*. He stressed the need for four different types of action.

1 Preventive action in situations where a dispute between neighbouring countries has the potential to erupt in conflict: the sending, by the Security Council but with the consent of both parties, to both sides of the boundary, of a force which might have the potential for military action.[7]
2 Similar preventive action in cases where both parties do not agree to the Security Council's intervention – the sending of a force only to one side of the boundary at the request of a country which fears invasion.[8]
3 (As, for instance, was contemplated in Cambodia and Angola at the time this is written), giving the peace-keeping forces the mandate to enforce the terms of a cease-fire agreement when one of the parties fails to comply with its terms.[9]
4 When economic sanctions under Article 41 of the Charter fail to have their effect, the restoration of peace by the use of force as prescribed in Article 42.[10]

In *Agenda for Peace* missions 1 to 3 are described as 'peace enforcement' activity, and his proposal is that UN members should create units of volunteers within their own armed forces, that they should be given special training for the kind of work such operations entail, and should be held in readiness for emergencies. These forces would be treated for Charter purposes as falling under the 'temporary arrangements' mentioned in Article 40, and they would be integrated in the structure of military organization created – outside the strict prescriptions of the Charter – for traditional

PKO activities – what Hammarskjold dubbed 'Chapter Six-and-a-half' activities.

Hence these activities would be considered separate from action to combat aggression under Article 42 – after the failure of economic sanctions (Article 41), and these forces would not be considered as the kind of UN force composed of member country units and acting under the Military Staff Committee such as is contemplated in Article 43.[11] (See the description in Chapter 4 of the efforts to implement that article in the immediate post-war period and how they came to fail.)

Nevertheless, the document does also call for the early implementation of Articles 42 and 43.

> The Security Council has not so far made use of the most coercive of these measures [specified in Chapter VII] – the action by military force seen in Article 42. In the situation between Iraq and Kuwait, the Council chose to authorize Member States to take measures on its behalf. The Charter, however, provides a detailed approach which now merits the attention of all Member States.[12]

One can only guess that the authors of the report judged it best to put the Article 42–43 provisions for the 'punishment of aggression' on hold and to seek to define 'peace-enforcement activity' (however logically difficult to distinguish from it) as an extension of the familiar 'peace-keeping activity', because they saw the expansion and strengthening of the present military command structure directly under the control of the Secretary-General as a better, or more feasible option to trying to create a new structure under a resuscitated Military Staff Committee. At any rate, most of the people who have written on the subject see no need for any kind of division of labour between two command structures. Take, for example, the proposals of the former American ambassador to Italy for a Rapid Deployment Force. He suggests that twenty to thirty countries should, through Article 43-type agreements, commit a battalion-strength force (2–3,000 men) for what is essentially UN peace-enforcement activity, give them a common training and common, or compatible, armaments, and suggests that the organization and training should be directed by the existing UN command structure.[13]

At any rate, the Security Council has gradually moved in the direction of strengthening and enlarging the functions of the existing command structure. As, during 1992, operations were mounted in Cambodia, Angola and Yugoslavia, and the number of men operating under the UN flag grew from eleven thousand to fifty thousand, it became clear that hasty *ad hoc* arrangements for the provision of troops were no longer enough. That is what lay behind the Security Council resolution of 29 October 1992 which urged member countries to report to the Secretary-General the military forces which they would be able to put at the UN's disposal.[14]

It also became clear that the existing administrative structure available to deal with these activities was quite inadequate to the tasks it had to perform.

The commander of the UN force in Bosnia is reported to have complained angrily that 'you can phone New York on Friday only to be told that there's nobody there and you should wait until Monday'. It is not surprising that the former NATO naval Commander-in-Chief should have proposed in a recent paper that the coordination of UN military activity requires a military planning staff capable of providing in advance for logistics, for the establishment of common communications systems and for training to uniform standards.[15]

And if organization is a problem, so also is finance. Hitherto each separate operation, once it has been decided on, has to be separately financed *ad hoc*. At Japan's initiative, in 1992 a trust fund was set up to make it possible for the UN to have cash to draw on to begin operations before financing negotiations had been completed. But the major problem is not just one of the means of collecting money but of the total amount. The estimated cost to the American forces of the Gulf operations was between 50 and 60 billion dollars (of which Japan contributed 13 billion). The sum total of UN expenditure on peace-keeping up to 1992 was a mere 8.3 billion dollars – of which 0.8 billion was promised but not yet paid up.

In *Agenda for Peace*, Boutros-Ghali writes: [16]

> Peace-keeping operations approved at present are estimated to cost close to $3 billion in the current 12-month period, while patterns of payment are unacceptably slow. Against this, global defence expenditures at the end of the last decade had approached $1 trillion a year, or $2 million per minute.

In pointing out the enormity of the 300-to-1 gap, Boutros-Ghali also makes the argument that expenditure on UN peace-keeping, in so far as it constitutes a contribution to collective security, is expenditure for the same purpose as national defence budgets, and it would therefore be logical for member countries to include such contributions in their defence, rather than in their foreign affairs, budgets. (Doubtless what he has in mind is not so much a matter of logical budgeting, as the fact that defence budgets are universally bigger and have more leeway.)

One could think beyond that to the possibility that member countries might be asked to contribute a standard percentage of their defence budgets to a UN peace-keeping fund. *Agenda for Peace* does not go that far. Doubtless 'one step at a time' is Boutros-Ghali's preferred strategy, or perhaps he is waiting for a cooperative country to make the proposal.

INTERNATIONAL CIVIL SERVANTS: THE CIVIL AND MILITARY BUREAUCRACY

'Bureaucratic' hardly counts as a term of praise in any country's vocabulary. And there are far too many grounds for the common accusation that the UN is riddled with the worst forms of bureaucratic behaviour. However

134 *The argument*

good the organizational structure might be on paper, unless it is operated by officials of high quality, it can do 'mankind' more harm than good. The common accusations made against UN officials include:

1 That the system of national quotas leads to far too many appointments under political pressure and far too many officials of low ability.
2 Salaries are too high. Newspapers reported that in Cambodia, the volunteers who were doing dedicated and dangerous work were under the supervision of UN officials living in safe zones and paid salaries several tens of times larger than their meagre allowances – and their 'supervisors' were often more obstructive than helpful.[17]
3 Perhaps most important of all is the question of loyalty – do UN officials see themselves as 'mankind's civil servants' or primarily as loyal citizens of their own countries? Recall the 1870s and 1880s in Japan, when the government was constantly accused of being a *hambatsu seifu* – a 'clan government' made up of men who were more concerned to promote the interests of the Satsuma or Choshu fief from which they came than to work for the interests of 'Japan'. There are far too many instances of Frenchmen, Russians, Japanese and Englishmen in the UN feeding privileged information to their own governments, and judging matters which should be regulated by impartial principles in the light of their own country's interests. It was noted in Chapter 9 that the IAEA inspectors in Iraq were accused of being agents of the United States, and it is no wonder that such accusations are common.

That the Japanese Foreign Office should currently have an official posted to Geneva whose job it is to offer, as may be needed, 'advice on diplomatic matters' to Dr Nakajima who heads the WHO and to Dr Ogata, the UNHCR, is perhaps understandable, given the fact that their performance in their office is rightly deemed to reflect on Japan's general prestige. How long will it be before 'what nationality was so-and-so?' is asked about a UN official only as a matter of mere personal curiosity – as one might ask in Japan 'what part of the country does the Vice-Minister for Transport come from?'

A long time yet. Nevertheless, there is something less than subtle about the way in which the Japanese Ministry of Foreign Affairs seems to treat Japanese officials of international organizations as 'representatives of Japan'. The British medical journal, *The Lancet*, reported as follows the background to the news that the thirty-one-member WHO governing body was about to re-elect Dr Hiroshi Nakajima as Director-General.[18]

> the organization seems to be suffering from a disturbing lack of fully competent leadership. This has resulted in abysmally low morale, with even regional directors telling the DG to his face that they had no confidence in him. Global travel has, not surprisingly, resulted in his being absent from headquarters 171 days so far this year. Particularly by com-

parison with Dr Halfdan Mahler, his predecessor, he is far from dynamic or articulate – even, according to his own countrymen, in Japanese. Apart from drumming up support for a second term, his visits to developing countries, have often been characterised, reliable sources say, by his giving little more than minimum attention to health institutions before turning to acquiring more artifacts, contemporary and antique, for his considerable collection amassed over many years. He has occasionally been accompanied by an aide who happens also to be highly expert in this field.

Although Nakajima is known to have old and influential friends in the ruling Liberal Democratic Party, the degree of support he enjoys from the Japanese Government has confounded Western diplomats. 'Never before in this context have we seen anything like it', one remarked. He said that a virtual task force, with as many as 18 people on occasion, has been deployed by Tokyo in a campaign using both carrot and stick – senior officials from various countries have been invited for VIP treatment; other countries, including Jamaica (coffee) and the Maldives (fish) have been tacitly advised that their exports to Japan might suffer should they fail to toe the line. . . .

When his election was finally confirmed, the *Asahi* newspaper reported the reactions of 'the Japanese government' under the headline: *General delight: 'Greater victory than expected'*, 'The government expresses relief that "Japan's contribution to medical cooperation has been internationally recognized."' On the other hand, '*the Government* [my italics] recognizes that among the criticisms that surfaced during the election battle 'there are points we should take to heart', and proposes to undertake a review of the management and policies of the WHO.'[19]

How far Dr Nakajima's management damages the WHO I am in no position to judge. But what does seem astonishing is the taken-for-granted nature of the assumption that Dr Nakajima – supposedly an international official – is no more than a representative of the Japanese government – or more specifically of the Ministry of Health and Welfare. Leave aside the simple equation of the reputation of Dr Nakajima with the reputation of Japan. The assumption that the management and policies of the WHO are the business of 'Japan', given that 'Japan' has captured the Director-Generalship, reveals a strange conception of the nature of international organizations.

What might be done to improve the quality of UN officials? In individual countries, two features seem to characterize the civil services of those countries – Japan, Britain, France, Germany, Korea, for example – where bureaucrats are generally acknowledged to be of high quality, not simply in the minimal sense of being intelligent and not taking bribes, but also in the sense of thinking seriously and honestly about the public interest. Those two features are that they have highly selective and competitive recruitment systems, and that those who enter the 'service' usually do so at a young age with the intention of making their life career in it. Their sense of being a small, and highly selected elite, their pride in membership in a small group of people with very special responsibilities for their country's destiny, is a precondition – or at least a facilitating condition – for the effort they put into the serious performance of their duties. They may give no outward signs of arrogant pride, but they probably feel it, and that pride and their willingness to do a loyal and responsible job are the two sides of the same medal.

Surely the international agencies could now begin to think of doing something similar. Of course, the more varied the national origins of international civil servants the better. But if, instead of national quotas, there were simply competitive entrance tests – careful and thorough entrance tests – for young recruits, the results would not appear immediately, but in twenty or thirty years' time the impact on the prestige and effectiveness of the UN should be considerably enhanced.

If Japan were to make such a proposal, it would do well, at the same time, to do something to make it easier for young Japanese men and women to choose UN careers. It might, for instance, increase the places available at the Diplomat Training School in the expectation that a fraction of those trained might choose a UN, rather than a Japan Foreign Ministry career. The Defence University might set up special courses for students preparing for a job as a UN military official.

ON QUESTIONS OF 'BASIC PRINCIPLE'

There are any number of questions a reader might expect to find treated in a chapter called 'an agenda of the issues' – the question of the composition and powers of the General Assembly, the role of NGOs, the somewhat Utopian notion of a directly elected 'world parliament' to gradually assume the powers of the General Assembly, new ideas about income transfers from the rich North to the poor South, the creation of UN trusteeships in areas which seem unable – at least temporarily unable – to govern themselves; all the problems of the environment, of international terrorism, of the AIDS menace, which clearly call for greater international cooperation. But of all these, the question of the UN's peace-keeping role seems to me the fundamental one. I have said something about the organizational problems, but of equal importance is the spirit in which organizations function, and the value systems they are intended to serve. Unless there is something like an international consensus on the principles which should define the role of the UN, the UN cannot function effectively. And no country is in a position to make proposals for the restructuring and strengthening of the UN with any hope of making its voice effectively heard, unless there is something like an internal consensus on the issues.

Translate the central 'principles' issue into concrete terms. Is it, or is it not, appropriate and reasonable to expect young men and women of one's national army to be sent to places where their lives will be at risk, not in the pursuit of any discernible national interest, but to save the lives of people of other countries or to build the basis for a peaceful international order?

And if the answer is: 'that depends', on what conditions, by what criteria, does one decide what is and what is not right and proper?

In Europe the significance of this 'principle' question has been brought poignantly to the fore by Yugoslavia. As this is written, in January 1993, the position of the United Nations (and of the European Community) can be roughly summarized as follows:

1 After the break-up of the Yugoslav Federation, the settlement of boundaries between the new countries should be peacefully negotiated, and therefore all arms sales to parts of Yugoslavia should be banned.
2 The wars which have nevertheless broken out have claimed countless innocent victims, for whom relief aid must be provided, and the delivery of that aid requires the protection of troops; hence the presence of British, French and other troops.
3 Of the combatants – principally the Bosnian Serbs and the Bosnian Muslims – the Serbs, inheriting the weapons of the former federal army, have used their strength to conquer more than half of Bosnian territory and look ever more clearly to be the aggressors. Hence economic sanctions on Serbia and a ban on military flights over the battle zones.
4 To bring the fighting to an end as soon as possible, the UN has appointed Cyrus Vance, former US Secretary of State, to work together with Lord Owen, appointed by the the European Community, to try to bring about a cease-fire and a lasting settlement.

But their efforts to mediate have met with little success; the fighting goes on and gets ever bloodier; the Serbs seem daily to be making helicopter flights in defiance of the UN ban, and are ruthlessly pursuing their objectives of gaining territory and ethnically 'cleansing' the territory they occupy. What anyone would count as war crimes are daily reported.

The reaction to these events in the US and in Europe has been increasing pressure for the international community to designate the Serbs as aggressors, to supply arms to the Muslim minority and to commit UN troops to their defence.

And if it did turn out that something like the Owen–Vance peace plan were accepted and Bosnia divided into a number of semi-independent states linked in a federation, many tens of thousands of troops would be required to keep the peace on the new, and inevitably disputed, frontiers. Either eventuality requires large numbers of young people from other countries going to places where their lives will be seriously at risk.

That is the background to the argument about principles which is currently proceeding in Britain. Two quotations will best give the reader a sense of the issues and the tone of the debate. The first is written by Dominic Lawson, editor of the *Spectator*:[20]

> Both the British troops [in Bosnia] and the American troops [in Somalia] are at the painfully sharp end of a strange experiment in Western foreign policy. That is the application of military force, and the inevitable spilling of Western soldiers' blood in regions where the West has no discernible strategic or political interest. Instead, we are told, there is a pressing moral need to intervene, to save one group of people or another from possible starvation and certain ruin.
>
> The Cold War, it is true, was always described by the West in moral terms. President John F. Kennedy spoke of paying any price in the pursuit and defence of liberty – but the real motivation was not moral, but self-preservatory; the West believed, in my view rightly, that it was the intention of the Soviet Union to subvert its political systems and security. . . .
>
> Britain, France and the US had supported the Iraqi dictator militarily not because they did not know what he was doing to his own people, but because he was seen as a secular bulwark against the spread of Islamic fundamentalism. Then he made a grab for the world's most prolific oil-fields, the ones we in the West most need to keep our cars on the roads and our airplanes in the skies. In this way, and only in this way, Saddam became, I think rightly, our enemy. . . .
>
> But there is no practical argument behind the sending of British troops to Bosnia. Arguably, if all the West is after is security in the region, it should give the Serbs a free hand to carve out discrete ethnic areas in the former Yugoslavia, however repulsive their methods. . . .
>
> The intervention is, as it claims to be, purely humanitarian, which is why the Foreign Office is so uneasy and hesitant in its handling of the affair; it has been dragged by a section of public opinion into a place where it would rather not be. I suspect that the same attitude of misgiving must pervade the State Department over the exposure of 30,000 troops in Somalia. But George Bush decided that food must get through to women and children who were starving.
>
> How were they starving? On peak-time US television, that's how. And where could John Major see the emaciated frames of Bosnians captured in Serbia? On British television, that's where. So now we know what the British and American troops will be chanting in Bosnia and Somalia: 'We're here because the networks are here.'

The second quotation comes from a newspaper article by Hugo Young, the author of a noted analysis of the Thatcher administration:[21]

> The British convoys in Bosnia fly no Union Jacks. If the flag is there, it is as a tiny symbol overshadowed by United Nations blue. . . . Soldiering is now the leading edge of internationalism. Yet, although this is an

observable military fact, the politics lags far behind. One large reason why... is the belief that while a soldier has been trained to die for his country, he should never be expected to die for any other cause. Revising this outdated axiom seems like one of the more worthwhile political tasks of the post-cold war era. Soldiers seem ready for it. Why not politicians?

[The leader of the Liberal Democratic Party is the only major British political figure to advocate intervention. The government seems to think that it is not 'wise' to respond with military force, however much the Serbs fly their aircraft in defiance of UN bans, however much they wreak aggression against a country recognized by the UN, however much they proceed with their ethnic cleansing.]

But another version of wisdom is available, if it could be articulated. It springs partly from humanitarian impulse; the assertion... that there are certain predicaments of mankind which we cannot stand and idly watch unfold to their hideous termination. But it also springs from self-interest; the assertion that the project of a Greater Serbia, imposed by vile bruality and illegal force of arms, imperils the peace across Europe. For what we are plainly witnessing is the collapse of the new world order before we even knew what it might be.

[Intervention would involve enormous difficulties. To intervene effectively, and with the minimum of casualties, would require the most thorough preparation. But the need to halt Serbian aggression is the decisive consideration.]

The soldiers of several nations are equipped to try and stop that, if the political will allows them. It is what they now exist for: to assert that the international community, in the shape of the United Nations, will not be defied.

Not, perhaps, what soldiers used to do; but among the many historic purposes for which they have entered a career of service and adventure, one as good as any other to die for.

A similar debate is proceeding in Japan over the dispatch of Japanese troops to Cambodia. But my impression is that the 'basic principle' issue gets overtaken by other issues. What will it do to Japan's image in Asia if Japanese soldiers take their guns and tanks on to the Asian continent again? Is it not in any case a breach of the Constitution to send Japanese troops abroad? Is the motive for sending Japanese troops to Cambodia really to help the Cambodians in a spirit of internationalism, or is it just that naive LDP politicians, when they go to America, want to be able to say: 'Look what a fine contribution we are making'? Etc.

But it seems probable that eventually this will change and the issue of basic principle will become central to the debate. As illustrated above, there is far from being any consensus on the issue in Britain. Nor will there be in Japan. But a lively national debate leading to some sort of consensus on the issue – what I have called above the 'basic principle' issue – does seem to me to be the key to resolving that question which *is* so much discussed – that of constitutional revision; and a precondition, too, for Japan to play a positive role in the work of restructuring the UN.[22]

Part II
Other points of view

Wanting to throw off a nasty burden, but suppressing the urge

Midori Yajima

[The original book concluded with a spoof 'folk tale' about the 'Yamato-ya' farm family (Yamato is an old name for Japan) which kept a fearsome dog that so devastated the neighbours' livestock that the big landlord family (Ame-ya, a *yago* house-name still found occasionally meaning the 'boiled-sweet makers') upped and killed it, and forced the Yamato-ya family to vow never to keep a dog again. Of course, later they do, but square it with their vows by never calling it a dog (*inu*) but always a *nui*. It is also a nice quiet dog, very unlike the one that was killed, and it is never allowed outside the garden. But the family is not a happy one. There are two brothers who bear old-fashioned Japanese men's personal names which derive from the ancient titles, Guardian of the Left Gate and Guardian of the Right Gate. They and their respective sons are engaged in constant debate about the dog which caricatures Japanese political debates about the Self-Defence Forces and their Constitution. In the end it is the 'womenfolk' of the household who force the denouement; a public declaration that of course they do keep a real dog, and that they'll now be happy to join in the organized hunts for the wild boar that devastate the village crops. The women say they simply can't stand the silly prevarication; they say that if they put things straight, everybody will be *sei-sei suru* – the 'feeling liberated of a nasty burden' of Ms Yajima's title.]

My position is that of the 'womenfolk' in Dore's splendid folk tale. On the one hand, I'm not fond of dogs = armies. On the other, it irritates me beyond measure that we should be the only house in the village that has this stupid convention of never calling a dog a dog. That feeling of irritation reached an all-time peak when listening to the sophistry of those parliamentary debates over whether sending the Self-Defence Forces to Cambodia was constitutional or not.

On the other hand, unlike most Japanese women I have had the experience of seeing the UN close at hand when I was an agency reporter in New York, covering the UN, between 1974 and 1976. This was a time when the third world countries, having become a majority, were increasingly vocal in their protests at the rich countries' economic domination, and when – at least at the verbal level – the General Assembly was coming to overshadow the Security Council. The arguments of that majority, however justified, came to nothing much in practical terms because of the obstruction and non-fulfilment of promises by the club of the rich countries, but, together with the growing strength of the forces seeking to break down the barriers of racial and gender discrimination, they did serve, I think, to produce some shift in ideas throughout the world. The experience of those years made me, while deeply aware of the gap between rhetoric and practice where the UN is concerned, nevertheless a supporter of the UN who expects good things of it.

And that is why I found Dore's book stimulating and informative. The only unfortunate thing is that it should have been Dore and not a Japanese to produce such a readable and lucid book, with such good arguments and good history, all spiced with a dash of humour. The trouble is, in the Yamato household, when it comes to anything to do with whether dogs are dogs, arguments always seem to turn into emotional shouting matches, or the rambling soliloquies of people who have long since given up all hope of ever convincing others.

There are a lot of points on which I find myself in agreement with Dore's persuasive arguments, but I would differ from him both as concerns what it is Japan should be proposing to the UN when it takes its initiatives, and on the question of what Japan should do internally to prepare itself for that initiative-taking – i.e. on the question of amending the Constitution. Reinforcement for my views has come both from the recent experience of UN intervention in Somalia and Bosnia, and from recent changes in the line taken by Japanese politicians – the nature of their preoccupation with Japan's becoming a 'normal country' able to take part in peace-keeping operations, and their assumption that there is nothing wrong with the Security Council except that Japan does not have a permanent seat in it.

The first point concerns the military structure of the UN and its interventions. Since the end of the superpowers' Cold War, armed warfare on our planet has mostly taken the form of civil war, ethnic and religious, or in the case of Rwanda, tribal conflict. Intervention by a peace-keeping force, or by a multinational force blessed by the UN, but usually not backed by any adequate understanding of the complexities of the local situation, has frequently had the effect of arousing hostility towards the UN itself, of deepening the original conflict, and moved the situation further away from, rather than closer to, solution (the former Yugoslavia, for instance). In Somalia, action in the face of strong local popular sentiment has only resulted in increased casualties. As the last remaining superpower, the US has (probably fortunately) played a spectator's role in Bosnia, and after the failure of its mission in Somalia has in general become much more reluctant to take part in UN operations. It looks as if, in future, UN interventions will be more and more determined by the close intertwining of high principle, and America's judgements of its own national interest.

In present circumstances, it seems to me, much more important than Secretary-General Boutros-Ghali's call in his *Agenda for Peace* for the evolution of peace-keeping towards peace-enforcement through the use of military force, is his emphasis on expanding the UN's fact-finding capacity. That is what I would like to see made the number one priority. There is a lot Japan could and should do to help in this by a clear offer to cooperate in providing resources and manpower.

Ideally I would like to see UN peacekeeping forces undergo what one might call a 'Japanese Self-Defence Forces transformation'. That is to say that their main purpose in life should be to respond with immediate aid for natural disasters – earthquakes, tidal waves, floods – which single countries cannot easily cope with. Their peace-keeping activities should be confined to the original minimum – i.e., monitoring cease-fires when there is agreement from both parties that they should do so.

Moreover, it is obviously desirable that these forces should be directly at the disposition of the UN and under unified command, with unified training and armament. Would it really be impossible to envisage something like the following? A force made up of units contributed on a quota system by member countries, with individuals signed on for three to five year terms, exchanging 'UN citizenship' and loyalty to the UN for their national citizenship and national loyalties while they do so. UN bases could be established around the world at which the soldiers of various nationalities would live and train together against the day when they are called out for emergencies at the shortest notice.

As for the structure and functions of the Security Council, discussions are currently going forward within the UN and seem some way from conclusion, but meanwhile the Japanese government has come out with clear statements to the effect that 'the candidates have been narrowed down to Japan and Germany', that there seems to be 'little objection' to the idea of simply increasing the number of permanent members with veto powers. (See the replies of the then Foreign Minister, Kakizawa, in the Upper House, as reported in the *Asahi*, 15 and 16 June 1994.) No thought is given to the problematic nature of the Security Council itself; attention is concentrated on seizing the chance to join the Great Power club, and one can easily foresee what follows: 'Now that our Great Power status has been recognized we must behave like a Great Power'; hence a step-up in military expenditure on the grounds that Japan must play its part in sending troops for UN operations.

Japanese public opinion is not strong on resisting *faits accomplis* and can easily bend. One has only to recall the way 'extended interpretations' of the Constitution have been used to sanction existence of 'the dog that is no dog' to imagine what a government could make out of interpreting 'cooperation with the UN' or 'the responsibilities of Great Powers'. What Dore calls with clearly apparent impatience the 'Peace-ists with their total introversion' ('the womenfolk' being a very important voice among them) have in fact acted as a brake on Japan's militarization, and one can only too easily see that the day might come when they are shut out of the media and lose all influence on the policy process.

If there is a real possibility that it is all 'sewn up' for the simple admission of Japan and Germany to permanent seats, now really is the time for making proposals to other governments for the restructuring of the Security Council. Since the Japanese government is unlikely to do anything of the kind, it falls to opinion leaders outside the government to take the initiative. The drawbacks of the simple solution are clear. In the first place, if Japan's foreign policy stance continues in the mould of the last half-century, it would mean one more vote for the United States. And secondly it would mean three votes for the European Union. The result would be an even more unbalanced composition than at present. There would seem to be much merit in Dore's suggestions that semi-permanent members should be elected for fixed terms, taking into account population size, regional and cultural bloc membership and contributions to the UN's work, and that there should be some limitations on the exercise of veto power.

Finally, on the question of creating the conditions within Japan for her to take initiatives *vis-à-vis* the UN, and to strengthen Japan's contributions beyond the merely monetary, how far is a revision of the Constitution necessary? And if so, what sort of revision?

Already, before coming across Dore's suggestions for the rewriting of Article 9, appalled at the prevarications of the parliamentary debate over the despatch of the Japanese contingent to Cambodia, this member of the Yamato-ya 'womenfolk' had come to a similar conclusion – that the best thing to do was to state clearly in the Constitution that the Self-Defence Forces do constitute the 'land, sea or air forces and other military potential' which the present Constitution says shall never be 'maintained', but to include in the revision of Article 9 provisions which strictly limit the uses to which they can be put. Was it not I.F. Stone, that lone-wolf American journalist who never relented in his unceasing critique of the exercise of power who once said: 'Every government is run by liars. Nothing they say should be believed'? Indeed, the whole history of those of my generation who happened to be born in Japan is a history of being lied to; before the war, during the war, and during the whole postwar period when we were supposed to believe that a dog is not a dog. If we go on like this we might well see the day when the Japanese government makes a nuclear attack on another country and blandly explains, in another of those 'extended constitutional interpretations' it is so fond of, that this does not amount to 'the use of force' by 'armed forces' and therefore does not breach the Constitution. This particular representative of the Yamato-ya womenfolk would at least like to be able to spend her old age not having to be in a perpetual rage at the apparently limitless process of expanded reproduction of untruth.

If one were to be guided by one's sense of exasperation to seek a revision of the Constitution, Dore's suggestions provide a good model, though I would disagree on one point. Whereas he would add to self-defence and disaster relief, as the third function of the armed forces, 'participation in peace-enforcement activities directly under the control of the UN', I would limit it to 'participation in peace-keeping activities'.

Would this lead to Japan being criticized for not accepting the provisions of the UN Charter and not being a fully cooperating member of international society? Not necessarily. If Japan were to take the consistent stance that it disagreed with the Great Power Club character of the present American-dominated Security Council, considered that any exercise of military force which resulted from the resolutions of such a Council had dubious validity, was prevented from taking part in such by its (present or revised) Constitution, and was consistently seeking what I called earlier the 'SDF transformation' of UN forces, the consistency and integrity of Japan's position would surely be recognized.

And that leads to a further reflection; if it were the case that members of the Self-Defence Forces who took part in peace-keeping activities were to suspend their Japanese citizenship in favour of UN citizenship, would there really be any need to amend the Japanese Constitution? The point is that, in the present situation in which influential politicians are seeking an amendment of the Constitution to increase Japan's 'international contribution' by which they mean obedient cooperation with the United States, any attempt to amend the Constitution, albeit for quite different motives, could simply play into their hands.

And that is why the womenfolk of Yamato-ya would do well, for the moment, to shut their ears to Dore's so very seductive arguments. That feeling that they would like to be rid of that lump which sticks in their gullet like a lump of petrified rice-cake, that feeling that it would be nice to feel free and at peace with the world again, they had better, for the moment, learn to suppress.

Tokyo, August 1994

Midori Yajima is a freelance writer, film critic and translator, formerly New York correspondent of *Kyodo Tsushin*.

Contributions, yes, but geared to the complex needs of a complex world

Yutaka Kōsai

I was impressed and jolted by this book. Impressed by Dore's idealism and his belief in progress, by the wide range of material and of historical facts which he has called in support of his ideas, many of which were a revelation to me. I was jolted in the sense that it made me reflect very seriously on Japan's international behaviour.

Let me first express my fullest agreement with the overall message: Japan should be ready to put forward constructive proposals for the rebuilding and maintenance of an international order. The book's suggestions about how and why, the concrete steps to be taken, I found very useful.

All that being said, I want to concentrate in these comments on three points. One, Dore's interpretation of Japan and of Japanese attitudes; two, Dore's view of what constitutes progress toward a new international order; and three, the restructuring of the UN and the revision of the Japanese Constitution.

Let me say that my proper business in life is the monitoring and analysis of the economy, and it is only as an interested amateur that I approach politics and international affairs.

JAPAN AND JAPANESE ATTITUDES

I respect Dore's analysis, but I would beg to differ on three points.

1 It seems to me that Japanese anxieties about her relations with neighbouring Asian countries colour her general perspective on international affairs far more than is recognized in this book. On pages 99–105,[1] in the analysis of the reasons for opposition in Japan to taking part in UN peace-keeping operations, what is missing is the recognition that it was not only left-wing intellectuals but many other people in Japan who were dubious about taking part in peace-keeping operations, and that these doubts sprang largely from fear of opposition to and criticism of such participation on the part of China and Korea and the other Asian countries. Japanese aggression and the history of colonization have left deep scars in the relationship of Japan with

neighbouring Asian countries. Many Japanese think it entirely right that Japan should show a concern for their feelings.

But to be guided solely by fear of what others might say surely shows a deplorable lack of identity, the reader might say; just get on with the business of improving relations with those countries. There is a lot in that. Prime Minister Hosokawa recently apologized for the havoc wrought by Japanese aggression – the least one can expect from a grandson of the Prince Konoe who bore major responsibility for the attack on China. But one cannot expect that those Asian feelings of hostility will be easily dissolved. And one can reasonably say that it is in Japan's national interest to take account of these feelings in order to maintain good relations with her neighbours. I personally was in favour of Japan's participating in the peace-keeping operations, but I think one has to recognize that this was one of the reasons for opposing it.

2 I was brought up short by the prediction/fantasy scenario on page 124: 'the main axis of world tension twenty years hence might be conflict between Japan/China on the one hand, and the US and Europe on the other'. I agree absolutely that the future development of China is of crucial importance, both for world society as a whole and for Japan. Also that Japan's past record of wars with China and its geographical proximity make it probable that she will go to great lengths to avoid conflict with China (this will sometimes mean getting out of step with the US and Europe, out of regard for maintaining relations with China). But, given precisely that history of tensions between Japan and China and the difference in their political and economic structures, and given also the immense importance of trade relations with the United States for both the Japanese and the Chinese economies, it is hard to think of Japan and China entering into an alliance relationship directed against the United States and Europe. It may well be, as Dore suggests, that there are differences in perceptions, East and West, about the nature of democracy and desirable patterns of authority, but the difference in political structures between Japan and China is also very great. That difference would disappear if China chooses to go along the path toward modern democracy. But if that happens, will this not eliminate the main cause of tension between Europe/United States and China? One shouldn't underestimate the importance of US relations for both China and Japan, and in Japan there are even those (of whom I am not one) who fear the development of a Sino-American alliance to exclude Japan.

The fact that Japanese opinion differs from that in Europe and the United States over the Tienanmen incident and the democratization of Hong Kong, owes something, to be sure, to a prudent diffidence toward a big neighbour and a desire not to be provocative; something also to a sense of being at a moral disadvantage *vis-à-vis* China, given past history. But it also owes something to some genuine sympathy for what the Chinese say about the harmonization of development and human rights and the interrelated principle of non-interference in the internal affairs of other countries. The Japanese are 'stage theorists' who believe that the proper interpretation of human rights and democracy is not fixed for all time, but depends on the level of development. They think that Japan, being now a developed country, has Western-style democracy and freedom, but it is unrealistic to expect identical standards for the countries of the South. With economic growth their societies too will become modernized. Doubtless this is a very convenient argument which enables one to dismiss the undemocratic blemishes on Japan's past history, but also I think it is true, as indeed is argued on page 7 of the book, that there is some correlation between technology and the values. But that correlation is something which a philosophical theory of natural rights that sees human rights and democracy as fixed and innate human values will never recognize. Such theories see freedom and individual rights as essential to human existence, as a basic necessity. To say that human rights and freedom come to be respected as economies develop, is to say that they are, instead, luxury goods with an income elasticity of 1 plus. It is worth noting that there is the same conflict between universal theory and a stages-of-development theory with respect to the role of the state in a market economy. For Japan, how this kind of conflict gets resolved is a matter of considerable importance.

To go back to China, China has apprehensions about a revival of Japanese aggression and Japan is anxious about the possibility of being swallowed up by China. I think it is in Japan's interest to maintain the presence of the United States and Europe (including Russia) in Asia, and to develop multiple relationships with those countries. And I agree with the book in suggesting that UN diplomacy can play an important role in this.

3 My third point concerns Dore's schematic map of Japanese internal political forces. In his delightful appendix/fairy story, 'The Dog at the House of Yamato-ya', he has the leadership in a change of policy coming from Sataro (the younger generation of the left) and the women. And Utaro, his right-wing cousin, is represented as an impetuous toughie. I see it a bit differently. Let's call his characters Young Leftie, Old Leftie; Young Rightie, Old Rightie. We can dismiss Old Leftie; he finds it understandable that the wild boars should ruin the corn crop, and would even help them at it. His self-righteousness leads to irresponsibility and complete intellectual bankruptcy. Young Leftie, on the other hand, is hardly discernible as a presence. However, that does not mean that Japan is to be left in the hands of Young Rightie as Dore depicts him. In fact, his Utaro has a much more reasonable younger brother, Ujiro, and I think it is up to the Ujiros of Japan; it depends on them whether internationalism develops in Japan.

If Japan is represented, as Dore represents it on page xxxix, as peopled by introverted peaceniks, economic animals and chauvinists, that is Japan's own fault and we should do something about it. But is it only wishful thinking on my part that there is a growing body of people in Japan who although conservative are also capable of taking a stand on democracy and open internationalism. The Japanese political map, the left/right divide, the conservative/radical divide, are changing. The Japanese left was so unrealistic that it has lost credibility among the Japanese people. If it is only from their bedraggled remnants that one can expect the seeds of internationalism to grow, then one would have to be very pessimistic about the prospects. But if those who at once are conservative and rational turn toward internationalism, one has far better grounds for optimism.

PROGRESS TOWARD AN INTERNATIONAL ORDER

I respect Dore's view of history, and he presents a lot of persuasive evidence to suggest that the conditions are there for rapid movement toward an international order. However, I have one or two doubts and questions.

Dore does not say a great deal when talking about international relations, about the interrelationship with domestic politics. Kant, in his *Thoughts on Perpetual Peace*, argued that peace would come only when all countries were republics. Fukuyama quotes him in *The End of History*. It is reasonable to assume that an important condition for the maintenance of peace is, indeed, that the major countries should internally be democracies. And reciprocally, the more peace is maintained the more democracy is likely to spread. The leading countries now *are* democracies, but it is important to ask whether one can be optimistic about the prospects for democracy in other countries that will become important in the future. How one thinks about international order depends very much on one's judgement about those prospects.

I raise this question because I for one find it difficult to make confident predictions about the future political structures of China, the former Soviet Union, and the other countries of the South (which are likely to become of increasing importance in the future). German Nazism has given us a twentieth-century example of a highly developed country which, having once experienced democracy, reverted to totalitarianism. In Japan too, the democracy of the 1920s was followed by the militarism of the 1930s. I think, or would like to think, that such an experience is unlikely to be repeated in Japan and Germany, but is the path for democracy in the world at large not likely to be a tortuous one? That being the case, might it not be wiser, instead of concentrating power excessively in the United Nations, to preserve some strength in those organizations which function as clubs of the leading democracies – the G7 Summit, OECD, NATO, etc. Democracy now seems triumphant in the world, but that may not always be so.

If one might put the matter in terms of development stages, we have the whole range: developed democracies capable of behaving in an internationalist manner, developing countries bent on the acquisition of national strength and the assertion of national identity, and yet other areas in which the civil state is barely emerging. Take China, where the constitution itself declares 'wealth and strength' to be the object of state policy. Japanese, recalling that the same slogan – 'rich country, strong army' – dominated the Meiji period and led finally to militarism, can only have complicated feelings about that, but I think that such national goals are probably helpful at certain stages of a country's development. The United Nations, even if under the oligarchic control of the leading countries, still has to embrace all these other nations too. And the UN, just as it survived the Cold War, has got to be able to survive future conflicts too. I would not go so far as Professor Nakanishi and say that the UN should get out of military action altogether, but I would suggest that the strengthening of the UN should proceed in gradual fashion. Instead of aiming for maximum power as soon as possible and the establishment of the right (duty) to intervene in internal affairs of countries, I would think it better to concentrate on the job of steadily building up concrete devices to promote peace (nuclear inspections and the prevention of proliferation), human rights (setting minimum standards), and environmental protection. I would be very much in favour of making the strengthening of the United Nations, on those gradualist lines, the pillar of Japanese foreign policy.

It is true that progress toward an international order has been striking. But it was so fast, that I am not entirely sure that it really is progress, rather than simply a situation change. As the book remarks, in the Gulf War deliberate attacks on civilians were avoided. Thinking back to my own childhood experiences, fleeing from the bombs and fires in the aerial attacks on civilian Tokyo, this is hard to believe. (I mention this only to explain my reactions, not to flaunt any 'victim consciousness' chip on the shoulder. Nothing can excuse the way the Japanese army involved civilians in the war.)

When Japan declared war on China in 1893 and on Russia in 1904 the imperial rescript made clear the claim that Japan was acting in accordance with international law, but those words did not appear in the declaration of the Pacific War. Maybe the jurists couldn't bring themselves to say it, given that Japan had already started in China a war that was not a war in accordance with international law. But was there not also this effect: when wars become holy wars, when their objectives are sanctified to an extreme degree, then war ceases to be a game played according to rules – it becomes total war in which all means are to be employed, even the total destruction of the enemy. This is the paradox of idealism, that it can sanctify inhuman cruelty. At present, the power difference between the leading democratic countries and the rule-rejecting terrorist countries opposing them is sufficiently great that conflict between them on a major scale is unthinkable, but there is no guarantee that this will always be so.

In this borderless age, the distance between New York and Tokyo is shorter than the distance between Edo and Satsuma at the end of the Tokugawa period, says Dore. It may seem odd coming from one of those economists who have popularized the notion of increasing 'borderlessness' but that may apply to technology, but not to values. Satsuma and Edo may have differed about whether to open up the country or drive out the barbarians, but they spoke the same language and they had the same sense of ethnic unity and shared the same Confucian culture. However borderless the European Community is becoming, monetary union seems a long way off. The fact that we have the technology to promote economic integration even if there is not integration in these other dimensions is characteristic of our modern age.

The book argues (pages 74–7) that one does not see 'progressive evolution' on the North–South development question, and that it will be necessary in the future to think of 'some form of welfare system for redistributing income on a world scale'. One can say that some kind of income distribution is taking place at the moment, but I differ somewhat on the initial judgement. The growth of Japan and Korea are past history, but now the wave of development has reached the ASEAN countries (though still with the exception of the Philippines), is sweeping China, and seems to have arrived also in India. In Latin America too, though recently so much under pressure from the debt overhang, many countries seem to have got back on track toward healthy economic growth. These countries seem to show that if one avoids excessive optimism, doesn't aim too high, and adapts carefully to the given environment, a surprising level of growth is possible. Skipping stages of growth is not easy, but moving from stage to stage at a fair speed is possible. That being the case, to say 'there's no hope for development, so provide welfare' is to show contempt for the developing countries' capacity for growth. One does, of course, have to make some provision for immediate needs, but it still basically is not food aid, but agricultural aid, not doctors, but medical education, that needs to be provided.

The section on 'principles' at the end of the book raises some extremely important questions. As someone who has had an economist's training, my reaction is to say that one should compare the prospective costs and benefits and determine how many resources to devote to international activity, according to where the indifference curve and the opportunity curve intersect. To deploy such arguments in matters of life and death such as these – wagging the moral dog by its utilitarian tail – may seem out of place. But surely one cannot make appropriate decisions without considering both cost and efficacy. The West tolerated Stalinist oppression for decades, and that was surely because the costs of intervention were obviously so high. If that is reality, then one needs to admit reality. Brave declarations which ignore reality in the end do not get carried out. And I do not find appealing loud claims to justice which are made only when the costs of enforcing it are cheap.

ON THE REVISION OF THE CONSTITUTION

I have explained why I cannot entirely share Dore's idealism and take a position characterized by realism and conservatism, but from that position I can still agree with his policy proposals. I don't think that one should make national honour the number-one objective of foreign policy, but I do agree that one should explicitly take it into consideration and I agree that Japan should take a much more positive role as a shaper and not just a taker of the international social order. My view of international order is a pluralist one: there are states, there are regions, there is the UN, there are alliances; variety is fine. And in that context the restructuring of the UN is an urgent matter. I also agree with the comments in the book on Russo-Japanese relations. I would especially endorse the suggestion on page 127 that Japan should not simply be seeking a permanent seat on the Security Council ('let me in the club, too') but that Japan and other countries should be seeking ways of restructuring the UN in order to make it capable of playing a more constructive role; also that there has to be some kind of balance within the organization between the oligarchic concept and one nation–one vote egalitarianism.

Reading through the UN Charter's provisions for the use of military force in Chapter 7 (the UN command, members' obligation to cooperate, etc.), my impression is that it reproduces the military command structure of the Allies during the war, and as such is somewhat too centralized for anything except dealing with a major enemy in total war. The arguments of this book have changed my view somewhat, but nevertheless I still can't help thinking that a somewhat looser form of collective action would be more useful for the United Nations. One doesn't want to be like the Emperor in Kyoto, totally lacking in military power and only able to issue proclamations demanding the punishment of outlaws. But it doesn't have to do everything itself. When, like the Italians in Somalia, a country disagrees with the UN's policy, how far should it be allowed to disobey orders? What sort of check and balance devices can one install? Security Council resolutions and supervision, etc. are surely necessary, but a military action can take a variety of forms: a rapid deployment force, directly under the UN; a UN force under the control of the Military Staff Committee; regional armies with delegated missions, etc. If there are sanctioning resolutions of the Security Council I am not sure one should rule out multinational forces on the Gulf War model. I wouldn't, like Mr Realist in Dore's dialogue, look forward to the emergence of a hegemonic Great Power, but nor would I, like his Mr Idealist, think the immediate establishment of a collective security system possible. I think there is nothing for it but to promote the activity and the effectiveness of the UN through the iterative process of continuous mutual constraint and mutual cooperation among the leading countries.

On the revision of the Constitution, I think we should seize a suitable opportunity (sheer opportunism again, I can hear somebody say) and write the recognition of the Self-Defence Forces and cooperation with the United Nations into the Constitution. Though whether one should specify that cooperation with the United Nations in peace-restoration activities should conform to Article 47 of the Charter is a different question on which I have not made up my mind. Dore's criticisms of our barrack-room lawyer approach to the constitutional issue really strike home. They made me feel personally the need for more intellectual honesty and courage. Even so, I have to say that I simply cannot envisage a situation in which Japan would move boldly forward to a solution of the constitutional issue that would leave everybody feeling 'clean, pure, and honest'. I am not entirely sure why, but if I had to own up to where I stand, I suppose I would have to stay closest to what Dore lists as position vii on page 105 – a sense of an obligation to the world at large rather than to the US, a sense that Japan will not be taken seriously until she is a full contributor, and a sense of the need to allay fears of a revival of Japanese militarism. Revision is 'not impossible', as Dore says, but it won't happen easily without a suitable opportunity.

Tokyo, September 1994

Yutaka Kōsai, director of the Japan Economic Research Centre, is a graduate of the University of Tokyo and Stanford University and a former professor of economics at Tokyo Institute of Technology. He has won the Suntory Prize (1980) and the Nikkei Prize for Excellent Books in Economic Science (1981) and is the author of *The Era of High-Speed Growth* (1986).

To die for high principle?

Shinsuke Yoshimura

The end of the Pacific War has left a deep imprint on the Japanese consciousness, and one constituent of that imprint is an acute scepticism about sacrificing one's life for lofty objectives.

Before and during the war, the Japanese people were taught that there could be no nobler end of man than to offer up one's life in patriotic devotion to Emperor and country; any sacrifice was justified by the objective of building the Great East Asian Co-Prosperity Sphere. The defeat showed the total emptiness of those claims. Never, ever again, would we allow ourselves to risk death for grand national causes. That determination, at least, was widespread and deep.

So what then *have* postwar Japanese been ready to give their lives for? Instinctive defence of wife and children against an armed robber, perhaps. And if one was unlucky enough to be killed, no one would count death in defence of loved ones foolish. Go beyond the family to the neighbourhood and local community. Most people would be more hesitant and more calculative; if they risked their lives for some public good dear to their hearts, what effect would it have on their family, would they be looked after?

The more the cause is remote from the concerns of those one is directly bound to by blood and neighbourhood ties, the more abstract the connection, the more postwar Japanese are 'cowards'. Never, under any circumstances, throwing away one's life for something as remote from private concerns as high national principle. How much less, therefore, to maintain world order through collective action in which one's nation is one participating unit.

Recently the Japanese have learned to call this, with a twist of self-mockery, 'one nation pacifism'. Going further back, twenty years ago, we talked of the 'my-home-ism' of the 'privatized' citizen who closed his mind to public concerns.

Behind this 'cowardliness' lies a deep visceral distrust of the state, and particularly a hatred of that most stark expression of state sovereignty, namely war and the deployment of military force. The idea that all war is evil has taken deep root. And this 'postwar pacifism' has resulted in what is surely a rare historical phenomenon: in half a century no single foreign solider has been killed or injured by Japanese troops.

This postwar pacifism has been decried as 'free-riding on the American security system' and denounced by right-wing forces in Japan as feeble idealism. But it remained the dominant sentiment.

Nothing happened to shake that stance, or the comfort the Japanese people derived from it, until the Gulf crisis of 1990 and the war which followed. America, for all its bitter experience of anti-war feeling at the time of Vietnam, was nevertheless prepared to take the lead in sending its young men to desert battlefields at the head of a multinational force. In the name of maintaining international order, civilized society was prepared to put lives at risk to deal with Iraq's lawless behaviour in invading Kuwait.

That war, and the fact that Japan could do no more than contribute $13 billion to its expense, forced the Japanese people to ponder on two unwelcome reflections. First, the prevailing postwar consensus held that all war was evil, but was not that war waged by the multinational force against an Iraq, clearly guilty of illegal aggression against a neighbour, a just war? And, secondly, if it was a just war, was it not cowardly not to be willing to sacrifice lives in that cause, along with other nations? The unease provoked by these questions, as the Japanese watched Desert Storm from a distance, has never subsequently left them. Dying for lofty national objectives was one thing, and clearly to be rejected. But for lofty world principles? Was that not something else?

The fact that, after much tortuous debate, a unit of the Japanese Self-Defence Forces took part in the UNTAC operation in Cambodia represents a subtle shift in Japan's 'postwar pacifism'. It is not too much to say, perhaps, that the idea has been gaining ground that, if one is a member of the United Nations, and sharing in its responsibility for world order, one has to accept it – in Dore's words in Chapter 8 of his book – 'as reasonable, indeed as a duty, to send troops, sometimes at the risk of their being killed, not to further some national interest but . . . to stop some human beings from doing unacceptably evil things to other human beings'.

And that clearly leads to discussion of revising the Constitution which at present lacks any provision which would clearly authorize Japanese participation in UN operations. Dore suggests a revision of Article 9 which would specify the limited uses to which the Japanese state could put its armed forces – including taking part in UN operations. There have been several other suggestions on the same lines. Ozawa Ichirō of the Shinseito argued when he was still in the Liberal Democratic Party that the concept of 'International Security' provided the solution: participation in UN peace-keeping was not an exercise of state power, and consequently did not require revision of the Constitution, though he would doubtless be in favour of a revision along the lines the Dore suggests. Nevertheless, at the grass roots of Japanese society, even if 'postwar pacifism' has been somewhat put into question, there is very little sentiment in favour of Constitutional revision – for, I think, the following reasons.

In the first place, advocacy of Constitutional reform, from the 1950s when it was part of the first post-Occupation 'reverse course' to recent discussion of the need for an 'international contribution', has been predominantly associated with the right wing of the Liberal Democratic Party. The fact that there are now some people in favour of 'revising the Constitution to preserve it' has not altered that association in the minds of the vast majority of the population, who remain allergic to the idea of touching the Constitution and suspicious of anyone who advocates it.

Second, many of those who have come round to the view that there are indeed just wars think that Japan's commitment to international peace-keeping should stop short of using military force, and believe that participating on that basis – as in Cambodia – can just about be justified under the present Constitution. There are some people in the scholarly and political community who advocate regularizing the situation, and clearing up ambiguities about the legal status of the Self-Defence Forces by enacting a quasi-Constitutional 'Basic Peace Law' which would establish the legality of the Self-Defence Forces while requiring them to be scaled down.

Third, after fifty years of 'postwar pacifism' the Japanese people have become genuinely 'peaceful'. Even if they recognize in principle that there can be just wars, they no longer 'have the courage' to take up the sword of justice against those who start wars that are unjust. Zapping an invisible enemy at the push of a missile control button, as in a computer game, is one thing; but killing and wounding visible enemies on the ground is quite another, and the Japanese no longer have the stomach – the 'roughness of spirit' – for that. That feeling, I think, is one reason why so many people, albeit a bit uneasily, argue that Japan should limit itself to non-military participation in peace-keeping.

Fourth, the actual prospects of a real UN military force seem – given, *inter alia*, America's reluctance to put its forces under any but American command – quite remote. Some people – the former Prime Minister, Miyazawa, among them – look forward to the perhaps even more remote possibility of creating a real UN army for international policing – one which people of any nationality could join as individuals. Then Japanese, no longer willing to die for the nation, would be able to choose to die for mankind but no question of the exercise of state power would be involved.

But there is no guarantee that all these considerations, dominant as they are at the present time, will always be so. The time will come when the wounds of the last war are healed. (Though the fiftieth anniversary and its disputes showed that it might be a long time coming.) There might be a second Gulf War, this time closer to hand. Attitudes could change. Much will depend on whether the UN really does acquire that peace-enforcement capability to wage just wars which is assumed in Dore's suggestions about revising the Japanese Constitution.

Tokyo, July 1995

Shinsuke Yoshimura is a leader writer on the *Tōkyō Shimbun*.

Economic and cultural rather than military contributions

Shinji Fukukawa

I entirely agree that Japan should 'take initiatives' and contribute to the shaping of a sound international environment, not just take it as given. But the initiatives need to be attractive enough, and to be modest and thoughtful enough, to find acceptance in other countries. The trouble is that the Japanese people are not yet internationalized enough, and we are not quite confident enough in our grasp of world affairs to be able to do this well. Moreover, Japanese are still learning how to express themselves effectively in international gatherings, and how to build up the personal network of friends and acquaintances which help to make their interventions effective. We have an urgent need, I think, to build up our cadre of opinion leaders who can do this – in government, in business and in the academic community.

I do agree that the organization and functioning of the UN is a topic of the first importance. I have expressed the view frequently in recent years that we are entering into the era of the Pax Consortis – in which, indeed, the UN can play a major role. The UN, in conjunction with the International Court of Justice and the GATT, can do a great to deal to bring greater justice, and greater cooperation in the relations among major countries. Dore's history of the UN and evaluation of its progress is an important part of the book and Japanese readers will gain a great deal from it.

I personally think that there is not yet a sufficient degree of support for Japan's becoming a permanent member of the Security Council, but we do need to reach a national consensus on the issue and decide exactly what role Japan would play on the assumption that we get such membership in the future. Given our history and the errors we have committed, I am of the opinion that we should keep the Constitution as it is and frame our UN involvement within the constraints it imposes.

A true security framework should have anticipatory, preventive mechanisms as well as *ex post* conflict-resolution mechanisms. The former, preventive, measures have a military side – the reduction in armaments, inspection of nuclear weapons, embargo on the export of large-scale destructive weapons, and improvement in the transparency of the conventional arms trade. They also have a non-military side – economic cooperation, technical assistance and balanced interdependency. Likewise the post-factum elements of the security system include both military and non-military elements – peace-keeping and joint military action under UN resolutions on the one hand, and economic blockades, or peace-keeping combined with assistance for postwar reconstruction on the other. The emphasis today is shifting towards the economic and cultural, rather than the military elements, and this makes it even more feasible for Japan to make great contributions to world peace even without any amendment of the Constitution.

Tokyo, September 1994

Shinji Fukukawa, formerly civil service head (Deputy Minister) of MITI, and Vice-Chairman of Kobe Steel. Currently Chairman and Chief Executive Officer of the Dentsu Institute for Humanistic Studies.

The need to wait for a generation change

Yukio Matsuyama

This is a highly readable and persuasive book. If I were an American or European Japan expert, or a man from Mars, I am sure I would have been nodding agreement from start to finish. The analysis of international politics, the directions for restructuring the UN and so on, show a breadth of vision, a sense of the *longue durée*, a logic and lucidity which give no grounds for complaint. 'Internationally', his argument is unquestionably a good deal easier to understand than the utterances of that succession of Japanese prime ministers who have declared themselves in favour of 'enacting a genuinely autonomous constitution', but renounced any expectation of seeing a revision of the constitution 'during my term', or than the pronouncements of all those Japanese newspapers which urge that defence expenditure should not be allowed to exceed one per cent of GNP.

Nevertheless, as someone who has been a journalist covering Japanese politics and foreign policy for forty years (more than eleven of them in the United States), someone who has seen the realities of Japanese politics and the flaccid faces of Japanese politicians at close quarters, I find myself thinking of the Japanese national character, of constitutional revision and of Japan's contribution to the UN, along a different vector from Professor Dore. I would like to respond to his request with a few words of – to use the language of minority reports by the American Supreme Court – 'respectful dissent', and try to throw some light on these questions from a rather different angle to his.

To be frank, at heart I am in favour of revising the Constitution. That a constitution enacted under the extraordinary conditions of the postwar occupation should be treated by later generations a half-century afterwards as golden words writ in stone goes against all my 'anti-feudal' instincts. What I particularly object to is, leaving aside the fact that the draft was produced by the occupying army, the fact that it was enacted as a revision of the Meiji constitution, referred to the Privy Council, and passed by the old House of Peers and House of Commons. The people involved were neither democrats nor liberals; many of them were very soon to be purged from public office. The Privy Council and the House of Peers were abolished.

Americans can stand tall and speak with pride of 'our founding fathers' – a sentiment we have never been privileged to share.

If one looks only at Article 9, on any straightforward reading there is no way to square the existence of the Self-Defence Forces with our 'Peace Constitution'. It is no wonder that sixty per cent of our constitutional scholars consider that those forces are unconstitutional. I have many times given talks at law schools in America and Europe, and when I read out the passage 'Land, sea and air forces shall never be maintained', inevitably somebody in the audiences titters or looks askance. Tell them about the tortuous interpretation which Ashida Hitoshi put on the opening words of the second paragraph – 'In order to accomplish the purposes of the preceding paragraph', and you can be certain of getting the same scornful reaction as Dore records – 'What a devious bastard'. This has become our Achilles' heel, a symbol of Japanese illogic.

The senior officials of the Cabinet Law Office and of the Foreign Ministry's Treaty Bureau have nearly all studied the constitution at first-class Japanese universities in their youth, and answered questions on it in their civil service examination. Not one of them will have written an answer which argued that the Constitution allowed the Self-Defence Forces to be sent abroad. And now they can say with a straight face, 'no question, but of course they can be sent abroad'. Legal interpretations change with changing circumstances, to be sure, but the current 'expanded interpretations of Article 9' are surely a bit much. This way we are on the road of transition from 'rule by law' to 'rule by decree'. If only to preserve popular respect for the law, I too sometimes think that the time has surely come to do something about revising the Constitution. No doubt, to use Dore's words, we should feel 'cleansed'.

Why, nevertheless, do I take the negative position that it is still too early to revise the Constitution? Because I know only too well the ideological background of most of the people who are in favour of revision.

Immediately after the war, the Americans, determined to make Japan 'armless and harmless', forced the enactment of the 'Peace Constitution' (and the vast majority of the Japanese people welcomed it). Then, as soon as the Korean War broke out, they switched rapidly to the policy of making Japan 'a bastion of anti-communism in Asia'. The Peace Constitution became an awkward obstacle. I have personally heard a senior Pentagon official speak regretfully of 'our great mistake in forcing that Peace Constitution on Japan'.

One cannot overestimate the extent to which postwar Japanese democracy has been poisoned by the 'tolerant' – or rather 'opportunistic' – attitude of the Americans who were prepared to treat anyone who cooperated in the rearmament of Japan, whatever their ideological background, as friends of the United States. When Kishi Nobusuke, former minister in Tojo's cabinet, became Prime Minister, Washington laid great store by his election promise to 'enact a genuinely autonomous constitution', and showed him every sign of friendship. How would the American government have acted if a member of Hitler's cabinet had become German Chancellor? Why did so few people in Europe or America have such a reaction?

Members of the older generation of Japanese conservatives – and their ideological heirs – are in my view nothing but 'accidental liberals'. They are people who fought against 'Kichiku Beiei' – The 'Anglo-American devils' – in the profound belief that liberalism and democracy were incompatible with the Japanese polity. Having been totally defeated by force of arms, they had nowhere to go but use their 'anti-communism' to become pro-American. That is what it is all about; acceptance of the ideas of Jefferson and Lincoln has nothing to do with it. If you want proof, just look at the series of 'unfortunate slips of the tongue' in recent years. Who are the people who have made these insulting remarks about America which they did not expect to get reported? Nakasone, Kajiyama, Sakurauchi, Watanabe – every one of them 'pro-American hawks' – Right-emons in Dore's fairy story.

As chairperson of the editorial board of the liberal newspaper, the *Asahi*, I have been blessed with the opportunity of experiencing all kinds of 'atmospheric pressure', and thereby observing just what are the values which animate these pro-American hawks. When does one see them hanging in there, pushing for a cause with their heart really in it? When it's a question of reviving National Foundation Day, making official visits to the Yasukuni shrine, singing the national anthem or flying the national flag in schools, keeping the old 'Year-period' system, keeping the Daijōsai coronation ceremony, enacting an anti-espionage law. For them, it is obvious, prewar Japan is not a past to be rejected. The acceptance of the Potsdam Declaration was not a rebirth of the Japanese nation; it was a mere change of regime. I wonder if politicians and generals in Europe and America realize with what critical dislike these people view the Tokyo War Crimes trials?

It is our tragedy that, in the words of Yanaibara Tadao, former President of Tokyo University, 'our postwar leaders have qualitatively been no different from our prewar leaders'; a paradox that – to quote the constitutional law expert, Professor Higuchi of Tokyo University – 'the people who have been most insistent that Japan belongs to the Western camp, have been the people most systematically hostile to the basic values of the Western world.' That is why I cannot go along with those who would ignore, or make light of those unfortunate facts and urge that we should 'change the Constitution in order to be able to make a contribution to international affairs just like any other country'. In terms of Dore's fairy story I am generally neither Left-emon, nor Right-emon, but Middle-emon; on the specific question of constitutional revision, I suppose I lean a little leftward of Middle-emon; Middle-left-emon, say.

In Europe and America, someone not capable of conceptual thinking is apt to be despised. In Japan, however, for politicians, and indeed other 'top people', conceptual thinking is not particularly necessary. Seriousness of purpose, loyalty, cooperativeness (and, sometimes, the ability to raise funds) are quite enough. In the world of politics, in the bureaucracy and in business, it's not a matter of 'Let's do this'; the mainstream thought is 'that's the situation, after all; better to go along and adapt'. Take initiatives, try to exert leadership, and you will find everybody treating you warily.

After many years in America I can understand exactly why people in the West get irritated by the Japanese lack of conceptual thinking, and I do indeed feel that we need to change – less adaptability, more positive initiatives. But this is a genuine cultural difference and, after all, should one really be so critical of the fact that the Japanese, having become 'over-conceptual' and got their fingers badly burned fifty years ago, have since become rather inclined to dithering? I'm more inclined to see danger the other way. If the Japanese, with their economic power and their technological power and, indeed, with their pride in their racial superiority, were really to ride forth into the world, look out!

But the fact is that this negativism does come out in Japan's posture towards, and behaviour in, international society, and we do get criticized for having 'no philosophy; no principles'.

The late Prime Minister Ohira used to lament that 'Japan is like a raft with only a pole to navigate the rapids'. I agree that the time has come to put an engine and a rudder on the raft. In that sense I agree with Dore's 'an end to this introversion'. Japan has the money, and the men and women and the ideas, and should come forth with them.

But when it comes to contributing personnel, I think one has to tread carefully. There is no guarantee that if the Japanese raft got an engine and rudder of a strongly military cast – if, that is to say, the Constitution were revised in what the proponents of revision call a way appropriate to today – the results would be something Western democrats and liberals would like. This is clear enough if you listen to what the Lower House MP Ishihara Shintarō is saying. Once start moving on that course, and the brakes will become hard to apply.

And if, at the present stage, the Japanese Self-Defence Forces were to go marching, the Rising Sun flag bravely flying, into the trouble spots of the world in Europe and Africa – and to start shedding blood – would there not be more apprehensive than grateful reactions from other countries?

However disappointing to those Japanese who want their country to be recognized as a Great Power, given Japan's recent past and the character of its people (particularly the conservative leadership), and thinking also of 'the women' who appear in Dore's fairy story, would it not be better, for a while, for us to stick to something like the role of Amanoya Rihei in the tale of the forty-seven Ronin – the one who did not take part in the midnight raid, but made significant contributions on the financial side. We should contribute personnel, but non-military personnel.

For better or for worse, there is a 'good-natured softie' side to the Japanese character. How otherwise would Japan – not a member of the Security

Council – have responded to its Gulf War resolutions with full cooperation and produced those $13 billion – at the cost of a hundred dollars in extra taxes for every member of the Japanese population? If America, Britain, France, Russia or China were in such a position, you can be sure they would have said 'no taxation without representation' and refused to give a penny. Would the Chinese or the French ever, in the first place, have accepted an invitation to join the United Nations as long as Article 53 – the so-called 'enemy country clause' – remained unchanged?

All the same, better a 'good-natured softie' than a 'bad-natured toughie' in my book. The fact that the Middle-emons and the Middle-left-emons and the Left-emons of Japan, while being favourably disposed towards America's ideals and culture, are nevertheless inflexibly resistant to American pressure, is because they do not trust America's 'bad-natured toughie' lawyer-like approach to things – the tendency to see everything in terms of short-term gains, to jump to simple black and white, friend and foe, divisions. In my years in Washington I saw at close hand just how much America's China-containment policy and Vietnam policy troubled the Japanese government. And later in New York I frequently filed reports describing how the American contempt for the UN was embarrassing other countries. They delayed paying their dues to the UN, they set out to harass the ILO and UNESCO – and now are telling us about the need to respect the UN. 'You've got a nerve!' is the only obvious reaction. Who was it that made up to Iraq and helped to build it into a military power? Whose responsibility is it that Cambodia got into such a dreadful state?

When Japan seeks to develop positive, forward-looking policies towards Asia, both domestically and abroad the cry goes up that Japan should first show proper contrition for its past behaviour. A positive, forward foreign policy should surely rest on proper reflection on past history. In that sense I think highly of Prime Minister Hosokawa's having, of all post-war prime ministers, come out very clearly with an acknowledgement of Japan's past misdeeds.

But in the same way, if America is going to take a forward-looking, positive policy towards the UN, it would become it to make frank admission of its errors in treating the UN so badly in the recent past.

There is one thing I would like to say to Western conceptual thinkers when they talk about 'justice' and 'human rights'. They tend to judge everything by Western standards. There are clear and present injustices in Tibet, in Myanmar, in our Northern Territories, just as much as there are in Bosnia and Somalia, but they do not seem able to give them much attention.

There is a neat Chinese phrase, *Hirihōkenten*, literally Wrong, Right, Law, Power, Heaven. Right triumphs over Wrong. Law triumphs over Right. Power triumphs over Law, and Heaven triumphs over Power. Americans are fond of Right, Law and Power, and try to settle matters quickly. For Orientals, who perceive that it is by slow historical processes that Heaven brings change to men and nations, they are altogether in too much of a hurry.

It was part of the greatness of President Kennedy that he got this right. I still vividly remember the strong emotions with which I heard him, just before his assassination, give his 'Strategy for Peace' address at the American University. In a Washington awash with lawyers and hawks, he said:

> History teaches us that emnities between nations, as between individuals, do not last forever. However fixed our likes and dislikes seem, the tide of time and events will often bring surprising changes in the relations between nations and neighbours. . . . We must, therefore, persevere in the search for peace in the hope that constructive change within the Communist bloc might bring within reach solutions which now seem beyond us.

How one wishes that Kennedy could have lived to see the fall of the Berlin Wall! In international affairs, patience is the necessary virtue.

Kenneth Boulding once said: 'The Japanese are the most continuous, non-revolutionary, non-dialectical people in the history of mankind.' There is some truth in that. But, as one sees in the birth of the Hosokawa government, Japan, too, is gradually but certainly changing.

In postwar Japan, it is the 'conservatives' who have been all for 'change', the 'radicals' who have defended the *status quo*, a curious 'intestinal inversion'. Fair is foul and foul is fair, in the words of Shakespeare. The conservatives have seemed radical and the radicals seemed conservative. There are many Japanese who, though desirous of change, have no desire to link up with conservatives who have yet to come to terms with the past. And yet, to move towards the radicals from sheer antipathy towards the conservatives with their prewar coccyx, their residual prewar tail, is to invite disappointment at their negative attitude towards any change in the postwar system. This is the tough dilemma which faces Japan's Middle-emons and Middle-left-emons.

My view is that only when a 'conservatism predisposed to change' really breaks loose from the prewar value system, and 'conservative radicals' really begin to consider rethinking the postwar settlement, can one really begin to think positively about constitutional revision. Instead of dividing, in Dore's terms, into the Messrs Realist and Messrs Idealist, we have all got to become idealistic realists or realistic idealists. Instead of seeking to promote political reform by means of constitutional revision, the right way is to reform our politics first so that we can produce founding fathers we can be proud of.

Let me finally once more stress how much the rough surgical treatment of an imposed constitution has left permanent wounds on the Japanese body politic. It must be extremely difficult for peoples who have never suffered defeat to apppreciate the pain that this involves. The greatest lesson this experience has taught the Japanese people is not so much 'Never lose a war', nor even 'Never start a war you are going to lose', but 'Never let yourselves fall prey to leaders, organizations, ideologies of the kind that start wars you are bound to lose'. That is why I insist; I await the day when those driven by nostalgia for prewar Japan vacate the arena of constitutional reform debates.

Tokyo, August 1994

Mr Matsuyama is a former leader writer, and former head of the Washington Bureau of the *Asahi* newspaper.

Limits on the spirit of self-sacrifice
Shijurō Ogata

The postwar Japanese Constitution should have been drafted by Japanese themselves rather than by Americans. Likewise, a book advocating an internationalist revision of this Constitution should have been written by some Japanese rather than a British scholar. However, it is Dore who has done it.

His intention seems to be two-fold. First, in response to the Ishihara–Morita book, *Japan That Can Say 'No'*, he has chosen his title, *The Japan That Can Say 'Let's Do This'*, to suggest that Japan should take initiatives with constructive proposals. Second, as the subject of such a proposal, he suggests a contribution to international peace through strengthening the United Nations. It is a pity that this did not figure in his title – at least with a subtitle such as 'In search of a more positive role for international peace'.

The historical analysis seems to me fair and useful in the distinctions it draws – between those who condemn any use of force even to preserve peace, and those who think that force sometimes has to be used, and between the two ways of enhancing national pride: the Israeli type and the Swedish type. I was struck also by his classification of three types of undesirable Japanese: inward-looking pacifists, economic animals concerned only with American reactions, and vain, presumptuous chauvinists. And also by his idealism and optimism. He tries to find evidence of some progress in international cooperation for peace in the United Nations even during the years of the Cold War, and some signs of evolution from a US-led hegemonic international order to a UN-centred democratic international order, even during the Gulf War.

Fundamentally, I agree with his views in general and with his proposals for the revision of Article 9 in particular. But I have one big reservation. Of course, I also think that we Japanese should be involved in international affairs even when our own national interests are not directly involved. We should formulate our own ideas, should take more initiatives and should not mind becoming trouble-shooters or coordinators when other countries are divided. For us to do these things is not very easy in view of our traditionally very passive attitude (*kanemochi kenka sezu* – rich men don't quarrel), but I do expect changes in that direction.

However, I am not so sure that we can revive the spirit of self-sacrifice, this time not just sacrifice for Japan, but sacrifice for the cause of international peace. The demilitarization of Japan by the Allied Occupation was so successful that, I am afraid, not only the inward-looking pacifists, but also even many of those who advocate our active participation in UN activities, are not ready to expose themselves to physical dangers for lofty causes. What Professor Nambara called at the time of the postwar parliamentary debate on the Constitution the ideal of 'establishing the eternal peace of the world by sacrificing our blood and sweat in order to protect actively freedom and justice for mankind' does not come easily to the present-day Japanese who are complacently pursuing a comfortable daily life.

The account of those debates is particularly interesting to me since they took place when I was a student. I remember Kisaburō Yokota, professor of international law, telling us that the new Constitution denied Japan's right of self-defence because Japanese previous invasions had been conducted in the name of self-defence – an argument similar to Prime Minister Yoshida's quoted in this book. For me it was an interesting discovery to learn about the original intention of Ashida's proposal to revise the beginning of the second paragraph of Article 9. I had been misled by him. I had assumed that he must have anticipated the future need for self-defence.

Dore has read widely and beyond academic writing, but even he misses a few things (see translation note 20 on p. 182) and gets some things wrong. For example, it is not the duty of Japanese diplomats posted in Geneva to 'give diplomatic advice in case of need' to top Japanese officials at WHO and UNHCR; they are Japan's representatives to international organizations headquartered at Geneva, and most of them tend to spend their time mostly on Japan's relations with GATT.

I was interested in the contrast between this book and another book of Dore's, written with Yūsuke Fukuda and published almost simultaneously, which takes a very positive view of Japanese-style capitalism. In the one he is urging the Japanese to change, in the other recognizing the strength of Japanese practices. This is not a contradiction, but the strength and the weakness must be interrelated. It may not be easy to correct the weakness while retaining the strength, but that is exactly what is desired.

Tokyo, September 1993

Shijuro Ogata is a former Deputy-Governor of the Japan Development Bank, and was co-chairman with Paul Volcker of the commission on the financing of the UN. He is currently member of several international commissions and a director of Barclays.

The advantages of diversity

Masahiko Aoki

We have a phrase in Japanese, *tenka-kokka-ron*, which means literally 'arguing affairs of state and empire' and carries images of callow youths, devoid of any experience of practical politics, convinced that they have the answers to all the world's problems. When Ron Dore sent me a copy of his book two years ago, the inscription said: 'Please *shōran* (read with deprecating laughter) my amateur *tenka-kokka-ron*'. I knew that, for all that modesty, Dore had already done outstanding work in a number of fields, but I was not prepared for what I found – Dore entering a new field and breaking fresh ground. I was impressed, and when asked for a reaction for the English edition didn't see how, even out of colleaguely good manners, I could refuse, for all the trespassing beyond my field of competence that would entail. But how even to get one's bat to touch such a hard ball? The book has been staring at me on my desk for two years, but I now finally have got down to writing this note, not just out of academic colleagueship, but because Dore has posed questions which it seems to me members of the Japanese social science community, even marginal members like myself, simply cannot avoid facing up to – however much they might be, like myself, real, genuine-article amateurs in the field of international relations.

I am an economist who, over the last five years, has gradually come to harbour doubts about the deductive methodology which counts as the discipline's orthodoxy, and to see the attractions in an evolutionary approach. I have always been interested in the comparison of economic systems, and my attraction to the evolutionary point of view derives from the questions that arise from such comparisons: how do different systems get to be different? Is there economic advantage to be gained from the coexistence in the world of a diversity of systems, or should the economy of every country conform to certain common rules in order to ensure fairness in international competition?

So, with this reason for sympathy with the evolutionary approach, it was entirely congenial to me to find Dore beginning his book with the contrast between evolutionary theory and cyclical theory and nailing his colours to the former mast. But as I began thinking about it, it appeared to me that, for all the differences in the subject matter treated, Dore's theme and my own scholarly interests deal in some fairly essential respects with an identical problem – and that there are some subtle differences between us. Let me develop those differences, even if in so doing I seem to be showing un-Japanese disrespect for a white-haired *daisempai*. But first let me make quite clear that, as somebody who from early youth has always considered himself an internationalist, my starting point in this discussion is very different from the assumptions of the variety of 'narrow' Japanese patriots whom Dore attacks with such vivacious wit.

The first chapter sets out a number of evolutionary propositions. Social systems are basically constrained by knowledge and technology, and the development and accumulation of the latter has brought about a rapid evolution of the former in modern times. In particular, knowledge being the common possession of an international cadre of experts, one consequence is that the principles by which it is possible to define what is 'universally' recognized as fair in the settlement of international disputes become gradually formulated, and appreciation of the need for a framework of international order which makes possible the enforcement of those principles, becomes more widely diffused.

So far I am almost a hundred per cent in agreement. (I say almost because, as will appear, I have some problems with the notion of 'universally fair' principles.) But, to put the matter squarely on the table, what I have doubts about is whether, from those premises, one can directly deduce 'UN-centrism' – the desirability of centralizing the settlement of disputes.

It is quite true that the bilateral settlement of the sort of disputes which arise in Japanese–American trade negotiations often leads to futile unprofitable argument and amplifies mutual distrust. The lawyers who negotiate on the American side believe that price competition is the only fair rule. They cannot understand that the long-term contractual relation, starting in the development phase, between automobile firms and their suppliers has the advantages of shortening the development cycle, improving quality and the timing of deliveries. But the Japanese bureaucrats, with the beam of over-regulation in their own eye, cannot put that counter-case effectively. So the argument continues on ever more barren ground with talk about reducing the trade imbalance on individual commodities – something which is as far removed from the notion of deriving mutual benefit from trade in different commodities as it is possible to get. But whether the problem would be solved if it were shifted from bilateral to multilateral negotiations is the question. It might stop the absurd attempt to make the reduction of bilateral trade balances the goal to be pursued, but it is unlikely that it would provide a panacea.

And the reason I say that is because I doubt whether free price competition can ever become a 'universal' economic rule. Economists are recently coming to realize that the market is not the only efficient institution. Organization, cultural norms and values, reputation, government regulation – the whole organizational complex of a society – cannot be ignored as factors which condition the economic equilibrium. If that were all that was involved it would not be worth talking about, but it has this following implication. Multiple equilibria can exist for an economy, depending on the history of its institutional evolution. Moreover, given the limited rationality of economic actors, there is no way of deciding in overall terms which institutional complex is the best. For example, the Japanese system seems to be very good at assembly industries like automobiles and at industries where the technological trajectory is already well established like memory chips, but the American system excels in fields like logic chips and multimedia where there is a need to create new technological trajectories and new industrial standards. That is to say that, whereas traditional Ricardian trade theory saw comparative advantage in international trade as a function of the relative endowment of countries with the basic resources of land, capital and labour, in the modern economy the organizational form of industry and firms is becoming the important factor determining the comparative advantage of nations or regions.

So it becomes an interesting question, which Dore explicitly raises, whether there is likely to be a convergent homogenization of different institutional economic systems on a world scale. And whether or not it is desirable that there should be. Dore says that it would be 'premature' to jump to such a conclusion, but that it is 'not beyond the bounds of likelihood'. And he does seem to judge that an evolutionary trend towards the formulation of a universal consensus and the formation of some kind of world government is desirable. To be sure, the focus of his argument is on the rational settlement of disputes involving armed force, and there is much to be said for his argument in favour of having an international body monopolize the means of exerting armed force. But it seems to me that, with the internationalization of knowledge, it is more likely that the world will move in the direction of recognizing a diversity of values, and that it might be better, in some fields, to try to build a structure which permits that – a structure which need not necessarily take the centralized form of an international organization.

Let us return to the example of trade disputes discussed earlier. It seems in fact that there is more economic benefit to be derived from the diversity of economic systems than from a situation in which every country – America, Japan, Russia, China – all had the same system. It is possible for countries to derive mutual benefits from trade based on their respective comparative advantages, as determined by their industrial structure, their reserves of natural resources and the level of their technological capacity. They can also, as Dore points out, gradually improve their organizations and institutions by learning from each other. But that learning is basically historically path-dependent; it proceeds in ways which still leave basic Chinese-type, Japanese-type or continental-European-type characteristics. For example, the Western advisers who tried to import the 'universal model' of neo-classical economics to Russia simply failed, but the Chinese, taking careful note of that experience, have been moving forward, feeling their way, trying to find their own mode of transition to a market economy which will be compatible with their historically conditioned circumstances. As they do so they are seeking also to learn from the institutional structures which served in the 'Asian model' economic development of Japan and other Asian countries. But in the end China will doubtless work out a specifically Chinese pattern of evolution.

To be sure, one cannot say that the diversity of economic systems is productive of nothing but good. It leads to all kinds of disputes of which the Japanese–American trade negotiations are a good example. But it is instructive to ask why these trade frictions seem recently to have died down. It may in part be because of the background emergence of the new GATT rules for the resolution of trade disputes, which caused both sides to moderate their excessively self-interested self-assertiveness. But I think it was also because problems with China – both trade problems and political problems – came rather sharply to demand attention. I believe that the Americans calculated that the cost of dealing simultaneously on both fronts with problems arising from system differences was just too great.

In short, the question I wish to pose is this. Should one say: 'institutional convergence is gradually taking place, and hence one should seek to centralize dispute-settlement mechanisms in international agencies'? Or should one say: 'There is intrinsic value in the fact that, for all the mutual learning, there remains diversity and distinctiveness in national institutional structures, and likewise there should also be diversity in methods of dispute settlement'? There may be circumstances in which centralized dispute settlement is most effective, but there may equally be other circumstances in which a more decentralized pattern of bilateral or regional settlement mechanisms is more cost-effective in terms of time and effort and cost of bureaucratic input.

Take, as another example, a field as full of uncertainties as the environment. Is it better for every country to act under the same rules and with the same information? Or under different rules and different information? There is no unambiguous answer. If all countries accepted the same rules and information and rushed off in the same direction the subsequent cost of any mistakes would be correspondingly greater. In situations of uncertainty, diversity can be a kind of insurance, a means of hedging, over the long term, against mistakes.

One can apply similar reasoning to, for example, the punishment of 'mistakes' by governments such as the Tienanmen Incident. Should every country concert its criticism and put up a solid front in refusing to let China sponsor the Olympics? Or is it better that there should be countries which take a somewhat ambiguous attitude and maintain connections? I would think there is no reason to suppose that, in the long run, the latter will not turn out to have been the better alternative.

So it appears that the real problem is whether an international organization can function in such a way as really to guarantee that we reap the advantages of diversity. It should not be impossible. And particularly if the reforms of international organizations of the kind Dore proposes took place, the prospects would be improved. But one cannot ignore the possibility that ultimately, instead of arriving at a single decision, under the given rules of a single organization, what would happen would be the vast expenditure of time and effort and bureaucratic maintenance costs on finding a compromise among conflicting views. And it is especially in such a process that the Japanese are notoriously bad at taking the initative of Dore's title and saying 'Let's do this', so much so that I find myself rather pessimistic about the probability of Japan making much of a contribution.

Which is not in the least to downplay the importance of the reforms of international organizations which Dore proposes. Nor is it to try to excuse the faceless anonymity of Japan's politics and diplomacy. But if Japanese experts and intellectuals are to expand their capacity to contribute to the development of knowledge as a common property of mankind, I rather think it is likely to be, not so much by contributing to the formation of universalist policies, but rather by helping to create a framework which permits, and derives benefit from, diversity, which helps write the menu from which men and women choose what knowledge to use and what ends to pursue in using it.

Stanford, September 1995

Professor Aoki is Takahashi Professor of Japanese Studies, Economics Department, Stanford University, and the author of *The Cooperative Game Theory of the Firm* (Oxford University Press, 1984), *Information, Incentives and Bargaining in the Japanese Economy* (Cambridge University Press, 1988) and numerous other works.

The fork in the road
Kazuo Chiba

Japan, among all the major powers of the world, seems to be most affected by the global changes caused in great part by the end of the Cold War, puzzling over which fork in the road to take. The comfortable ways of the past, the politico-military anonymity of the repentant war-loser – itself a protective adaptation to a hostile post-World War II environment – is no longer possible in these days when Japan has enormous economic clout and is faced by raucous calls from the victors of a half-century ago to shoulder global political responsibilities and leadership – and cannot avoid the nagging suspicion that any attempt to take them at their fickle word would bring down bitter criticism of 'presumption' and new convulsions of Japan-bashing. Beset by a faltering economy, large-scale natural disasters and unprecedented criminal action aiming at mass murder by poison gas and other loathsome means, and facing a period of indefinite political drift, the certainties of the Cold War days, when the left- and right-leaning were in a sort of ballet-like equilibrium, are gone for ever. Who knows that excessive Japan-bashing might not precipitate a completely new nationalistic reaction, neither the irrational jingoism nor the blustering militarism of the past, but something coldly calculating and Machiavellian, cleverly putting unpleasant pressure on perceived tormentors?

It is disturbing that Arnold Toynbee's observation, seemingly out of fashion among the British, that Orpheus would sooner or later change into a snarling drill sergeant, appears to be reflected in the now-familiar American 'trade hawk', hurling epithets left and right. To replace the long-familiar 'low posture' with a high leadership posture which is bound to draw fire (more often 'friendly' than hostile) frightens Japanese of many hues.

Here Ron Dore comes, offering good advice, while fully aware of Japanese sensibilities, advice not untinged with satire as in his little story about the Self-Defence Forces, the 'dog not called a dog'. Basing his arguments on the need to strengthen the United Nations as an instrument for mankind to surmount the post-Cold War world, he suggests that the Japanese desire for an honourable place in international society might be fulfilled by contributing to, and eventually attaining a leading position in,

UN efforts to safeguard peace, perhaps as a permanent member of the Security Council. His call to harness the proven energies of the Japanese in strenuous but benign activities on a global scale, the now-despondent reading public should surely find reassuring and revitalizing. He combines this basic appeal with pragmatic suggestions on how to handle the all-important yet ultra-sensitive American relationship, as well as many other practical (and practicable) measures.

I have only one quibble – the phenomenon of regionalism and the transformation of the significance of the sovereign state in the developing structure of the world could have been delved into a little more, as East Asia develops at breakneck speed, with China rapidly looming large in the international scene. For Japan and the Pacific Ocean states, including the US, shaping a viable regional grouping as an integral part of the global structure will without doubt be of the utmost importance. The Japanese would respond better to the clarion call if shown a bit more clearly the direction to be taken.

Tokyo, July 1995

Ambassador Chiba is a former Japanese ambassador to the Court of St James, London, and currently Advisor to Mitsui and Company.

Notes

PREFACE TO THE ENGLISH EDITION

(Japanese authors are cited surname first, for works in Japanese, and surname second, for works in English.)

1. See Wakamiya, Yoshibumi, *Sengo hoshu no ajia-kan* (Conservatives' Views of Asia since the War), Tokyo, Asahi Shimbunsha, 1995, for a detailed account of the views of prominent LDP members who have tried to block any expression of official apology for the war.
2. Thanks to Chikao Tsukuda for guiding me to the discussion of Thucydides' observations in Donald Kagan's excellent *On the Origins of War and the Preservation of Peace*, New York, Doubleday, 1994.
3. Takashi Inoguchi, 'Japan's response to the Gulf crisis, 1990–1991: An analytic overview', *Journal of Japanese Studies*, 17, Summer 1991, 257–273.
4. Ozawa, Ichirō, *Nihon Kaizo Keikaku* (A Plan for Japan's Reconstruction), Tokyo, Kodansha, 1993.
5. For details see Takashi Inoguchi, 'Japan's United Nations peacekeeping and other operations', *International Journal*, 50, ii, Spring 1995, p. 325–342.
6. Miyazawa, Kiichi, *Shin Goken Sengen* (A new 'Protect the Constitution' Declaration), Tokyo, Asahi Shimbunsha, 1995.
7. New York, Twentieth Century Fund, 1995.
8. Takashi Inoguchi, 'Peacekeeping' and Akihiko Tanaka, 'UN Peace operations and Japan–US relations'; Chapter 3 of P. Gourevitch, Takashi Inoguchi and Courtney Purrington, eds, *United States–Japan Relations and International Institutions after the Cold War*, San Diego, Graduate School of International Relations and Pacific Studies, 1995.
9. See E. Childers and B. Urquhart, *Renewing the United Nations System*, Uppsala, Dag Hammarskjold Foundation, published as the first 1994 volume of *Development Dialogue*.
10. Yoshio Hatano, in *Look Japan*, vol. 41, no. 475, October 1995, p. 11.
11. Nishikawa, Yoshimitsu, *Funsō-kaiketsu to Kokuren, Kokusaihō* (The UN, International Law and the Settlement of Disputes), Tokyo, Koyo Shoten, 1996, p. 249–251.
12. See Takashi Inoguchi, 'Dialectics of world order: A view from Pacific Asia', Hans-Henrik Holm and Georg Sorensen, eds, *Whose World Order? Uneven Globalization and the End of the Cold War*, Boulder, Westview, 1995.
13. Miyazawa, *op. cit.*, p. 91.
14. Harada, Katsuhiro, *Kokuren kaikaku to Nihon no yakuwari* (Reform of the UN and Japan's Role), Tokyo, Nihon Keizai Shimbunsha, 1995, p. 247.

15 Maeda, Tetsuo, in *Asahi Shimbun*, 18 April 1996.
16 Kuriyama, Shōichi, 'Nichibei kankei no zentaizō o', *Gaikō Forum*, 93, June 1996, p. 10.
17 Wolf Mendl, *Japan's Asia Policy: Regional Security and Global Interests*, London, Routledge, p. 158.
18 Nobu, Noda, 'The dangerous rise of Asianism', *Japan Echo*, 22, i, Spring 1995.
19 Keizai, Dōyūkai, *Anzen-hoshō mondai Chōsakai, Anzen-hoshō mondai chōsakai hōkokusho* (Report of the Committee for Examination of the Security Question), 8 April 1996.
20 Mushakōji, Kinhide, *Kokuren no saisei to chikyū minshushugi* (The Rebirth of the UN and Global Democracy), Tokyo, Kashiwa Shobo, 1995.
21 Mogami, Toshiki, *Kokuren shisutemu o koete* (Transcending the UN System), Tokyo, Iwanami Shoten, 1995.
22 Koseki, Shōichi, et al. 'Kyodo teigen: Heiwa kihonhō o tsukurō', *Sekai*, April 1993 An English translation has been published by Gavan McCormack, *Peace and Regional Security in the Asia-Pacific: A Japanese Proposal*, Australian National University, Research School of Pacific Studies, Working Paper No. 158.
23 Takashi Inoguchi, 'Japan's United Nations peacekeeping and other operations', *International Journal*, 1, ii, Spring 1995, p. 336.
24 *Yomiuri Shimbun*, 3 November 1944. An English summary – together with reactions from other newspapers – may be found in *Japan Echo*, Spring 1995.
25 Ozawa, Ichirō, *Nihon Kaizō Keikaku* (A Plan for Japan's Reconstruction), Tokyo, Kodansha, 1993.
26 Miyazawa, op. cit., p. 103.
27 Wolf Mendl, op. cit., p. 156.
28 See Chikako Takeishi, 'Japanese national identity in transition. Who wants to send the military abroad?', *International Sociology*, 11, ii, June 1996.

PREFACE TO THE JAPANESE ORIGINAL

1 Number 45, June 1992, p. 6.
2 *International Herald Tribune* (Rome edn) 9 March 1992.
3 Trans. note: A story recently told in fascinating detail by Robert Wade, 'Japan, the World Bank, and the art of paradigm maintenance: *The East Asia miracle* in political perspective', *New Left Review*, 217, June 1996.
4 Trans. note: But succumbing to the pressures of international financial markets – allowing the financial tail to wag the economic dog – seems more likely than it did. 'Superior efficiency' is also called into question by the American recovery of the technological lead in a number of fields, but on that the evidence is still conflicting.

1 PHILOSOPHIES OF HISTORY

1 *Asahi Shimbun*, 9 March 1992.

2 THE EARLY STIRRINGS OF INTERNATIONALISM

1 D.P. Moynihan, *On the Law of Nations*, Cambridge, MA, Harvard University Press, 1990, p. 156.
2 Hugo Grotius, *De jure belli ac pacis*, 1625.
3 R.O. Keohane and J.S. Nye, Jr., eds, *Transnational Relations and World Politics*, Cambridge, MA, Harvard University Press, 1971.

180 *Notes pp. 21–42*

   4 G. Dante, *Monarchia*, c.1310. The following attempt at a potted history of thinking about international organization derives almost entirely from F.H. Hinsley, *Power and the Pursuit of Peace*, Cambridge, Cambridge University Press, 1963. The bibliographical references to early works are also lifted straight from Hinsley.
   5 N. Machiavelli, *Il principe*, 1513.
   6 E. Crucé, *Nouveau Cynee*, 1623.
   7 W. Penn, *Essay Towards the Present and Future Peace of Europe*, 1763.
   8 Hinsley, *op. cit.*, p. 39.
   9 J.-J. Rousseau, *Extrait du projet de la paix perpetuelle de Monsieur L'Abbe de Saint-Pierre*, 1756, and *Judgement sur la paix perpetuelle*, 1756.
10 I. Kant, *Thoughts on Perpetual Peace*, 1795; H. de Saint-Simon, *De la reorganisation de la societé européenne*, 1814; J. Bentham, *Plan for a Universal and Perpetual Peace*, written 1786–1787, published 1843.
11 J. Mill, 'Law of Nations', in *Encyclopaedia Britannica*, 1820.
12 Hinsley, *op. cit.*, p. 96.
13 Hinsley, *op. cit.*, p. 98.
14 National Association for Arbitration and Peace, founded in Britain in 1882.
15 Hinsley, *op. cit.*, p. 261.

3 THE BIRTH OF THE UNITED NATIONS

   1 S. Howson and D. Moggridge, *The Wartime Diaries of Lionel Robbins and James Meade, 1943–45*, Macmillan, 1990, p. 193.
   2 Christopher Thorne, *Allies of a Kind: The United States, Britain and the War Against Japan, 1941–45*, Oxford, Oxford University Press, 1979.
   3 R.B. Russell and J.E. Mather, *A History of the United Nations Charter*, Washington, Brookings, 1958, pp. 34–39.
   4 *Ibid.*, p. 419.
   5 *Ibid.*, p. 419.
   6 *Ibid.*, p. 55.
   7 Brian Urquhart, *A Life in Peace and War*, New York, Harper and Row, 1957, p. 99.
   8 Hakubun, Itō, *Commentaries on the Constitution*, Tokyo, Igirisu Horitsu Gakko, 1989.

4 THE USE OF ARMED FORCE

   1 Russell and Mather, *op. cit.*, p. 937.
   2 Hugh Thomas, *The Armed Truce: The Beginnings of the Cold War*, New York, Athenaeum, 1987, p. 173.
   3 Russell and Mather, *op. cit.*, p. 937.
   4 D.P. Moynihan, *op. cit.*, p. 146.
   5 D.W. Bowett, *United Nations Forces: A Legal Study*, New York, Praeger, 1964.
   6 Russell and Mather, *op. cit.*, pp. 256–259.
   7 *Ibid.*, pp. 470–472.
   8 United Nations Participation Act, 20 December 1945 (C583, 59 Stat, 619).
   9 Russell and Mather, *op. cit.*, pp. 468–470.
10 SWNCC 219/8, 27 February 1946.
11 *Office Memorandum: Conference with Senators on SWNCC 219/8*, 2 April 1946, State Department 501BC/3.246.5-1BC/4, 2346.

12 Joint Chiefs of Staff to US Representatives on Military Committee, 24 May 1946, in *US Foreign Relations*, 1946 vol. 1, p. 799.
13 Stettinius to Acheson, 16 May 1946, State Department BC/5-1646, Box 2134: Byrnes to Stettinius, 28 May 1946, same box.
14 F.A. Lindsay to B. Baruch, 21 October 1946, in *US Foreign Relations*, 1946, vol. 1, pp. 955–959.
15 Johnson to Acheson, 30 July 1946, State Department, 501 BC/7-2946.
16 Department of State, position paper SD/S.734, in *US Foreign Relations*, 1946, vol. 1, pp. 955–959.
17 The Soviet proposal is described in Knoll to Johnson, 18 September 1946, State Department 501 BC/9-2146.
18 Security Council, Second Year, No. 43, 138th meeting, 4 June 1947, p. 956.
19 Security Council, *Official Record*, Second Year, no. 43, 138th meeting, 4 June 1947, p. 956.
20 Security Council, *op. cit.*, Second Year, *Supplement 13*, Annex 36, 30 June 1947.
21 Security Council, *op. cit.*, Second Year, no. 52, 142nd meeting, pp. 1169–1171.
22 G.F. Kennan to the Secretary of State, 29 June 1948, Policy Planning Staff, PPS/34 (Summary Compilation, p. 297).
23 Trans. note: Since this was written an excellent study of the MSC has appeared. Jane Boulden, *Prometheus Unborn: The History of the Military Staff Committee*, Ottawa, Canadian Centre for Global Security, Aurora Papers, 19, 1993.
24 Hugh Thomas, *op. cit.*, p. 179.

5 THE ENACTMENT OF JAPAN'S PEACE CONSTITUTION

1 Shimizu, Chu, ed. *Chikujō Nihonkoku Kempō Shingiroku*, Tokyo, Yuhikaku, 1962, vol. 1, p. 14 (9 July, Lower House Committee).
2 *Ibid.*, vol. 1, p. 42, 24 June, Lower House Plenary.
3 *Ibid.*, vol. 2, p. 14, Speech by Hayashi Hirauma in the Lower House Committee.
4 *Ibid.*, vol. 2, pp. 65–67, 13 September, Committee of the House of Peers.
5 *Ibid.*, vol. 2, pp. 81–82.
6 *Ibid.*, vol. 2, p. 15–16.
7 *Ibid.*, vol. 2, pp. 41–42, 28 June, responding to Nosaka Sanzo's argument for retaining the right of self-defence.
8 *Ibid.*, vol. 2, p. 112, 9 July, Lower House Committee.
9 *Ibid.*, vol. 2, p. 109, Lower House plenary session.
10 *Ibid.*, vol. 2, p. 102, Lower House Committee.
11 *Ibid.*, vol. 2, pp. 19–23, 27 August, exchanges among Nambara Shigeru, Shidehara Kijurō and Yoshida Shigeru in a plenary session of the House of Peers.
12 *Ibid.*, vol. 2, p. 91, 26 August, House of Peers plenary session.
13 *Ibid.*, vol. 2, p. 97, 13 September, House of Peers Committee.
14 *Ibid.*, vol. 2, p. 92, 26 August, House of Peers plenary session.
15 *Ibid.*, vol. 2, p. 108, 13 September, House of Peers Committee.
16 *Ibid.*, vol. 2, p. 97, 13 September, House of Peers Committee.

6 FROM THE WORLD'S UNITED NATIONS TO THE UNITED NATIONS AS NO MAN'S LAND

1 This account of events from Korea to Suez derives predominantly from D.W. Bowett, *United Nations Forces: A Legal Study*, New York, Praeger, 1964, pp. 21–26.

2 Michael Howard, 'The UN and International Security' in A. Roberts and B. Kingbury, eds, *United Nations, Divided World*, Oxford, Clarendon Press, 1988, p. 35.
3 I translated this sentence, written in 1992, on a day of ambiguous significance – the day of the arrival of Russian troops in Sarajevo!
4 T.M. Franck, 'The functions of the Secretary-General' in A. Roberts and B. Kingbury eds, *United Nations: Divided World*, Oxford, Clarendon Press, 1988, p. 91.
5 D.P. Moynihan, *On the Law of Nations*, Cambridge, Harvard University Press, 1990.
6 D.P. Moynihan, and S. Weaver, *A Dangerous Place*, Boston, Little, Brown, 1978.
7 T.J. Farer, 'The UN and human rights' in Roberts and Kingbury, *op. cit.*, p. 138. Nearly all of the foregoing discussion of human rights is drawn from this first-rate paper.
8 *Sekai*, July 1991.
9 P.M. Roth, *Independent*, 8 December 1992.

7 THE REVIVAL OF THE UN

1 Sir Antony Parsons, 'The UN and the national interests of states', in Roberts and Kingbury, eds 1991, p. 56.
2 G.R. Berridge, *Return to the UN: UN Diplomacy in Regional Conflicts*, London, Macmillan, 1991, pp. 43–45. Much of what follows comes from the same source.
3 *Ibid.*, p. 85.
4 M. Gorbachev, 'Realities and guarantees for a secure world', *International Affairs (Moscow)*, November 1988, quoted in Berridge, *op. cit.*, p. 165. Petrowski himself, as a member of the Russian delegation to the UN, made similar proposals in a memorandum to the General Assembly. (UN COC A/43/629, 22 September 1988.)
5 Berridge, *op. cit.*, p. 27.
6 *Facts on File*, 9 December 1988.
7 *Facts on File*, 9 December 1988.
8 *New York Times*, 4 August 1990, A6.
9 *Ibid.*, 8 August 1990, A1.
10 *Ibid.*, 8 August 1990, A8.
11 *Ibid.*, 10 August 1990, A11.
12 *Ibid.*, 13 August 1990, A8.
13 *Ibid.*, 14 August 1990, A9.
14 *Ibid.*, 15 August 1990, A6.
15 *Facts on File*, 1987, p. 930 (16 December).
16 *New York Times*, 20 August 1990, A7; 22 August, A12; 23 August, A1.
17 *Ibid.*, 24 August 1990, A1.
18 *Ibid.*, 26 August 1990.
19 G. Rozman, *Japan's Response to the Gorbachev Era: A rising superpower views a declining one*, Princeton, Princeton University Press, 1991.
20 Trans. note: On this I was clearly wrong. Professor Sadako Ogata – now the UN High Commissioner for Refugees – wrote an article in an influential monthly which took a very positive view of the effect of these developments on the UN. 'Kokuren o saisei saseta Gorbachov' ('Gorbachov brings the UN back to life', *Chūō Kōron*, February 1989).
21 *Financial Times*, 15 December 1992. 'Scare tactic by Russia stuns conference'.

8 JAPAN'S INTERNATIONAL ROLE AND THE CONSTITUTION

1. Quoted in Fukuda, Yūsuke, *Reimei no seiki*, Tokyo, Bungei-shunju-sha, 1991, p. 9.
2. Trans. note: Perhaps I am wrong about this. 'As a means of settling international disputes' needs, perhaps, to be amended to 'as a means of furthering national interests'.
3. Trans. note: One probably needs to add something like, 'or successor clauses of the same intent'.
4. Shimizu, *op. cit.*, vol. 2, p. 42.
5. Furuseki Shōichi, *Shinkempō no tanjō* (*The Birth of the New Constitution*), Tokyo, Chuo-koronsha, 1989.
6. *Ibid.*, p. 245.
7. Shimizu, *op. cit.*, vol. 2, p. 11, Lower House Committee, 21 August 1946.
8. *Ibid.*, vol. 2, p. 66, House of Peers Committee, 13 September 1946.
9. Furuseki, *op. cit.*, pp. 244–245.
10. Kanamori, Tokujirō, 'Kōwa in akogareru, ichishimin no kokoro' ('Waiting for the peace treaty. The thoughts of a Japanese citizen') *Chūō Kōron*, November 1950.
11. Fukase, Chūichi, *Sensō no hōki* (The Renunciation of War), volume 3 of *Bunsen senshu: Nihonkoku Kempō* (The Japanese Constitution: Selected Readings), Tokyo, 1977.
12. The Naganuma case had been deliberately framed to involve individual rights.
13. Fukase, *op. cit.*, p. 14. It is unfair to hold Professor Fukase up to ridicule, when I have profited so enormously from his splendid work in pulling together in these volumes so much valuable material on the Constitution. I crave his forgiveness but know no better way of making the point.
14. *Financial Times*, 10 February 1993.

9 A UN-CENTRED FOREIGN POLICY AND BILATERAL RELATIONS

1. Trans. note: Compare the Clinton administration's recent discovery of 'soft power'.
2. *International Herald Tribune* (Rome), 9 March 1992.
3. See the uncomfortable passage in the preface on 'learning lessons'.
4. Trans. note: $100 per Japanese, financed by an increase in gasoline taxes, cuts in university budgets, etc. See preface.
5. As quoted in Joseph S. Nye Jr., 'What new world order', *Foreign Affairs*, Spring 1992, p. 83.
6. Trans. note: In fact, of course, the Clinton administration started off with several expressions of a much more positive evaluation of the UN, and a much greater willingness to defer to its role. The small residual contingent of US troops in Somalia was – for the first time in history – put under the nominal command of a Turkish general. Then, in the summer, the CNN cameras switched from the distended bellies of starving children to the image of a wounded American airman being dragged through the streets of Mogadishu by an angry mob. Repeated refusals to commit ground troops to Bosnia crystallized in ever more clear declarations that US troops would never be sent abroad except in pursuit of national interests – finally elevated to the status of doctrine in Presidential Decision Directive, No. 25 of 6 May 1994.
7. Trans. note: After a long period in which the island issue had receded from prominence in public discussion, the present Prime Minister, Hashimoto, seems bent on bringing it to the forefront again.

8 Trans. note: A much disputed calculation; some would argue that, using a purchasing power parity exchange rate for the comparison, the present gap is a good deal less.

10 THE RESTRUCTURING AND STRENGTHENING OF THE UN

1 Shinyo, Takahiro, 'Kokuren no saikasseika o motomete' ('In search of ways to revitalise the UN'), *Gaikō Forum*, No. 46, p. 20.
2 *Ibid.*
3 'Learning from the Gulf', *New York Review of Books*, 7 March 1991, p. 36.
4 UN General Assembly, A/43/629 22 September 1988.
5 Boutros Boutros-Ghali, *An Agenda for Peace*. United Nations DPI/1247 June 1992, p. 22.
6 *Ibid.*, p. 14–15.
7 *Ibid.*, p. 18.
8 *Ibid.*, p. 18.
9 *Ibid.*, p. 26.
10 *Ibid.*, p. 24–25.
11 *Ibid.*, p. 26.
12 *Ibid.*, p. 24.
13 Richard R. Gardner, 'Collective security and the "New World Order": What role for the United Nations?' in J.S. Nye, Jr. and R.K. Smith, eds, *After the Storm*, Lanham, New York and London, Madison Books, 1992, pp. 39–41.
14 *Financial Times*, 30 October 1992.
15 Admiral Sir James Eberle, *Agenda for Peace; Military Issues*, mimeo, 1992.
16 *op. cit.*, p. 28.
17 *Independent*, 27 January 1993.
18 *The Lancet*, vol. 340, 5 December 1992, p. 1399.
19 *Asahi Shimbun*, 22 January 1993.
20 'Lives risked by humanitarianism', *Financial Times*, 9/10 January 1993, p. xxii.
21 'A cause, rather than a country, worth dying for', *Guardian Weekly*, 20 December 1992, p. 11.
22 Trans. note: The issues outlined here were the subject of a conference held at Siena in the summer of 1994, and attended by scholars, journalists and diplomats predominantly from Germany, Italy and Japan. The documentation for that conference, substantially revised and updated, has since been published as a book of readings: P. Taylor, S. Daws and U. Adamczick, *Documents on the reform of the United Nations*, Brookfield Vt., Dartmouth, 1997.

PART II

1 All page references in Part II refer to this edition.

Index

absolute monarchy 22
Acheson, D. 181
adaptive learning 7
Afghanistan 12, 65, 81, 83, 85, 89
Africa 24
Agenda for Peace xvii, xxviii, 130–3, 145, 184
aggression 61, 114, 132; definition of 45, 65
AIDS 136
Akashi, Y. xvix
Akhmatova, A. 93
Albania 17
Alexander I 23, 25
Alsace 20
Amanoya Rihei 165
Analects 8
Angola xviii, 81, 83, 100, 131
Anti-Slavery League 72
Aoki, M. xvi, 171
Arab countries 89, 119
Arab–Israeli War 62
Arafat, Yasser 89
arbitration 20, 24, 26, 27
Armacost, M. 103
arms trade 160
Asahi Shimbun xxvii, xxviii, xxx, 135, 179, 184
Ashida, H. 53, 107, 163, 170
Asian model of economic development 174
assassinations 53
Atlantic Charter 32
Attlee, C. 34, 60
automobile industry 7

Baker, J. 14, 43, 68, 90, 117
Bandung Conference, 1957 64
Bank of Japan xxxiii
Baruch, B. 181
Basic Peace Law xxvi, 158

Bentham, J. 22
Berlin 31
Berlin blockade 81
Berlin Wall 167
Berridge, G. 182
biological weapons 113
blood and sweat 57–8, 170
borderlessness 153, *see also* globalization
Bosnia xvii, 118, 137, 143
Boulden, J. 181
Boulding, K. 167
Boutros-Ghali, B. xv xvii, xviii, xxviii, 120, 130, 145, 184
Bowett, D. 180, 181
Boxer Rebellion 40
Brady Plan xxxiii
Bretton Woods Conference 29
Britain xii, xxxvi, xxxvii, 13, 28, 62, 82, 127, 138
Buddhism 4, 8
bureaucracy, meanings of 133
Bush, G. xx, 116, 117, 119, 138
Bushido 97
business cycles 3

Cambodia xv, 58, 67, 84, 100, 131, 139, 143, 157, 166; volunteers in xxxi
Canada xxxvi 49
Canning, G. 23
capitalisms, diversity of 6
Carter, J. 71, 73
centralization of power 13
chemical weapons 113
Chiba, K. xix, 176
Childers, E. xviii, 178
Chile 73
China ix, x, xvi, xviii, xiii, 13, 17, 21, 104, 127, 128, 148.151, 152, 166, 174; and founding of UN 33; and Gulf War xxxvi, 90; and Military Staff Committee 42ff; and non-interference

80; and UN membership 60; attitudes to Japan xxii; GNP 123–4; 'loss of' 68; Tienanmen xxxvi, 91, 124, 149, 174; trade with US 149; US bases in 46; US–China relations xxiii–xxiv, 123–5
Choshu 134
Christianity 8
Christopher, W. 117
Churchill, W. 32
Clinton, W 117, 183
CNN 183
Cold War xv, xxi, xxxv, xxxvi, 14, 31, 42ff, 61, 81, 85, 92, 122, 127, 138, 152, 163, 176
collective security arrangements xxii, xxx, 14, 23, 27, 29, 38, 53, 55, 57, 115; in Asia 123
comfort women xxvii
communications 14, 114, 152
Communist Party xxvi, 107
Condorcet 4
Confucianism x, 4, 124, 128, 153
Congress of Vienna 22
conservatism 151
constitutional monarchy 19
containment 48, 166
Crimean War 12
Crucé, E, 21, 22, 180
Crusades 20
CSCE 123
Cuba 11, 83
Cuban Missile Crisis 78, 81, 87–8, 128, 136, 172–5
cultural hegemony 83
cyclical theorists 4, 11

Daijosai 164
Daimyo 12
Dante, A 20, 179
death 8
defence expenditure 133
defence technology xxiii
democracy 13, 19, 124, 149–52
democratization 74
dignity *see* honour
disarmament 66
Disarmament Conference, 1932 41
dispute prevention 129
disputes and threats to peace 38
diversity, advantages of 173–5
diversity, value of 154, 173–5
Doko, T. 7
Dostoevsky, F. 85
Dulles, J.F. 92, 122
Dumbarton Oaks 29–36

East Bengal 80
eastern values x
Eberle, J. 184
economic development 149
Eda, S. 5
egalitarianism 3
El Salvador 66
elitism 136
Emperor xxix
environment 136, 152
Ethiopia 21, 28, 81
European Community 153
evolutionary economics 171
evolutionary progress 3–15, 152, 172

fairness *see* justice
Falk, R. xxvi
Falklands war 68
FAO 76
Farer, T. 182
Financial Times 182, 183, 184
Finland, xxviii, 90
fishing rights 123
foreign policy, aims of xii, xxxiv, 96; agenda-setting 105
France xii, xxxii, xxxvi, xxxvii, 13, 28, 62, 82, 90, 91, 127, 138
Franck, T. 182
Franco–Prussian War 25
frankness, in diplomacy 43
French Revolution 23
Friedman, M. 9
Fukase, C. 110, 183
Fukuda, Y. 170, 183
Fukukawa, S. xix, 160
Furuseki, S. 108, 183

G7 summits 69, 82, 151
Gaiko Forum xxxii
Gardner, R. 184
GATT 16, 121, 160, 170, 174
generation change 162
Germany xviii, 93, 111, 127, 146; and Russia xxxvi; and UN xxxvi; Basic Law 111
Ghana 76
globalization 6, 12, 19, 59, 113; and convergence 173
Golan Heights xviii
Gorbachev, M. 84–9, 121, 182
Great Depression, 1930s 28, 29
Greece 42, 48, 66
Grenada 11
Gromyko, A. 43–7
Grotius, H. xxxix, 17, 21, 26, 179

growth rates 123
Guardian Weekly 184
Gulf War xiii, xxviii, xxxii, xxxiv, xxxvi, 11, 15, 31, 67, 78, 89, 103–4, 106, 111, 114–19, 133, 152, 154, 157, 166
gunboat diplomacy 11

Hague convention 10, 26
Hague Peace Conference 25
Hammarskjold, D. 40, 63, 68, 130
Hara, S. 55
Harada, K. 178
Hashimoto, R. xxv, 183
Hatano, Y. 178
Hayek, F. von 9
Hegel G.W. 4
hegemony 17, 19, 114–21
Helsinki Declaration 74, 81
Hideyoshi, T. 14, 114
Higuchi 164
Hinsley, F. 21, 179
Hirauma, H. 54, 181
Hitler, A. 164
Hogen, S. 92
Hong Kong 149
honour 96–9, 154
Hosokawa, M. 149, 166, 167
House of Lords 114
Howard, M. 182
Howell, Secretary of State 41
Howson, S. 180
human nature 114
human rights 35, 71–4, 87, 149, 152, 166; and economic development 149
Hungary 62
Hussein, Saddam 119

Iacocca, L. 7–8
IAEA 86, 119, 134
Ichii, S. xxxviii
Ichiro, O. 157
Idi Amin 80
ILO 27, 74
IMF xxvi, xxxii, xxxiii, 31
imperialism 11, 17, 19
Independent 79, 184
India 80, 120
individualism 7
INF Treaty 87
Inoguchi, T. xxvii, 178, 179
International Association for Arbitration and Peace 24
international conferences 23
international court 22–6

International Court of Justice 10, 16, 26, 27, 38, 69–71, 82, 86, 122, 160; jurisdiction of, 39
International Herald Tribune 179, 183
international law 10, 16–19, 24, 69–71, 78, 152
international order 87, 151; types of 16–19
international organizations 9
International Postal Union 25
international professional communities 8–10
international relations, and domestic politics 151; study of 78–80, 83, 97
international society 78; as status system xix, 52, 96–9; *see also* cultural consensus
internationalism xix, 29, 37, 41, 49–50, 57–8, 103, 139, 172
Inter-Parliamentary Union 24
Iran 17, 42, 69
Iran–Iraq War xii, xxxiv, 91
Iraq 15, 89, 113, 119; air exclusion zone 94
Ishihara, S. xvi, xxiv, xxxii, xxxv, 98, 105, 165, 169
Islamic countries 50, 129
Islamic fundamentalism xiii, 67
Israel xxviii, 62, 98, 169
Israeli–Egyptian war, 1973 81
Italy xxxvi, 28
Itō, H. 35, 180
Itō, K. 92
Itō, S. 99
Izvestia 90

Jamaica 135
Japan,
    American occupation x
    and Asia xxiii–xxv, 123, 148
    and Cold War 92
    and Gulf War xiii, 89
    and peace-keeping operations xiii, xxix, 103–5, 139, 180
    and racial equality x
    and UN xii, xiii, xx, 101–5
    appointments to UN 134–5
    arms exports xxiv
    as 'normal' country xxii, 107, 144
    as aid donor xii
    as Number One xii
    as victim 101
    at Versailles Conference 26
    'burden-sharing' xii, 176
    civil code x

Index

consensus politics xxx, xxxvii, 165
conservatism and radicalism 164, 167
Constitution 1889 35, 102
Constitution 1947, xi, xii, xvi, xxv, xxvii–ix, 30, 52–9, 100–11, 126, 144–7, 154–5, 157, 161, 162, 167–8, 169
corporation structures xi
defence expenditure xii, xix, 145
Defence University xix, 102, 136
democracy xxv, 163
dependence on American market xi
Diet 52–9
economic competitiveness 6
economic growth x, xi
elite 102
equality with US ix
fascism xii, 102
foreign aid
foreign policy x, xi, xviii, xxxii; Foreign Ministry xxxii, 136, 163; initiatives xxxiii; characteristics of xxxiv; political background xxxix; UN-centred 95
form of capitalism 170, 172
generational watersheds, xxxi
Imperial Conference 53
Imperial family ix, xxix, 54, 102, 154
imperial legacy 148
international contribution xxxiii
international status x
internationalization 160
judicial system x, 109
Koreans in 73
labour relations 27
land reform x
left-wing intellectuals 103
liberals x, 27
Liberal-Democratic Party xii, xiii, 158
Marxists xi, xii
militarism xi, 102, 152, 158, 165, 170
national character xxxiii, 97, 162
nationalism x, 176
negativism 165
New Harbinger Party xxii
nuclear weapons xx, 146
opening to West ix
Official Secrets Act xxvii
pacifism (*heiwashugisha*) xxvi, xl, 53, 100, 156–9
political attitudes 150
postwar reforms x, xii
racial sentiments xxxii
relations with China ix, 123–5, 149
relations with Russia 122
relations with US ix–xvi, xviii–xxiii, xxxiii, xxxviii, 104, 113–21, 146
remodelling of ix
renunciation of war, 52–3
'reverse course' xi, xii, 103
Self-Defence Forces xv, xix, xxii, xxvi, xxvii, 9, 101–11, 143, 147, 155, 157, 163, 165, 176
Socialist Party xv, xxv, 5
Supreme Court 110
Tokugawa period xxxviii, 13, 69, 88
trade unions xi
trade with US xxxii
troops abroad, xxx
views of Russia 92
war guilt 148
withdrawal from League 28
youth volunteers, xxxi
Japan-bashing 96, 113, 176
Jefferson, T. 164
just wars 65–7, 157
justice 10, 84, 166; vs. peace 38

Kagan, D. 178
Kagoshima 11
Kahn, H. xii
Kajiyama, S. 164
Kakizawa, H. 145
Kanamori, T. 58, 109, 183
Kant, I. xxvi, 4, 22, 151, 180
Karens 66
Keizai Dōyūkai xxv, xxviii, 179
Kennan, G. 48, 181
Kennedy, J.F. 138, 167
Kennedy, P. xxxviii, 11
Kenney, General 44
Keohane, R. 179
Khozylev 93, 121
Khrushchev, N. 67, 85
Kimura, H. 92
Kingbury, B. 182
Kishi, N. 163
Kissinger, H. xx, 96
Kita, R. 56
Kohl, H. 111
Kondratieff cycles 3
Konoe, F. 149
Korea xviii, xxvii, 76, 124, 148
Korean War 48, 60–3, 163
Kosai, Y. xxiii, xxx, 148
Koseki, S. 179
Kurds 66
Kuriyama, S. 178
Kuwait Government xii

Lancet 134, 184
Large Retail Stores Law 121
Lawson, D. 138
League of Nations 10, 26–8, 31, 34, 64, 74, 93, 126
Libby, F. 37
Lincoln, A. 164
Lindsay F. 181
loyalty 134

MacArthur, D. 60
McCormack, G, 179
Machiavelli, N. 20, 180
Maeda, Lord 9, 14, 178
Magna Carta 13, 114
Mahathir, M. xxiv
Mahler, H. 135
Major, J. 138
Maldives 135
Manchuria 28
Mandelstam, O. 93
Marxism 4, 8
Mather, J. 180
Matsuoka, Y. 27, 93
Matsuyama, Y. x, xii, xxvii, xxx, 162
Mendl, W. xxiv, 179
military force, uses of 12
Military Staff Committee 89–91, 114
Mill, J. 22, 180
MITI, xxxii
Miyazawa, K. xix, xx, xxix–xxx, 123, 158, 178, 179
modernization 5
Mogami, T. 179
Moggridge, D. 180
Monroe Doctrine 42
moral principles 136–40
Morgan, L. 4
Mōri family 88
Morita, A. ix, xvi, 105, 169
Moynihan, D. 69, 179, 180, 182
Mozambique xviii
multilateralism 121, 125, 172
Murayama, T. xxv
Mushakoji, K. 179
Myammar 166
my-home-ism 156

Naganuma judgement 109, 183
Nakajima, H. 134–5
Nakanishi, T. 78, 100, 129, 152
Nakasone, Y. 164
Nambara, S. 57, 170, 181
Namibia 41, 83
Nanking, rape of 12

Napoleon 22
national armies, purpose of 137
National Association for Arbitration and Peace 180
National Council for the Prevention of War 37
National Foundation Day 164
national identity 72, 85, 87
national interest 96, 117
nationalism 20, 66, 122
NATO xvii, xxi, 133, 151
natural selection 6
Nazism 4, 151
neo-classical economics 171
neutrality 58, 82
New Information Order 75
New Left Review 179
New World Information Order 75
New York 143
New York Review of Books 184
New York Times 90, 115
NGOs xxvi
Nicaragua 39, 66, 82
Nicholas II 25
Nintendo xxiii
Nishikawa, Y. 178
Nitobe, I. 9
Noda, N. 179
Non-Aligned Countries 64
non-interference, principle of 35–6, 65, 67, 71–4, 79, 128
North Korea xxi, xxii, 17, 43, 104
Northern islands dispute 69, 92, 122, 166
North–South relations 75, 77
Nosaka, S. 56, 107, 181
Nuclear Non-proliferation Treaty xix
nuclear weapons xii, 30, 48, 60, 65, 104, 113, 115, 152, 160
Nye, J. xxi, xxii, 179, 183, 184
Nyureyev, R. 87

OECD 151
Ogata, Sadako 134, 182
Ogata, Shijurô xix, 169
Ohira, M. 165
Oil crisis 75
Okinawa xxi
original sin 4
ostracization 100
Owen, D. 137
Ozawa, I. xiii, xxviii, 103, 116, 178, 179

pacifism 21–4, 37, 38, 59, *see also* **Japan, pacifism**
Pakistan 80, 83

Index

Panama 11
Pan-American Conference, 1889 25
Parsons, A. 182
patriotism 14, 28, 95, 156
Patten, C. 124
Pax Americana xii, 11, 88,
Pax Brittanica 11, 88
Pax Consortis 160
Pax Japonica xii, 11, 88
Peace Keeping Operation Law xxix
peace process 68
peace, nature of, 57; enforcing 131; peace-keeping xxxii, 131
Peninsular War 9
Penn, W. 21, 22, 180
perestroika 92
Pérez de Cuéllar, J. 83
periodization 17
Persia 21
Petrowski, V. 86, 130
philosophy of history 3
Poland 47
police forces 10
Pope 21
Potsdam Declaration 53, 56, 164
prestige *see* honour
Privy Council 114
protectionism xi
Prussia 19
Pushkin, A. 93

Quakerism 21–4, 100

race and status 128
race, and human rights 73
racial conflict 64
racial differences xxxv
racial equality 26, 64
rationality 173
Reagan, R. 39, 71, 82
realism 78
regulation, proliferation of 9
religion 8
Rhodesia 63–4
Righter, R. xvii
Robbins, L. 29
Roberts, A. 182
Rockefellers 98
Roman Empire 20
Roosevelt, F. 32, 50
Roosevelt, T. 20, 37
Roth, P. 182
Rousseau, J-J. 21–2, 180
Royal Institute of International Affairs 107
Rozman, G. 92, 182

rule of law 14, 69
Rusk, D. 49
Russell, R. 180
Russia xii, xxxi, 23, 29, 69, 74, 83, 151, 152, 174; and Gulf War xxxvi; and Military Staff Committee 42ff; and Security Council xxxvii; attitudes to UN 84–94, 122–3; education system 85; foreign policy post 1990 93; nationalism 93; transformation of 85–6
Russian threat xxi
Russo–Japanese War 152
Rwanda xvii

Saint-Simon 22
Sakamoto, H. xxxii
Sakurauchi 164
SALT 81
San Francisco Conference 28, 100
San Francisco Peace Treaty xi, xxxi
Sase, M. 92
Satsuma 134, 153
Saudi Arabia 89
Sawada, U. 54
Scandinavia xv
Second Hague Conference 25
Second World War xxxvii, 14, 28
Security Council 10, 19, 33, 38–40, 160
Sega xxiii
Sekigahara 14, 88
self-defence, right of 45, 56, 170
Self-respect xxxv
Self-sacrifice, justification for 156, 170
Serbs 93
Sheverdnadze, E. 43, 90, 121, 129
Shidehara, K xxxiv, xxxv, 53ff, 93, 108, 181
Shimazu family 88
Shimizu, C. 181, 182
Shinyo, T. 184
Shogun 20
Sino–Japanese War 152
slavery 74
Smith, R. 184
social evolution xvi, 4, 5–10
social mobility 97
social movements 99
socialism 25
Somalia 78, 80, 100, 101, 117, 120–1, 143, 154
South Africa 63–4, 72–3
sovereignty xxix, 12, 17, 26, 28, 35, 41, 65, 71–4, 77, 96, 113
Spain 23, 46
Spectator 138
Spencer, H. 4

Index 191

spy satellite 119, 131
Stalin, J. 66
Star Wars 85
state, role of 35
Stetinnius, P. 181
strategic studies 78
Suez crisis xxviii, 62
Sunagawa Incident 109
Sweden 98, 169
Switzerland 58, 82
SWNCC 180

Taiwanese elections xxi
Takayanagi, K. 58
Takeishi, C. 178
Tanaka, A. 178
Tanaka, K. 69
Tanzania 76, 80
technology, accumulation of 5; social 9; and social structure 7–8; and values 7–9
Teheran Conference 37
television 77
terrorism 136
Thai–Cambodia dispute, 1959 68
Thatcher, M. 3, 9
The Japan That Can Say 'No' xxxii
The Times 22
Third World 5; debt xxxiii; development 153; and UN 64, 143; Russian policies towards 84, 86
Thomas, H. 50, 180, 181
Thorne, C. 180
Thucydides xii
Tibet 166
Tojo, H. 163
Tokyo Shimbun 108
Tokyo War Crimes trial 164
Tolstoy, L. xxvi, 93
total war 152
Toynbee, A. 4, 5, 176
trade theory 173
transnational corporations 19
transnational organization 25
Treaty of Chaumont 23
Treaty of Portsmouth 20
Truman doctrine 48
Truman, H. 50, 60
Tsukuda, C. 178
Turkey 21, 24
TV, and politics 138

Uganda 80
United Nations,
 and development 74–7
 and Japan's constitution 52–9

and use of armed force 37–51
as instrument of US policy 61, 91
birth of 29–36
Charter, Article 41 90; Article 42 90–1; Article 51 57, 89; Atomic Energy Committee 43; Chapter 7 14, 41, 36, 38–51, 78, 89, 100, 131, 154; Chapter 8 123; 'enemy country' articles 32, 52–9; revision xvi, xxxvii–xxxvi
choice of name 33
contempt for 78
disaster relief 77, 145
Economic and Social Council 72
Fiftieth anniversary xv
financing of xxxviii, 65, 87, 127, 166
General Assembly xxvii, 61, 64, 87
humanitarian interventions 80
Japan's contributions to 112
Japan's membership 58
mandatory sanctions 34, 38, 48, 63, 65, 90, 127
military activities, role xxxvi, xxxviii, 37–51, 60–7, 78, 100–5, 144, 147; command structure 45, 89, 144; common training 44, 132–3; financing of 133; force strength, 44, 47–8; rapid deployment force 46, 132; standing army 41, 145, 158; volunteer force, 132, 158
Military Staff Committee x, 37–51
need for xxiii
progressive trends 62–80
relaunch xxxv
Russian proposals for reform 86–7
Secretary-General 34, 40, 45, 60, 63, 67–8, 83, 120, 130–3, 145
Security Council xv, xviii, 14, 16, 19, 60–8, 82, 83, 87, 91, 118–20, 126–33, 144, 146, 154, 177; composition 127–9; veto powers 33, 34, 41, 42, 44, 67, 91, 126–9
staff xix, xxxviii, 34, 50, 74, 76, 87, 133; loyalty of, 134
Trusteeship Council 66
Uniting for Peace Resolution 61
US attitudes to 64, 78
UN University xxvi
UNCTAD 74
UNDP 74
UNEF 62
UNESCO 74, 77, 82, 84
UNHCR 77, 134, 170
UNICEF 77
UNIDO 74

United Nations Participation Act, 1945 41
United States Congress 26, 27
Universal Peace Congress 1889 24
universalism 88, 172–5
UNRRA 33
UNTAG 41
Urquhart, B. xvii, 129, 178, 180
United States 138; and Britain, as allies 30; and Cold War x; Congress xi, 14, 39, 41; Constitution 162; and Gulf War 89; hegemony 147; international status xxxv; and Iran 69–71; isolationism 28; Jewish lobby 64, 82; military capability 31, 116; and Military Staff Committee 41–9; and Namibia 83; occupation of Japan xxxii; Panama invasion 118; Pentagon xxxii, 13, 115; presence in Asia 150; relations with China, xxii–xxiii, 124, 149; relations with Japan 104, 113–21; relations with USSR 30; Security Treaty with Japan xi, xxvi, 92; State Department xi; trade with China 149; trade negotiations with Japan 172; and UN xvii, 82, 84, 117, 144, 166; as world policeman, xvi
USSR *see* Russia

Vance, C. 137
Vandenburg, Senator 41
Venice 21
Versailles Conference x, 26, 64, 126
Vietnam x, 12, 63, 66, 81, 85, 96, 157, 166

Wada, H. 92
Wade, R. 179
Wakamiya, Y. 178
Wakon yosai 14
Watanabe B.J. Governor xxxiv, 126
Watanabe, K. 164
Weaver, S. 182
Wellington, Duke of 9
West Point 117
western technology x
western values 128
WHO 74, 76, 134, 170
Wilson, W. 26, 27
women, and politics 143
World Bank xxvi, xxxiii, 31
world federalism xvi, 35, 120
world order xxix, 16–18, 115–18
WTO xxvi

Yajima, M. xxviii, 143
Yamagata, D. xxxviii
Yamazaki, I. 56
Yanaibara, T. 164
Yasukuni shrine 164

Yeltsin, B. 93, 121–22
Yokota, K. 170
Yomiuri Shimbun xxviii, xxix, 179
Yosano, A. 101
Yoshida, S. xxvii, 53ff, 107, 181
Yoshimura, S. xix, xxviii, 156
Young, H. 138
Yugoslavia 66, 67, 100, 122, 137, 143,
Yusin, 90

Zionism 64